The Best Friends' Guide to

Babies

A Note on the Author

VICKI IOVINE is the happy and chronically overwhelmed mother of four children (five if you count her husband, and what wife doesn't?). Along with being a mother, Iovine is the celebrated author of the highly successful Best Friends' Guide series that immediately found its niche with the hip and innovative *The Best Friends' Guide to Pregnancy*, which has been reprinted forty-one times and translated into twelve languages. It was followed by the equally beloved *The Best Friends' Guide to Babies*, and, keeping up with Vicki's own life experience, *The Best Friends' Guide to Toddlers* was published just in the nick of time for those on Vicki's reproductive timeline. To offer her no-holds-barred stories of women trying to reenter the 'real world' of careers, compromises and, of course, love and sex after the kids were in school or day care for at least four hours a day, *The Best Friends' Guide To Getting Your Life Back* was the fourth in the series.

While raising four kids is full-time work, Iovine has been a columnist for several magazines including a monthly column in *Child*, a bi-monthly column for *Redbook* and a weekly column devoted to family life in the *Los Angeles Times*. She was also the parenting contributor for *Today*, a frequent guest host on *Later Today* and has appeared several times on *Oprah, Good Morning America* and *The View*.

The Best Friends' Guide to

Babies

Wise and witty advice on everything from coping with postnatal mood swings to salvaging your sex life to fitting into that favourite pair of jeans

Vicki Iovine

BLOOMSBURY
LONDON · BERLIN · NEW YORK · SYDNEY

This book is dedicated to Grandma Gladys:

Thank you for teaching me to love books (and for my snotty attitude!). I miss you, Grandma.

XO

First published in Great Britain 1999
as *The Best Friends' Guide to Surviving the First Year of Motherhood*
This edition published 2011

Bloomsbury Publishing Plc, 36 Soho Square, London WID 3QY

First published in the USA 1997
A Perigee Book published by The Berkley Publishing Group, a member of
Penguin Putnam Inc., 200 Madison Avenue, New York, NY10016

Author's note: some of the Best Friends' names have been changed to protect their privacy . . . but Friends, you know who you are

A CIP catalogue record for this book
is available from the British Library

ISBN 978 1 4088 1426 0

10 9 8 7 6 5 4 3 2 1

Typeset by Hewer Text UK Ltd, Edinburgh
Printed in Great Britain by Clays Ltd, St Ives plc

MIX
Paper from
responsible sources
FSC® C018072

www.bloomsbury.com

contents

Acknowledgements

Last night, in that supportive way that children can have, one of my own asked mopingly, 'Mum, when are you going to stop all this writing so that you can be with us?' Since I work in our house, I asked her what she wished I was more available to do. She said, 'Drive me to school every day, mornings and afternoons, and watch all of my dance and gymnastics classes instead of just dropping me off.' Well, my little babies, Mummy is back behind the wheel. I know that I took a lot of time away from us to write this book, but you were very sweet and generous about it. I just hope that all four of you grow up to find something in your life you enjoy as much as I enjoy this. I love you all soooo much, and I promise to take you to McDonald's real soon.

To the best, funniest, most loving and understanding man in the world, my husband, Jimmy: thanks for letting me renegotiate our parenting agreement and for taking over the tap dance and baby gym duties. I owe you a t-ball practice and a spring sing. I promise I will now try to honour our No Working at Weekends pledge, no matter how much my computer flashes at me. Most of all, I love you madly. Oh, yeah, and I promise not to get pregnant again or buy a new puppy without consulting you first.

To Ray Manzella, who has been such a good friend for so many years, who helped me see what I could accomplish and who, in spite of being a handsome manly-man kind of guy, could almost be a Best Friend: thank you for giving me the glasses to see what's on the horizon.

To the folks at Putnam Berkley Books, and especially Phyllis Grann and Chris Pepe: from the moment I walked into your offices and met you, I knew that I was home. Phyllis, I want to be you when I grow up! And Chris, I want to watch you keep bringing those beautiful babies into the world! Thanks to you both for looking after me so well, and, Chris, allow me to be the first to use the word *wunderkind* in writing to describe you and your talent. (P.S.: Now that we have got the writing out of the way, let's go hang out and sip martinis at the Four Seasons.)

To Jody-Girl, thanks for being here for me every day, for being here for my kids and their friends, for being here for all repairmen, baseball coaches and karate and piano teachers, and thanks for listening to me moan every afternoon when I can't think of one more thing to write. Our family is your family.

To my Best Friends, and you know who you are: thank you for teaching me over and over again that the good times are better shared with friends, and the hard times are bearable (sometimes even hysterically funny) when shared with friends, especially when the friends are such extraordinary women as you. I love you guys.

Foreword

Motherhood: It's more than a Job - It's an Adventure!

Here it is, YOUR BABY! And here you are, A MOTHER! It's enough to take your breath away. A real, honest-to-goodness miracle has occurred in your life, the greatest event you will ever experience (even if you are still a little too sore and tired to believe me right now). Sure, people have had babies before, but that doesn't diminish by one watt the awe and humility you feel when it happens to you. Nobody ever said that meeting an angel is less heavenly because it's happened before.

Congratulations!

We Best Friends have been hovering around, waiting for this moment when we could all crowd in and welcome your little darling. We promise not to touch or breathe on her! You're right, she *is* the most beautiful baby we have ever seen! You look pretty good yourself – maybe a little puffy eyed, but nothing time won't fix. So, now that the baby is here, the hard work is over, right?

'Why?' you screech. Why didn't we tell you about what it's really like to have a baby? Well, first of all, we knew you wouldn't have believed us, and second, we didn't want to scare you. All prospective mothers, whether pregnant or adopting or ordering through a catalogue, carry in their hearts a rosy picture of motherhood. They've been perfecting it and polishing it since they were little girls: a sort of composite of the mothering they received, the mothering they wished they'd received and a large helping of too much television. Odds are good that the rosy picture didn't include the stitches, bruises, sore bones, broken capillaries and God help you. And I guess it's safe to assume you didn't know there'd be so much *leaking*, either. There's milk or colostrum coming from your breasts, some bloody horror from your vagina and probably lots of tears, from joy and fear (often simultaneously), dripping from your eyes. Hanging over everything like a fog is the nagging suspicion (which, by the way, is correct) that life as you knew it is over.

All through your pregnancy, you assumed that gestation was a nine (ten)-month experience of life in a parallel universe, but that you would reenter the real world upon delivery. Now is the time for those of us who love you (and who know better) to let you know the truth. Normal, as you knew it, is gone. Poof! Out the window! Think of it this way: having a baby is like entering a carnival fun house, except this fun house is your new home. It's a thrilling adventure, even if you do look a little distorted in all the mirrors, you have no sense of direction and have to feel your way along in the dark, and even if every once in a while something pops up that you didn't expect and scares the heck out of you. You can fight it by running around looking for the exit or you can just exhale and remember, life is a carnival, old chum. This first year of motherhood is a lot about making yourself comfortable in your new home.

You will be feeling the aftershocks of the Great Motherhood Quake for years to come and in areas too numerous to mention so early in this book. (Don't worry, we'll get to everything eventually.) Aftershocks, big and little, will be felt in everything from your psyche to your sex life, your shoe size to your bra size, your career to your car. Nothing will be the same. It may be more difficult, it will certainly be more wonderful, but it ain't gonna be the same; that we Best Friends can tell you for certain.

Let's start with the most important information: YOUR BABY WILL NOT ONLY SURVIVE YOUR MOTHERING; HE WILL THRIVE AND LIVE TO BE YOUR LORD AND MASTER. Don't spend one more calorie of energy worrying about what an amateur you are at parenting and whether you are capable of taking care of an infant. It's a pretty safe bet that you will sacrifice yourself on all levels to protect your enchanting little dictator's every comfort.

It's *you* the Best Friends are concerned about. Most mothers wouldn't hesitate to bite off their own arm if it would provide comfort to their crying babies, but ask these same generous women to treat themselves to a bubble bath or an afternoon nap when they are hysterical and stupid-tired, and they quickly think of a million reasons not to resort to such wimpy indulgence. Just as *The Best Friends' Guide to Pregnancy* let pregnant women in on the secret that no awards are passed out in hospital for those who deliver cheerfully and drug free, *The Best Friends' Guide to Surviving the First Year of Motherhood* wants you to know that there are no marks for your performance as a mother. That's because no one knows when the job is done and ready to be evaluated. It's like the caucus race in *Alice in Wonderland*; you just keep running and running in a big circle; there is no start or finish line. Our advice is to pick a nice easy jog for your parenting pace because this race is going to last longer than you ever imagined, and we're only dealing with the first year here. Take a break now and then (maybe even that bubble bath); the race will continue without you and you can rejoin later when you're rested.

The first year of motherhood knocks all of us mums off balance, and often the only thing that keeps us from falling flat is another mother standing right beside us. That's what your Best Friends are for, so feel free to lean against us as you wonder how you will live on little or no sleep, how a person with the secret inner life of Pippi Longstocking can ever become Carol Brady, how you'll ever get this breastfeeding business worked out (or if it's worth the effort anyway), why your partner just doesn't seem to be suffering as much as you are and how (and *why*) you will ever let that man be intimate enough with you that you might have to go through pregnancy and delivery AGAIN!

Now quick! Lie down, and do so every time you reach for this book. The most critical advice we can give you today is simple:

Don't stand when you can sit, don't sit when you can lie down and don't stay awake when you can sleep.

why I wrote this book

Walk down the baby-and-child-care aisle in any bookshop and you will notice the shelves groaning with the weight of countless books on how to care for babies, how to make them smarter, how to make them sleep through the night, how to teach them party tricks like drinking from a cup or using the potty and how to keep them from blaming you to their psychiatrists when they grow up. (As if!)

Now check those shelves more closely. Do you see one *single* book for us, the mothers? No fair counting those books that tell us how to eat well to provide healthy milk *for our breastfeeding babies*! I'm talking about a book that deals only with *us* and the stunning fact that our lives have changed forever with the arrival of motherhood. Don't bother looking any longer (since you are a new mum, you have probably already forgotten what you were looking for anyway).

This is that book: the book for those of us who thought having a baby would be something like getting a very, very small flatmate. Even better than having a flatmate because you won't have to share the bathroom with it for the first couple of years. This is the book for those of us who weep when we hold our baby, but we're not always sure whether it's because we're overcome by adoration or terror. It's for those of us who secretly suspect we may not be up to this job, but don't want to give the baby back. It's for those of us who cherish breastfeeding our babies in bed and falling asleep together, but who yearn to talk to real grown-ups who read newspapers and have seen at least one of the films nominated for this year's Academy Awards. It's for those of us who wouldn't have missed parenting for all the world, but who wonder if while we're parenting we're missing the rest of the world. It's for those of us who rush past a mirror and think for a moment that we just saw our mother, and spend the rest of the day in tears.

Trust us when we tell you that this is your hardest year (leaving aside adolescence for the time being). If you can get through this, *and you can*, you will be an old pro by the time you're throwing the baby's first birthday party. The Best Friends are back to offer encouragement, information, anecdotes and advice as you rise to the challenge of being a mummy. When in doubt about the baby's well-being, read Dr. Spock or Miriam Stoppard, but when in doubt about your own well-being, read *The Best Friends' Guide to Surviving the First Year of Motherhood*. We've all suffered the utter cluelessness you feel, the irrational fears about nearly everything and the pain of having your heart break every time you imagine you have let your baby down in some way, whether it's because you've gone back to work or, most heinous of all crimes, you've decided to have another child and dilute your love proportionately.

We also know an even juicier secret: your life feels so much more *significant* than ever before because you are a mother.

Take heart because the womenfolk have arrived. Our stretch marks are worn with the pride all soldiers have about their stripes. We may pee when we laugh or forget midsentence what we were talking about, but what we've got we'll share. We're here for the next year to share every single bit of information, every clever trick, every hour of guilt and uncertainty and every moment of bliss, and before you know it, we'll all be moving, ever so capably, into planning the baby's first birthday party. 'A piece of cake!' you'll declare (with the pun intended). Then we'll sit down to congratulate ourselves, only to leap back up before our bottoms have touched the chair, because by that point the baby will be **walking** and that's a whole other fish to fry.

Top-Ten Biggest Shocks of Childbirth

10
How big you really got during pregnancy.

9
How fat you still are when you leave hospital.

8
How messy childbirth and recovery are.

7
How frightened you are of ever having a bowel movement again in this lifetime.

6
How fat your face looks in the delivery room videos and photos.

5
How certain you are that you will never want sex again.

4
How irresponsible the hospital was to have released this precious baby into your care, considering you'd never even changed a nappy until yesterday.

3
How complicated breastfeeding a baby really is.

2
How overwhelming your devotion and enslavement to the baby are already.

1
How nobody ever told you how much it REALLY hurts to have a baby.

1

IN HOSPITAL

Hospitals are scary places, largely because they are strange, big and generally unfamiliar to healthy people. Aside from the odd appendectomy or tonsillectomy, most of us new mummies have never really been an official hospital patient. Knock wood and spit on the ground that hospitals should always have such beautiful associations as the arrival of new babies. Entering the world of maternity provides enough surprises on its own.

If you give birth in a hospital (which the Best Friends unanimously endorse for first-time mums, and which I endorse for absolutely everyone every time), the hospital itself shouldn't freak you out. This chapter of the *Guide* lets you know what to expect: who is who, how you check in, how you get out and what might happen at any point along the way. Forewarned is forearmed, so you will find your hospital stay more pleasant if you heed our warnings. (Besides, we suspect that several of you are reading this book a tad prematurely and your hospital visit is still several weeks away. It's fine to skip ahead, since you'll have more time to read while you're pregnant than you will after the baby comes; just don't get mad at us if you learn more than you wanted to know at this point.)

HOSPITAL ETIQUETTE

There are countless hospital procedures and rules that, to us silly mummies, seem to be more inflexible and illogical than the Inland Revenue is about deductions. For example, it will almost certainly prove to be folly to ask just anyone in an official-looking uniform to bring you some food after you have endured twenty hours of labour and delivery with nothing more than ice chips and lemon swabs for sustenance. Food is handled by food services, thank you very much.

Clean nightgowns and sheets are handled by laundry services, and vacuuming incessantly in the middle of the night is handled by housekeeping services.

Then, in a category all their own, are the blessed nurses. It is they who provide a modicum of comfort to you in your bruised and battered state. They don't mind practically *carrying* you to the bathroom for your first postnatal visit, they know exactly where to put the ice packs and, most important, they are the only people on the planet who can teach you in under two days everything you need to know about caring for a tiny baby. Don't waste their time (or incur their disdain) by whining about needing fluffier pillows or not liking the cafeteria French toast. Keep in mind that nurses are there to help you, but they don't work for you. If you aren't polite and respectful, don't expect a quick response to your call button (unless your family name is on a wing of the hospital). Remember, these are the keepers of the keys to the kingdoms of Successful Breast-Feeding and Clean Belly Button Stumps. YOU NEED THEM AND YOU NEED THEM BAD!

Your 'Honeymoon Suite'

Don't think of the hospital where you deliver your baby as a temporary holding pen for the two of you until you are released to your ever-so-much-prettier, cleaner, quieter, more familiar home. We Best Friends suggest that you try thinking of the maternity ward of any good hospital as a sort of 'Honeymoon Suite'. After all, newlyweds don't go directly from saying their vows to picking up their dry cleaning or polishing their bathroom fixtures. They adjust to their new life conditions by taking a few days to honeymoon and gently ease their way back into society. New mothers need some time to adjust, too. If you ask any mother on this planet, she will tell you that, compared with having a baby, the stress of matrimony is piffle, especially now that you can have a no-fault divorce. If a wedding requires a week or two of vacation, then childbirth should entitle all new mothers to lifetime memberships at the Golden Door or some other such sublime indulgence. Since that isn't going to happen (and even if it did, you wouldn't be able to get a good sitter to cover for you anyway), we who love you and care only for your safety and happiness beseech you to stay in the hospital as long as you can after you have a baby. Sure, the food sucks, the service would flunk any Marriott Hospitality Test and there is precious little peace and quiet to be found, but hospitals still have one thing that ranks them right up there with the finest five-star hotels:

THEY ARE ABSOLUTELY BRIMMING WITH PEOPLE WHO KNOW ABOUT BABIES AND NEW MUMS.

This feature alone beats twenty-four-hour room service, orchids on pillows or fax machines in every room for the typical terrified, tired and titillated brand-new mum. Months from now you will think back on those days in hospital/Honeymoon Suite with deep longing. You will think about lying in your bed (sure it was narrower than most picnic benches, but who cares?) with your baby curled up on your chest while you ate all the chocolate that your best friend brought up from the gift shop.

- The baby starts to cry. Quick, ring for a nurse; she'll know what to do! Even if she doesn't, she can make the baby go away for a while until you compose yourself.

- What? Your stitches hurt too much to bend over the isolette to change the baby's nappy? Don't trouble yourself, Mummy Dearest; a nurse who's changed a thousand squirming babies if she's changed one is just a whimper away.

- Having trouble getting the baby to overcome his insistence on breastfeeding only from one breast and in danger of watching the neglected one explode? The Breastfeeding Specialist will be right there, awash in the glory of her competency and her utter (udder?) lack of self-consciousness when grabbing your breast in one hand and jamming your nipple into the crying baby's mouth with the index finger of the other. Granted, her uncontainable enthusiasm about the countless benefits of breastfeeding your child until he is old enough to walk up and unbutton your shirt all by himself can be mildly irritating, but irritation is peanuts to pay for a satisfied baby, the avoidance of the cracked nipples and the granite boobies of an engorged woman.

- In desperate need of fresh ice for that pack you're keeping between your legs to relieve the soreness and swelling from all that stretching and stitching? In your nicest voice, ask the nurse to bring you some *when she is finished with anything more important that she may be doing.*

Even if it takes her till tomorrow, you will still be getting what you need sooner and more precisely than if you were at home and asked your partner to get it for you.

(Note: While we're on this subject, I must confess that I still seethe when I think of when I was confined to bed for the last four months of my first pregnancy, and, near starvation (or at least during a very strong craving), I asked my otherwise competent and attentive husband to bring me a bowl of cereal. He brought it all right: a big bowl of Cheerios, no spoon, no napkin, NO MILK. Nine years later, we're still finding those little toasted o's and pieces of that bowl in the darnedest places.)

Even people who have spent a good deal of time in hospitals are usually overwhelmed by them. Their size alone, especially the bigger metropolitan hospitals, completely confounds any internal sense of direction. Without a map or coloured lines painted on the floor to direct you, you can quickly get lost forever. That's why you must heed Rule Number One of Hospital Survival:

SIGN UP FOR THE TOUR OF THE MATERNITY WARD, NO MATTER HOW BUSY YOU ARE, HOW DORKY IT SEEMS OR HOW SICK TO DEATH YOU ARE OF THE BLISSFULLY UNINFORMED EAGER BEAVERS IN YOUR ANTENATAL CLASS.

This tour might be a regular part of your classes or you may have to sign up for it on your own. The single most important bit of information you will get from this tour is this:

YOU WILL BE TOLD THE SECRET OF HOW TO ENTER THE HOSPITAL WHEN YOU ARE LABOURING LIKE YOU'VE SWALLOWED A BUCKING BRONCO WITHOUT GETTING MIRED IN THE QUICKSAND OF THE ACCIDENT AND EMERGENCY DEPARTMENT AND HOW TO PROCEED DIRECTLY TO THE RELATIVE CALM OF THE LABOUR AND DELIVERY WARD.

The last thing a labouring woman needs when she could explode with absolutely no warning is to be seated in the accident and emergency room between a compound fracture and a gunshot wound.

The second cardinal rule in Hospital Survival is this:

MAKE SURE ALL YOUR PAPERWORK HAS BEEN DONE IN
ADVANCE.*

Your obstetrician's office will probably give you a simple little pre-admission form sometime in your second trimester. They will then forward it to the hospital for you or tell you how to send it in yourself. It wouldn't hurt to call the hospital about a week after submitting this form to see if it has been received and if there is any additional information you can give them that will make your arrival as smooth as it can possibly be. Partners, listen up! Women in labour are notoriously short-tempered, and if you want to see one go Friday-the-Thirteenth, tell her, as her amniotic fluid is making a puddle on the floor between her feet, that you just need to fill out a couple of forms before she is allowed to go to a room. Better still, ask her if she has a pen you can borrow.

what Happens after check-In

There are generally two paths into a delivery room. The one you will take is largely determined by whether your midwife has admitted you into a labour room after examining you and concluding that your rocket is on the launch pad, or if you have come directly to the hospital without first being examined. Many larger hospitals are a little selfish about their labour and delivery rooms, especially those nice new ones with homey furniture, stereos and lights that dim, and they won't give you one until somebody with a rudimentary knowledge of obstetrical biology has given you the first of countless internal-exams-by-complete-strangers. Sometimes this exam is performed in a holding area called *triage*. If your labour looks like it is progressing toward a dilated cervix, you will be awarded a labour room. If it's questionable or if your cervix is still tightly closed, you might be sent home for a few hours to see if anything develops. Keep in mind that there are special circumstances – like the fact that your water has been dribbling out for several hours or, like my Best Friend Sondra, you have the doctor by the throat and are screaming that they'd better give you something to get things moving in there because there is no way you are leaving this hospital without your baby in your arms – that can get you into a

---

* This does not apply in the UK. If you are in labour and not close to the hospital you have chosen, you will be seen – any formalities can wait.

labour room a little sooner than otherwise might happen. In a case like Sondra's, a wise resident will usually get your regular midwife on the phone and ask to be excused until he or she arrives.

Labour Rooms

As hospitals have realized that they have to compete with one another for the ever-shrinking pool of consumers, many have completely redesigned their maternity wards. For example, my mother laboured in a room with several total strangers in beds right beside her. When it was time to deliver, she was wheeled into a room that was outfitted for any garden-variety surgical procedure (that is, if you overlooked the stirrups hanging from the ceiling). When I had my first baby nine years ago, I had the good fortune to be able to skip labour entirely (scheduled Caesarean), but with my second, I laboured in a private room where no one but my husband and my midwife could hear me whimpering. It was a dingy, tiny room, but it was mine, and since the labour progressed smoothly (at least from the midwife's point of view), I was able to deliver my baby there, too. Of course, after the baby was born, my husband disappeared for an eternity while he announced the great news via a pay phone since the room had no such convenience. I just stared at the doorway in hopes that someone one would come in and rescue me, since I was all alone and didn't even have a TV for company.

All during my third pregnancy, I was reassured that the local hospital had remodelled everything and that I would labour and deliver in a room nearly as comfortable and spacious as my own at home. Yeah, well, no one ever warned me that those fabled rooms were issued on a first-come, first-served basis! When I was admitted, I was evidently one of the last to come and, therefore never served. I spent a good deal of labour on a trolley in the corridor, waiting for some other inconsiderate mum (probably having her sixth kid and, therefore, in no need of any special comfort) to hurry up and push her baby out and free up a bed. Finally, by the last pregnancy, I got the deluxe treatment. (Thank heavens, I could finally call an end to this gestating obsession.) It was just like I'd dreamed; there were windows, a television (I love *Wheel of Fortune* when I'm labouring), a working telephone and enough room for nearly every Best Friend I have to come in and gossip across me while I quietly begged for an anaesthetist. There was even an uphol-stered chair that converted to a bed for the partner or birth coach or whatever. Considerate as it was to provide that chair, I have to confess a certain resentful feeling toward it to this day. Maybe it has something to do with the fact that my husband had converted that chair to a bed, stolen my security blanket from my suitcase and assumed the resting position before I had even changed into my hospital gown, and he was nearly asleep by the time the foetal monitors were hooked up to me. I suppose I'll get over this with time, or the right trinket.

If you have a scheduled Caesarean, then you'll miss this little *House Beautiful* tour, and if foetal distress or another complication is detected, then it's right into a surgical suite for you, Missy. Believe me, if you are having a C-section, there is enough going on to distract you – you won't miss the stereo or cable television for one instant. If you have a C-section, and between 5 and 10 percent of us do, don't waste any time with an over-romanticized longing for the birthing room experience. The truth is, the bed is still hard and crackly, the floor is still covered with industrial-grade linoleum and it's so hard to get an outside line that the telephone is practically useless. Look at it this way: you may not get mood lighting, but you get morphine after delivery and, really, which would you rather have?

The maternity ward

One other difference between delivering vaginally and by C-section is that, since the latter is major surgery, you will need to spend some time in a recovery room where surgical nurses can monitor your blood pressure and other vital signs. After a couple of hours, you will be moved yet again, this time to your real Honeymoon Suite, the room on the maternity ward where you will get to know your baby and recover for a day or two before reentering the real world. Even if you delivered vaginally and without incident in a birthing room, you'll be moved shortly after. Don't get attached to that stereo or the size of the room because you will have to clear out. Be considerate of us mums on trolleys in the corridor, and get a move on.

Maternity wards, like Disneyland, are 'the happiest place on earth'. The heartbeat of the ward is the nursery, with all the beautiful (at least to their mothers) new babies lying in clear plastic bassinetlike beds called *isolettes* and wrapped up so tight they look like papooses.★ There

---

★ Most nurseries in UK hospitals are fairly empty, as more and more mothers opt to keep their baby with them at all times.

may be a little more traffic on this ward than you would normally like, especially during visiting hours, but don't be too quick to complain because these people are usually the new grandparents or close family friends, and to them, in their rapturous state, *all* mothers, including complete strangers, are goddesses. When you are feeling up to it, take a stroll down to the nursery windows where they are lined up peering at the babies; you'll practically get a standing ovation, and, if you point out your little angel in the crowd, you will drown in their exclamations of his or her extraordinary beauty and obvious intelligence. Rarely does motherhood include such moments of congratulation and appreciation, so seek them out and savour them now.

If the hospital has been laid out with any forethought whatsoever, the mums' rooms will be near the nursery. I know there are some exceptions, however, because nine years ago, when my Best Friend Mindy was recovering from the C-section birth of her daughter, one of our bigger earthquakes struck Southern California. Imagine poor Mindy, hunched over her stitches, trying to run to the other end of a fairly large hospital to get to her precious baby in the nursery. I hear they've recently remedied that situation, so I won't embarrass the hospital by naming names. By the way, Mindy made it to her baby's side before the shaking stopped, but you knew she would.

The trend seems to be moving toward semiprivate and private rooms for new mummies. As you can imagine, the rooms have gotten smaller and smaller as they have gotten privater and privater, but that probably won't inconvenience you unless you plan to do a lot of entertaining, which is never a good idea. Actually, privacy is a funny concept in the context of childbirth and recovery. It seems that anyone who is so inclined can come in at any time, whether you are sleeping, breastfeeding or in a coma, and check your sanitary pads and stitches. You will be numbed to this humiliation early on. Now I know why women of childbearing age or older never seem to mind the communal dressing rooms in clothes shops – they lost their modesty during childbirth.

If creature comforts are important to you, there are a few things you can take with you to hospital or ask a partner or Best Friend to pick up. At the top of that list should be your pillow from home. The standard-issue hospital pillow feels like it is stuffed with Styrofoam popcorn and smells like disinfectant. Your own pillow will not only feel softer; it will smell like home, and that can be very reassuring. Just remember to put an old pillowcase (or two) on it because there is a lot of spilling and leaking going on around you right now. If you have a blanket, a throw or a shawl that you love, take that, too. Not only will it be cosy to wrap up in, but it also can look pretty draped over your shoulders when people come to visit. I am an advocate of wearing the bottom-baring gown the hospital gives you until you are ready to go home because any pretty new nightie will soon look like you were slaughtering chickens in it. As I have told you before, that little 'discharge' some books tell you to expect is much more like a flash flood. If you just can't accept this advice and the shawl/blanket idea makes you feel deprived, then consider a bed jacket; that way you'll look lovely from the waist up and keep your frills well above the messy parts. After all, no one will see your legs if you're in bed because the blanket covers them. If you have to stand, simply ask everyone to clear the room. (It's a good way to adjourn the visit anyway.)

The Best Friends agree that it's a good idea to take a comfortable bathrobe and flat-soled slippers (no little black mules with maribou feathers yet!). Consider both of these items in bigger-than-normal sizes. Even though you are no longer pregnant, fluid buildup in your feet can make them look like Fred Flintstone's and your belly will still be large and swollen. In the last fifteen or twenty years, some medical genius decided that getting a woman up and walking soon after delivery speeds her recovery, even if she has had a C-section. Don't be surprised if, just as you were about to gingerly roll over and take a nap, a nurse enthusiastically marches in and announces that it's time for a stroll around the ward. You C-section Best Friends can complain that your incision hurts too much, but chances are she'll just hand you a pillow to hold against your tummy and help hoist you up. Once you're walking, it is actually kind of nice, and most important of all, it helps to stimulate your intestines and bladder to get back to work after the trauma of childbirth. I always forgot between births how hard it was to pee after having a baby. Let's not even talk about making No.2 yet!

Bottled water is another little luxury you might take to your room. The water they leave in those little pitchers beside your bed tastes just like the plastic the pitchers are made of. You will need LOTS of water, especially if you are breastfeeding, so ask someone to pick up a six-pack for you and leave it within arm's reach. Oh, by the way, there is one other beverage you might want to take to the hospital: champagne! We Best Friends admire certain French traditions and one particular favourite is a champagne toast after giving birth. If you have been a temperate pregnant woman, it has probably been a long dry spell since you've tasted the bubbly. Soon after the baby is born, and before your milk comes in, congratulate yourselves on a job well done and thank the heavens for the gift of a perfect baby. The hospitals are so used to this little ritual that they usually even offer to refrigerate your champagne for you if you bring it in when you're in labour. For those of you who have decided that alcohol should play no part in this celebration, you can at least pretend with some sparkling cider or mineral water. Then again, you could go to sleep.

Bring your own hair dryer, Best Friend. Most hospitals offer nothing, and even the most luxurious ones just have those silly wall-mounted dryers that offer about as much wind as it takes to blow out a candle. Unless you were born with thick rich cascading curly hair or Asian-straight floss, your hair will absolutely need to be washed and repaired after labour and delivery. Presentable hair is important for two reasons: it makes you feel refreshed and, more important, it helps you look decent in the billions of photos that will be taken in the next twenty-four hours.

One last item that you will appreciate having on hand is lip balm. Chapped lips are the consequence of all that mouth breathing that you did to get the baby out. Go for the good thick stuff, preferably with little or no scent because the baby will be hyper-sensitive to anything that doesn't smell like Mummy.

Do *Not* Bring Any of the Following:
1. Candles (they are fire hazards).
2. Jewellery, for you or the new baby (it is certain to disappear, probably through your own absentmindedness).
3. Birth announcements or thank-you notes (if you spend one moment of this precious recovery time meeting social obligations, your status as a Best Friend is seriously jeopardized).
4. Any toiletries in glass containers (the bathroom floor and shower are not very cushiony, and your grip may be weaker than you remember).
5. Your favourite pair of old jeans (sorry, you won't be fitting into them for quite some time still).

The Nursery

In most cases, even after a C-section, you will have some time right after birth to count your baby's fingers and toes and introduce yourself. Your midwife may even put the baby on your chest right after she has emerged and before the umbilical cord is cut. Don't be surprised by the gunk she's covered with. Before she has time to get a chill, the midwife will give her a good wiping off and wrap her in a blanket. The midwife will usually weigh and measure the baby in your presence, often while her colleagues are doing any necessary repair work on you or the doctor is closing your C-section. Then the baby seems to disappear.* I have foggy recollections of four births followed by being left alone in the delivery room. The daddy traditionally goes to the nursery with the baby, the doctor traditionally goes home to sleep and the midwives traditionally move on to some other labouring woman who will depend on them for their survival and the same compassion they showed you a couple of hours ago. If you are lucky, the hospital staff will have a bed on the maternity ward ready and waiting for you, and you will be quickly moved to your Honeymoon Suite.

I wondered for the longest time where in the world my husband and the babies went without me after delivery. After our third child, it finally occurred to me to hold tightly to the baby until somebody in charge explained exactly where they were taking him, how long he would be there and what they were going to do to him. This is what a nurse explained to me as she gently loosened my grip on the baby's receiving blanket:

The primary function of the nursery staff is to observe the baby for the first few hours after his birth. Statistically, most serious health problems that are not identified immediately after delivery will become apparent within the first twenty-four hours of life, with the first hour being the most crucial. There are also several tasks to be performed on your little sweetie during his first visit to the nursery. One of the first may be the bath. The babies are usually not cleaned with any water in the delivery room because there is too great a risk that they will get chilled. In the nursery, however, the temperature is nice and toasty, and a nurse will start with the matted hair on their little heads and scrub down to between their itsy-bitsy toes. He or she then gets the standard-issue uniform of newborns: a T-shirt, a disposable nappy and the optional accessories of a knitted cap and booties (often in designer colours of pink for girls and blue for boys). The baby will then be swaddled, which means wrapped up tightly in a blanket with all the corners tucked in. (Haven't you been wondering what that meant ever since they taught you in Sunday School that Jesus was wrapped in swaddling clothes?)

---

* In the UK, your baby is usually with you throughout your hospital stay – unless you ask for a break.

Another procedure that will be performed, and which your baby will find even more annoying than the bath, is the application of antibiotic drops in his eyes.* This is done to kill any stray bacteria that the baby may have picked up as he exited your body, particularly gonorrhoea. Of course we don't mean to imply that you have a sexually transmitted disease, but this is just another example of how hospitals apply rules generally and really don't care to hear one word about why you should be an exception.

I always thought that there was one particular reason why it was just as well that the mothers didn't get wheeled into the nursery with their babies – they wouldn't have to see them get their first shot. Yes, they get a shot of vitamin K at most hospitals, and a blood test! You can make yourself faint by just *thinking* about taking your darling baby to the doctor for his first vaccination in a few weeks. You are most definitely not ready for this kind of trauma right now.

Babies also receive identification bands in the nursery. Most hospitals seem almost fanatical about preventing 'swapped at birth' incidents, and we mothers love them for it. No one does a thing with a baby until they have read the baby's band and your band and established a match. By the time my last (yes, LAST!) baby was born, there was a new procedure in effect. Every baby was tagged with one of those plastic tags that stores put on merchandise to prevent shoplifting. (Don't worry, not the kind with the big tacks in them.) There was a sensor at the entrance to the maternity ward that would sound alarms if any baby was taken through it. That may sound like overkill to some people, but to new parents, it sounds like the greatest invention since the ear thermometer.

After all this poking and prodding, the baby will be put into a clear-sided plastic bassinet and parked alongside all the other new babies. If you walk down to the nursery to look at all the little angels, you may notice some of them sunbathing under glaring contraptions called *bili lights*. This is the standard treatment for babies who are jaundiced and it doesn't hurt a bit (although a tiny pair of Ray•Bans might be cute).

At some hospitals, there is another nursery for babies with health problems that require special attention or treatment called the Neonatal Intensive Care Unit. If your baby should happen to spend time there, just try to be thankful that you have access to such miraculous lifesaving equipment and medical care, and remember, it won't be long before the baby is strong enough to go home with you and keep you awake all night.

---

* This is not common practice in UK hospitals.

ROOMING IN

Most hospitals now allow you to keep your baby with you at all times if you are capable of caring for her yourself; in other words, you're not feverish or high on painkillers. This practice is called *rooming in* and it is quite fashionable for expectant mothers to insist that they will allow nothing but rooming in after their baby is born. I don't want to generalize, at least not on every page, but these rooming-inners are usually the same women who are marching behind the natural child-birth banner. In other words, these are women setting rules and standards based on no actual familiarity with having a baby. Not a good idea.

Give yourself the option of keeping the baby with you all the time or letting the nursery staff care for him while you attend to such luxuries as a bath or sleeping for more than forty-five minutes. We Best Friends implore you to rest as much as you possibly can for your way-too-brief stay in hospital because you will not be allowed to lie down and be cared for again until you have your next baby, and by then you'll be feeling too guilty about the firstborn to enjoy it. You may think that you are fine and that caring for the baby is a breeze, but THIS IS A TRAP! You are high on a cocktail of adrenaline and infatuation, and your baby is going to wake up in a few days, never to close her eyes again (or so it will seem). Your only hope, aside from a full-time nanny, is to hoard sleep now.

One of the most commonly expressed fears mums-to-be have about turning their babies over to the care of the nursery is that the nurses on duty secretly disdain your insistence on breast-feeding and will, disregarding all orders to the contrary, sneak some formula into the little one when the viewing room shades are drawn. I can understand this fear completely, and several of my Best Friends say they have evidence that it is true. Breastfeeding can be hard enough to master, and the last thing you want is a baby who's not really hungry or who is developing a secret preference for the bottle because it's a lot less work for him. In an attempt to cut through the maternal hysteria, I went directly to my Best Friend DeeDee's sister, who just happens to be a nurse in the maternity ward of a large and well-respected hospital. And guess what; IT'S TRUE! but not all the time. According to DeeDee's sister, the babies are often given sterile water from a bottle when they seem to need help quieting down. And, yes, there are nurses who are pained by the thought that a child might be hungry because she and her mum haven't quite got this breastfeeding thing down and who can't resist feeding her on the sly.

So, where does this leave us? If you ask me, nine years after the birth of my first child and three more births after him, I can give you a laundry list of things that can happen to your child that are a lot worse than being slipped a little formula. But I'm jumping ahead, and you're entitled to experience each maternal neurosis for yourself. My only words of wisdom are to make your decision about rooming in after considering your needs as well as the baby's. Remember, no Perfect Mummy Awards are presented until your child has been accepted at Oxbridge, and even then they can be revoked if he eventually flunks out or she becomes a politician, so don't exhaust yourself this early in the game.

Another justification for rooming in is to get to know your baby and to practice your mothering skills within the safety of a medical setting. This is a very wise and pragmatic choice, especially if you allow yourself to send the baby back to the nursery for a few hours if the responsibility is still too much for you. Just thinking about sleeping in a hospital bed with their tiny baby tucked up against them or watching her sleep in her little techno-bed for hours on end can make mothers weep. The wonder and amazement at finally meeting this perfect being is dumbfounding. You can watch her breathe or flutter her eyelashes with the same fascination a football fan reserves for the Super Bowl. And the smell! Your little baby's unique perfume is intoxicating. In fact, my Best Friends with older kids tell me that we will continue to love how our children smell right up until puberty gives them B.O. and stinky sneaker feet . . . but I'm getting off track here.

One of the most compelling reasons to keep your baby with you in your room for long stretches of time is to let the other parent (whom we'll call Daddy for nostalgia's sake) get some significant hands-on time. Newborns can be strange and intimidating to people who haven't handled them before, and Daddy will probably feel much safer if his first experience is under the tolerant supervision of a nurse or doctor. Some people, especially those who happen to be men, feel inhibited about going goo goo over a baby when other people are watching. The privacy of your room can be the perfect setting for Daddy to try out the baby talk and cooing that are probably second nature to you already. One of the most sublime experiences of sharing parenting with someone else, be he or she father, lover, grandparent or therapist, is watching each other watch the baby. For the rest of your life, you will be inspired to nudge someone and say, 'Oh, look at the way she wrinkles her nose when she makes poo poo!' or some other equally poignant observation, and this hospital honeymoon is a nice time to begin.

Other services

Like a good hotel or a Carnival Cruise, your hospital will probably offer other services or activities to make your stay more fulfilling. As soon as you are coherent, ask a nurse whether they offer any infant care classes*, and if they do, limp on down to one. Right now, you don't even know the right questions to ask, let alone the answers, so a class that systematically goes through what the professionals consider the most important information is just what the doctor should have ordered. If Daddy can come, too, better still because you can't possibly remember everything in your condition (or ever again, for that matter). Besides, he is expected to carry his weight in this parenting thing, too. Go through the channels on the television in your room, too, because many hospitals offer something like a Baby Channel that is full of all sorts of pertinent information.

If you intend to breastfeed your baby, you might find the assistance of a Lactation Specialist tremendously valuable. I don't want to be Eeyore here, but you shouldn't be surprised if breastfeeding is more difficult that you imagined it would be. I, personally, am astonished that the human race has survived this long depending on all mothers to know instinctively how to suckle a baby. I found breastfeeding as frustrating as learning to ride a bike and much more painful. Thank heavens for the maternity and lactation nurses who insisted I keep taking my nipple out of my babies' mouths and reinsert it until I finally got them to 'latch on' properly. I thank them even more for warning me in advance not to try to take a baby off my breast by pulling away without first breaking the suction by sticking my finger in his mouth. These knowledgeable people will also give you numbers to call after you've gone home because some of the most exciting breastfeeding emergencies occur long after you've left the hospital.

A hospital service that is not so crucial, but appreciated nonetheless, is a photographer who takes those kitschy newborn pictures. They are

* Less common in UK hospitals, although baby care is usually covered in antenatal classes, and a midwife may show you how to bath and change your baby. Help with feeding is also on hand.

wonderful to have because your newborn will never look that way again. The pointy head, the splotchy skin and the swollen eyes will soon disappear and, if you have more children, chances are that you will have to read your notes on the back of the photo to identify which baby is in the picture. So great is our rapture with our own babies that we almost universally fail to see them as anything short of beautiful. It is that intoxication that inspires some of us to use the hospital newborn picture on our birth announcement. If this is what you choose to do, we Best Friends unanimously applaud your decision, but trust us when we tell you that your baby will be *even more beautiful* in a few weeks, hint, hint.

Before you leave hospital, ask whether they have a 'hot line' that you can call if you have questions or concerns after you get home. Many hospitals and birthing centres have advisers taking phone calls twenty-four hours a day to help new parents. Not every 'crisis' requires a sprint to the doctor. Sometimes reassurance and advice are all the medicine you need, and both are readily dispensed by these hot lines. Best of all, they have a direct-dial number so that you don't have to go through the hospital switchboard when it's 3:00 A.M., your baby has a rash and both of you are crying.

visitors

There is absolutely no way you can know in advance how you will feel about having visitors after the baby is born. Some women love having people come by, particularly if they bring gifts or flowers! They love hearing the congratulations and revel in telling their very own delivery room story. If this is how you feel, then have yourself a party because there is no better reason to celebrate than the birth of a baby.

Many other women feel anxious, overwhelmed or disappointed about their birthing experience. The last thing they want at this moment is to have to put on a party face and amuse guests. There is such anticipation and expectation leading up to delivery, and when it's over lots of women feel let down or just plain tired and sore. People will understand if you don't receive guests until you are feeling better, and if they don't, who cares?

Daddy plays a crucial role in this visitors scenario. He should be in charge of all traffic control. He can be the master of ceremonies for those of you who feel like partying. He can call people and invite them to come by, he can pass out cigars or whatever substitute is politically correct and he can try to round up more chairs for your visitors because most rooms have only one. If you feel like being quiet, he can answer the phone for you and pretend that you are sleeping when you're not in the mood to talk. He can keep a lookout in the hallways to make sure that no surprise drop-ins are approaching. Keep your door closed and let him explain that you are learning to breastfeed right now and can't be disturbed. If he's really good at his job, he might even be able to keep your mother-in-law or mother out of sight, but not for long.

souvenirs

Before you check out, take some time to ask someone with authority which 'stuff' you are allowed to take home with you.★ Be assured that all the toiletries, from bedpan to mouthwash, will be billed to you whether you use them or not, so take them. Some of the most immediately valuable supplies that hospitals often provide are water bottles to rinse your sore little vagina (especially after going to the bathroom if even the expensive toilet paper feels as rough as an S.O.S. pad), Dermaplast or some other topical anaesthetic spray to squirt on your privates when those paracetamols aren't quite enough, some good strong (prescription, maybe?) haemorrhoid cream and/or suppositories and if you are lucky enough to have been given a donut pillow to sit on, throw that sucker right into the suitcase without even asking permission. (It's so humiliating to have to go buy one in your local pharmacy.)

Even if you have brought a 'going home' outfit for the baby to wear, ask if you own the little T-shirt and blanket that he wore in the hospital because they make good keepsakes. Nappy bags, albeit made entirely of vinyl and emblazoned with the name of the hospital or some formula manufacturer, are also common give-aways. I've even heard of hospitals giving away infant car seats, but I'm sure that the cost is buried somewhere else, like in the $10 box of tissues.

The single most important thing you can take home from the hospital, aside from the baby, of course, is the nasal aspirator.† This is the little rubber bulb, often blue, that you use to suck mucous out of the baby's nose, and it's a marvellous thing. It's not until you actually have a baby that you realize that he can't blow his nose or even sniffle yet. The only relief for his stuffy nose must be provided by you. Yes,

★ Most NHS hospitals do not give away a great deal, due to their methods of funding.
† Not common in the UK.

you can buy a nasal aspirator at most drugstores, but the ones at the hospital are usually better.

Another thing to stock up on is a package or three of the obstetrical pads* many nurseries use to clean the baby during a nappy change. Here's something else about baby care that nobody told you about during pregnancy: you don't use nappy wipes on newborns because the chemicals are too irritating to their skin. A clean flannel that has been dipped in tepid water works great, but the clothlike paper squares called obstetrical pads are even better. They are soft on the baby's bottom, but they are thrown away after they are used. Remember, you will be changing a lot of nappies, and who needs to be washing all those flannels?

If your baby is a little boy and if he was circumcised, you will also need a good supply of gauze squares to protect his penis until it heals. You can get them easily enough at the drugstore, but you never know how long it will be before you feel like doing any shopping. Might as well take those, too, if you can get your hands on some.

The Paperwork†

As you might expect, no human being is allowed to enter this universe, at least not the United States part of it, without being documented. The delivering doctor will begin the process of registering your tiny human when he fills out the certificate of live birth. Then later, when you are in your room, several papers will be given to you to fill out. Don't feel that you have to do all this paperwork now; it can be taken home and completed. Just don't throw it into your suitcase without looking at it because you may be inadvertently packing your breakfast order form, and don't lose it because you will live to rue the day.

The paperwork that is of the most immediate concern is all the stuff that has to be signed before you are allowed to leave the hospital. The biggest concerns seem to be:

1. Whether you understand the fundamental rules about caring for a newborn (which includes being able to demonstrate that you have a car seat to take her home in), and
2. Who is going to pay for all this?

---

* Not common in the UK.

† You are free to discharge yourself at any time after the birth, but should take medical advice before doing so. You must register your child's birth before he or she is six weeks old. When you have registered the birth, your child will be given an NHS number.

Fortunately for you, this part of childbirth is traditionally handled by Daddy or someone else authorized to act on your behalf, so you can relax while he wanders around trying to find the person to release you.

Did you know that you also need to get a Social Security number for your little darling in order to declare him a dependent on your tax returns? Gone are the days of relative anonymity from the IRS until you got your first job. Uncle Sam wants your baby, and he wants him now! You will also need the baby's Social Security number to open a savings account in his name, always a wise move if you have the kind of family that understands the charm of cash gifts for birthdays, brises, christenings and so on. Some states make registering with Social Security easy by letting you apply for it by checking a box on the form for the Certificate of Live Birth. Others require that you apply separately. Just what you will need this first year, an excuse to go wait in lines at the federal building nearest you. Ask your nurse if she can give you the forms.

Well, you're about ready to leave this little bubble. It's been way too short, I know, but the real adventure awaits you at home. Besides, the honeymoon is over, Best friend.

2

GOING HOME

Going home with your new little family unit is thrilling. You have been waiting for this moment for nine (ten) months, and you are probably eager to begin this new chapter of your life. You get to do terrific things like show the baby her room, introduce her to the beloved family dog (not too close, please), lay her on your bed and take her picture and try out the rocking chair that wasn't in your budget but you bought anyway. You will feel as if you've been away forever and the siren song of your own bed and your own refrigerator will be calling to you. I just hope that you have asked a couple of Best Friends to put fresh sheets on the former and several casseroles in the latter because, once you get home, you won't leave again for several days if you can help it. That also means that someone other than you should dash out to the store to stock up on such things as nappies, sanitary pads, bottled water, toilet paper, juice and tabloid newspapers (the preferred reading of every overweight, overtired and housebound new mother).

Going home with your baby is like moving into a cocoon and sealing the silks up behind you. It will be quite some time before you feel a part of the outside world. Its rhythm won't be yours, its concerns won't be yours and its citizens' germs certainly won't be yours, if you have any say in the matter. If you don't feel like having visitors during this cocooning period, you are completely normal and well within your rights. You may need to devote all your attention to getting to know this new human being who has settled in your midst, without having to make yourself presentable or offering a little something to eat to guests. You need to rest, recover and adjust for the next couple of weeks, so put your Filofax in the drawer and let the answering machine take all calls, at least until you are down to using only one sanitary pad at a time. We'll get back to you later in chapter 5, 'Blue, Baby, Blue' to let you know when too much cocooning is too much of a good thing.

Making Your Getaway

Let us warn you right now that the process of going home from the hospital will take you much longer than you could ever have imagined. You can see why when you read this list of the typical events leading up to walking in your own front door:

1. You will need to shower and get dressed.

If you haven't taken a shower since the baby was born, take our word for it when we say it feels great, but it can leave you exhausted. Allow an extra half hour in this part of the progression to allow for falling asleep wet on the bed or for trying not to faint after touching your swollen and stitched labia. (Better still, don't touch anything down there for a few more days.)

If you feel up to putting on makeup and styling your hair, knock yourself out. If you don't, at least try to dry your hair and consider a little under-eye concealer and/or lipstick. We are not suggesting this because we care one way or another how you look; we love you no matter what. It's just that you will have your picture taken many times, and you might not appreciate having a whole photo album in which you look like Poppin' Fresh. A discernable mouth couldn't hurt.

A new mother's thermostat is out of whack for several weeks after the baby is born, and the most common indication of that is perspiration. It might be a good idea to wear a soft cotton knit fabric home from the hospital because it is likely that you will work up a serious sweat just dressing yourself.

2. You will need to get the baby ready.

If dressing yourself didn't make you sweat, dressing the baby is sure to. Truth be told, you really *don't* have to put a special outfit on the baby; she wouldn't mind at all if you just let her stay in the familiar stuff the hospital gave her. But that's no fun! So we start in with the bodysuit, the stretch sleepsuit, the sweaters, the hats, the booties and so on. All the while we are excruciatingly nervous about breaking the baby's neck, touching the soft spot on top of her head or dislocating her arms as we struggle to slip them into sleeves. Here's my secret for dressing the baby and not stressing out: have your mother or mother-in-law do it for you. They know what they are doing and they will love having the chance for a closer baby inspection.

3. You will need to find a porter.

No matter how terrific you may feel or how much you hate feeling like a spectacle, you may not be allowed to walk out of hospital. You may be paraded out in a wheelchair.* You can try to argue about it if you want, but that's usually about as fruitful as trying to talk a meter maid out of giving you a parking ticket. The hospital's insurance policy may require that they make every effort to keep you from falling down or dropping the baby while you are still on their property. That means wheelchair. Not just anyone can push you in that wheelchair, either. That job belongs to the porter or nurse's aide. Before you start complaining too bitterly, look around your room and notice how much junk you have to take home with you. There's no way your partner can carry your suitcase, your nappy bag, your pillow, your handbag, your flowers and your sheaf of papers by himself, and your arms will be full of baby (by the way, ALL outings will feel like this for a while). So your challenge is twofold: not only must you locate an available wheelchair, but you must also find one with a legitimate operator attached. There always seemed to be ten other new mums checking out and one wheelchair on the days that I was leaving with my babies. Allow up to an hour for this part of the progression.

4. You will need to feed the baby.

Even if you have only a five-minute car ride home from the hospital, it will be the longest five minutes of your life if you have a crying, hungry baby in the car with you. Since check-out day often coincides with the day the baby decides to wake up and have a good meal, you cannot expect him to stay satisfied and full for any extended period of time. I don't care how many people tell you that a baby will usually go for two to three hours between feeds; that rule doesn't apply today! Consider feeding your baby in the car before you get all strapped into car seats and seat belts and BEFORE THE CAR MOVES EVEN ONE INCH! Once he's full, he just might sleep the whole ride home.

5. You will need your pain medication.

I've seen those TV commercials where the brand-new mothers say that, after their C-section, their doctors gave them paracetamol for the

† This is not the case in the UK.

pain, and I want to yell at them, 'You foolish wimp!' I speak for myself here, but the only thing sold without a prescription that would have relieved my pain would have been a mallet. The jostling of the car ride can be more uncomfortable than you expected, and sitting there in the backseat, hovering over your little baby, can make you a tad sore, too. If you are, indeed, taking something for pain relief (I must show my integrity here by adding that this should only be under the supervision of your doctor, whether the medication is prescription or over-the-counter), make sure that you have taken one (or two) at least forty-five minutes before leaving the hospital. Unlike the baby's feeds, most pain medication *can* be relied upon to last for two to three hours.

6. You will need a car seat.

I don't mean to hammer this nail to death, but it is truly so important to put your baby in a car seat AND to position the car seat correctly that I am willing to annoy you for a moment. No hospital should allow a baby out of its care without first making sure that the parents have a suitable car seat in working order and that it is fastened properly in the seat belt, but I'm going to walk you through it one more time because the stakes are very high and humans are prone to err.

By suitable car seat, I mean one that is designed for newborns. Remember, tiny little babies cannot sit upright and they cannot support the weight of their own heads. They need seats that keep them in a semi-reclining position. Do us all a favour and read the manual that comes with the seat BEFORE you use it for the first time; they are more complicated than you'd think. In fact, it wouldn't hurt to install the car seat, or its base if it's the pop-out kind, before the baby is born and get familiar with it without the stress of a tiny, fragile baby strapped in. Of tremendous importance is knowing exactly how the car's seat belt fastens to the car seat. I am constantly amazed by how many competent and intelligent people run the seat belts through the car seats in such a way that they prevent the car-seat safety belt from automatically locking in the event of a fast stop. Another common mistake is failing to use any clips the manufacturer has provided to connect the shoulder and lap belts before running them through the car seat. Not all car seats require this, but if yours does and you have thrown the clip away with the packaging, there is a chance that the car seat will shift or tip when you turn sharply or stop.

Infants must always sit facing the back of the car, no matter how much you think they would prefer seeing the scenery as it approaches rather than as it leaves. Keep in mind, they are brand-new and don't yet know they have options. (A good habit to establish right from the beginning is, don't feel obligated to consult your children about everything. Sometimes there is only one way and it's Mum's way.) If your car has passenger-side air bags, DO NOT PUT YOUR CHILD IN THE PASSENGER SEAT. As a frantic mother, I know how irresistible it will be to put your baby up front beside you so that you can talk to him and encourage him to breathe, but you'd have to live under a rock not to know by now that the explosion of an inflating air bag can seriously injure a baby or small child. Put the baby in the backseat, preferably in the middle, and install an extra rearview mirror on the inside of your wind screen so that you can keep an eye on the top of his head. If you get really concerned about the baby, you can always reach back and hold your hand above his nose to feel his breath. If that doesn't give you reassurance, pull over and take a look. (If desperate, you *could* also give his hair a gentle little motherly tug and see if you can make him whimper a bit, but I'm not suggesting anything.)

7. You will need a spit-up cloth.

Have a barf towel or blanket at the ready. Remember, you probably just fed the little one before leaving the hospital, and a burp is inevitable, especially in this new semi-sitting posture. If the baby spits up, don't get too alarmed (yes, I KNOW this entire journey is like Disneyland's Mr. Toad's Wild Ride, but this spitting up should barely register on the Richter scale of a new mother's quaking life). Spitting up does not generally mean that the baby is car-sick and that you will have to walk her the rest of the way home. Clean her up and carry on. By the way, feel free to use this cloth to dab at any tears rolling down your face; they're sanitary enough.

8. You will need a dummy.

Hysterical crying, however, can have significant seismic influence on the Mummy Richter scale. No parent, especially a brand-new one, is humanly capable of continuing to drive a car in a focused and calm manner with a wailing little creature piercing his or her eardrums from the backseat. If you need to pull over to regain your composure, by all means do so. The first thing the 'baby attendant' should do is try out one of those dummies that you swore you'd never use but bought because your Best Friends insisted. Put it in the baby's mouth with the flattened part of the tear up against the roof of the baby's mouth, since that's how nature intended them to suck on your breast. You will have to be somewhat forceful at this stage because they will not just open their mouths in joyous anticipation of the dummy; they will initially see it as an intrusion since they are probably still uninitiated into the calming, soothing feeling that sucking on one of those little things can magically provide Admit it, even now, at your age, an occasional tug on the old dummy sounds rather lovely . . . but I digress. If you have succeeded in getting the dummy into the baby's mouth and she is sucking away like a little grouper, you might have peace and calm for the rest of the ride home. I don't know why, but most experienced Best Friends gently tap the end of the dummy with their fingertip if the baby seems to be losing interest in the thing. Perhaps making it vibrate makes it more attractive to the baby or maybe the mothers are just manifesting some primordial need to make a physical connection with everything that goes into a new-born's mouth. Let's just call it a 'Mummy Thing'; you know, like preferring to hold an infant with its head over your left breast or knowing just the right cadence to bop or sway a fussy baby into a sleeping baby.

One last note about dummies, at least for the time being: just because you have soothed your newborn with a dummy during a single car ride does not mean that your baby will ultimately become one of those timid four-year-olds who are so dependent on one that they look like they have been corked until their vintage matures. All four of my kids had dummies while I breastfed them; otherwise I would have had them gnawing on my very sore nipples twenty-four hours a day. If they weren't hungry, I was very grateful to have a chance to air-dry my beleaguered boobies – maybe even button my shirt up for the first time all day. Anyway, all four gave up the dummies when they moved on to milk or formula in a bottle. Of course, getting them to give up the bottles was no day at the beach, but, hey, you won't have to face that particular challenge for another couple of years. Besides, if you DO find yourself with a four-year-old who needs a dummy, you'll have gained a tolerance and wisdom by then to understand that anything a child can do in this crazy world to make it more hospitable, short of petty crimes and drug use, is a gift from God.

9. You will need self-control.

If the baby is still wailing, it might be time to feed the little thing. Even if you just fed her as you were checking out of the hospital, she may need to have her tank topped up. Digestion in little babies is amazingly quick, particularly if they are breastfed, and this is way too early to be thinking about feeding your baby on any schedule other than the one she improvises from hour to hour.

The first thing you must do is STOP THE CAR. A little privacy is nice and some shade is always appreciated, but any safe parking position will do. You must stop the car because you will need to take the baby out of the car seat to feed her properly, whether it's by bottle or breast, and YOU MUST NEVER TAKE THE BABY OUT OF THE CAR SEAT WHEN THE CAR IS MOVING, NO MATTER HOW DESPERATE SHE IS TO BE PICKED UP. A CHILD IS NEVER SAFE IN HER MOTHER'S ARMS WHILE THE CAR IS MOVING, NO MATTER HOW CAREFUL AND PROTECTIVE YOU MIGHT FEEL. As a matter of fact, your baby could be more seriously harmed in the event of a collision by Mummy's body providing more 'thrust' than the baby's own body would have if it were just lying unrestrained on the seat. You know we Best Friends almost never boss you around or lecture you, but an exception must be made here because nearly every day I *still* see women in the front seats of cars with babies or toddlers on their laps, mistakenly trusting that they're safe if they are sharing the adult seat belt. WRONG!!!

After you have come to a halt, liberate the baby for a good cuddle and a snack. For obvious reasons, they will greatly prefer this position to the infant car seat, but after eating and having their nappy checked, they may be ready enough for a nap that you can successfully put them back into their space capsule for a quiet ride home. While you have the baby out of the car seat, check her head and hands. We all have an irresistible impulse to wrap our babies so warmly that any climate outside of the Arctic feels like a sauna to them. Loosen or peel off a layer or two and see if that provides relief. Your little honey might have been crying simply because she was feeling steamier than a Turkish bath. Between you and me, I would consider taking the little knit cap off her sweaty head, but my mother-in-law finds this akin to child abuse, so leave the cap and booties on and strip the baby down to her nappy and undershirt if the temperature is above seventy degrees. I should add, however, that all my kids were born in Southern California and I realize some of our traditions border on ridiculous, so feel free to reject my advice out of hand.

If you've tried everything and nothing will convince this little being to relax into her perfectly engineered car seat that snaps out and becomes a baby carrier, then you are going to have to suck it up and get through this bit of bumpy road with the help of your cool head and inner reserve of calm. PUT THE BABY BACK IN THE CAR SEAT. Then, take a swig from the water bottle that should always be within reach for the next year, because you must be parched by now. Take a deep breath and repeat this mantra: 'Crying never killed anyone, crying never killed anyone.' It certainly won't do anything to the baby but make him tired (which is a good thing), and while it may give you a migraine and reduce you to uncontrollable weeping, you, too, will survive.

Turn on the radio. Melodic classical music may help relax the tension that has turned your shoulders into cast iron and shrunk your neck by several inches. Louder rock music might actually calm the baby since they instinctively react to harsh droning noises, like vacuum cleaners and hair dryers, by going right to sleep. This is known in the trade as the 'shutdown mechanism'. Keep it in mind for any inconsolable crying that may pop up in the next few weeks. Many a screaming baby has fallen into angelic slumber when Mum wore him in a front carrier and started vacuuming energetically.

If you and your partner (whom I will assume is probably driving) feel certain that you have recovered your wits sufficiently to continue, then resume driving home. Look at it this way: you can't just live in your car, so you may as well bite the bullet and forge on to the promised land full of things like cribs, food, a clean and familiar bathroom, and if you're lucky, a grandma or other pair of loving arms (be they related to you by blood or hired through the nanny grapevine) standing in the doorway, eager to take that fussy baby into her arms, coo to her and smell every delicious inch of her.

10. You will need confidence.

At some point during your journey from hospital to home, you will be struck by the certainty that you know more about lubricating a car than you do about caring for a baby. Suddenly, you will feel your neck tingle and your hairline moisten with perspiration. This is a mistake! You can't be trusted with this baby! And as ignorant as you may be, chances are your partner is even worse! Quick, turn the car around; you can drop the baby off at casualty and speed away before the police find you!

Here is the truth, Best Friend: you may not know much, but you know all that you need to know today, and tomorrow you will know more, and still more with every day that comes. Get used to this feeling of being on the verge of out of control because it's a chronic state for parents. You are never really prepared for any situation; you just learn to go with your gut, ask for advice and make it up as you go. (Not to mention the ferocious fights you'll occasionally have with your partner over parenting styles!) That's why grandmothers are often better mothers to our children than we are; they got their learner's permits with their own children, and now, with the arrival of our kids they are fully licensed.

Take a deep breath and a sip of the water that you should be carrying in your car or changing bag at all times. You are going to be magnificent. Your baby is going to think you are the centre of the universe. You're a hero. You'll do what's best as often as anybody else does (and any gaps you leave eventually will be filled in by your child's therapist). YOU ARE SOMEONE'S MOTHER!!!

Before you walk into your home with your new baby, stop and mentally photograph this house or apartment building so that you can keep it in your heart forever. In this mobile society of ours, there's a good chance that your child will not live in this place till he goes away to college. You may move two or three more times during his childhood, especially if you find you like this mothering business and have more kids. But this will always be Bethlehem to you, the place where your family was born. You may not know it yet, but your most precious memories are about to be created here, and in years to come you will have forgotten if it had bad plumbing or funny shag carpeting. It's where you brought your first child. Welcome home, Best Friend.

3

ASSESSing the Damage

'I Feel Like I've Been Hit by a Truck!'

OUCH! It really does hurt to have a baby, doesn't it?! Throughout your pregnancy, you had a pretty good idea that getting the baby from inside of you to outside of you was going to be problematical, but I'll bet even on your most hysterical days you didn't imagine that there would be so much stretching, bruising, tearing and bleeding. These are the small details that we veterans reserve for *after* you have the baby. If we had told you before, you would have spent your entire pregnancy trying to find an escape clause. But now you're in the thick of it and you don't have to waste any energy anticipating the worst because it has already happened. Of course, the best has happened, too, because you now have your beautiful, perfect baby, but let's get back to *you* for a minute or two. If labour and delivery have left you none the worse for wear, congratulations. It happens. My Best Friend Sondra had her daughter, took a shower in the hospital and then went home to cook a big breakfast for all her family, much to the annoyance of the rest of us. But if you feel like you'll never be able to pick up all the pieces of your body and assemble them into anything even resembling your former self, the Best Friends are here to help you appraise the damage and begin the repairs. This is just a cursory evaluation. We will deal much more specifically with the various aspects of your recovery as we move through the rest of this *Guide*.

Inventory: From Top to Bottom

Your Head

Start with your head, since it is surprisingly one of the most victimized parts of your postnatal body. Your hair, of course, is a mess, but you will probably have the chance to wash it sometime before you leave hospital, and it doesn't really become an issue for several more months, when it starts falling out in clumps. But more about that later. Many of my Best Friends noticed their faces swelling up like Cabbage Patch dolls in the first twelve hours after delivery. Their cheeks got even rounder than before and their eyes were so puffy that they had no peripheral vision. My poor Best Friend Monique thought she was going to explode, and no one bothered to reassure her that she wouldn't spend the rest of her life looking like a float in the Macy's Thanksgiving Day Parade. I know, I know, you're supposed to start *losing* water weight after having a baby, and you will, but just not for another day or so. In the meantime, every time someone dressed in white passes by your hospital room, beg them to bring you two ice packs; one for between your legs and one to put over your eyes. Better still, ask your mother or partner to bring you some of those blue gel ice packs (prefrozen, of course) in a small cooler to keep by your bed. When you get home, plastic bags of frozen peas work great to bring down swelling.

The eyes can be delivery casualties in another way. My sister-in-law and Best Friend, Janet, pushed so hard to get one of her sons out that she broke blood vessels in the whites of her eyes. With the red eyeballs and the general swelling and bruising, she looked just like some friend of Lestat. (★There, I've told you one of my scary delivery stories. I have been waiting ten months to get to shock you with it, but I wanted to be a good Best Friend and wait until you could handle it.)

Keep in mind that little blood vessels and capillaries are concentrated on your face, too, and you may notice that you have constellations of these little starbursts on both your cheeks. For now, use a good concealer. Later, most of the spots will clear up, and those that don't can be easily zapped into oblivion by a dermatologist.

As full of water as your facial tissues may be, your lips and mouth will almost certainly be as dry as old loafers. You are deprived of water from the minute you enter the hospital, so it may have been hours since you've had anything cool and wet to drink. And those of you who remembered and used various breathing techniques in a valiant attempt at pain management probably now find yourselves with lips so cracked they threaten to curl up and fall right off your face. Keep a good lip balm at your side so that you can apply it to your lips whenever you happen to glance at it. Even more important, get someone to bring you something to drink. I particularly loved fruit juice that first day because it helped get my blood sugar level back up after hours of hard work and no food.

At this point, we have to ask, 'Have a headache, Best Friend?' If you do, it surely isn't a surprise, what with having endured labour, not eating for countless hours, receiving pain medication that can leave you with a hangover headache, and then there's the small matter of becoming someone's mother, which can be a migraine in itself. Sleep and food are our first prescriptions, but fluids are right up there, too, because you will be waging a constant battle against dehydration throughout your recovery and longer if you breastfeed, and the first sign of dehydration is usually a headache. If you didn't have the foresight to bring your own water and snacks to the hospital with you, send a friend or relative out immediately for a supply. Send your partner only as a last resort because he, too, is probably very hungry, and he may not be able to resist the temptation to sit down to a nice breakfast for himself in the hospital cafeteria before bringing you a measly cereal bar and a banana after he has had his third refill of coffee.

NOTE: If you have had a Caesarean delivery, you will be taking your meals through an IV, then moved gently from liquids to solids as your intestines get over the trauma. You may be hungry, but if you're lucky, you'll be too medicated to notice.

You know that thick head of hair that pregnancy gave you? Let's see, how can I break this to you gently? It isn't yours to keep. Mother Nature has yet another practical joke up her sleeve: she makes your hair fall out in clumps, usually when you are most discouraged by your looks anyway. It happens at different times to different women, but sometime between next week and next year, you may find your hairbrush beginning to look like a puppy or that you have to get your shower drain snaked a lot more often than before. While the fallout can seem massive, relax; you won't go bald, I promise. In fact, some of my Best Friends lost clumps at a time and my keen eye couldn't notice any difference in their appearance. That's because you are not really going bald; your body is just releasing the hair follicles that it held on to so tightly during pregnancy. In other words, those weren't your follicles, anyway. They were the baby's. Expect to go back to the same volume of hair that you had in your prepregnancy days. Anything more dramatic than that could signal some other problem, like a vitamin deficiency, and you need to speak to your doctor about that right away.

While it is fair to assume that you won't be robbed of your hair's original volume, any other assumptions about your hair after having a baby are ill-advised. I would guess that one out of three mothers I know insists that her hair used to be blond and turned brown in pregnancy, or that her hair was straight as a board until the baby came and now it's curly, or any other imaginable variation on that theme. They aren't crazy; it really happened. Unfortunately for me, I never ended up with a halo of ringlets or straight flaxen hair. All I have noticed is that my roots show up more quickly (even though I am capable of living with them for disgraceful periods of time) and I never seem to have a good haircut when I need one.

The source of greatest discomfort for your head right about now is probably the emotional whiplash you are feeling. One minute you are euphoric over your accomplishment, then you are besotted by your adoration for the darling little angel heaven has dropped in your lap, then you come crashing from those highs with feelings of certainty that you will never be able to keep track of where you have laid the baby down, let alone be able to nurture it into an Olympic gold medallist or Oxbridge graduate. And I haven't even mentioned that nagging little voice in the back of your head that says, 'I've changed my mind. I've changed my mind. I've changed my mind.' This emotional fracas is so vast and varied that we Best Friends discuss it more thoroughly in later chapters. In the meantime, suffice it to say, you are registering high on the normal-meter if you have more personalities than Roseanne right about now. It's chemical, it's hormonal and it's rational, in its own charmingly irrational way, so don't fight nature; She always wins.

Your Neck and Shoulders

Lots of us Best Friends carry our tension in our neck and shoulders under the best of circumstances. That proclivity is compounded after childbirth by sleeping in a hospital bed with one of those cardboard pillows (if you ignored us when we told you to bring your own), holding a newborn that seems more fragile than Dresden china, learning to breastfeed her (or not), not to mention the slightly higher level of stress you might be feeling right now. One of the kindest things your partner could do for you now, and for the next several years, is learn to give a good shoulder massage. Inspire him to take it seriously by suggesting that it may enhance the eventual recovery of your libido.

I'm sure you can still recall that particular quirk in heterosexual men of doing nearly anything to get sex. Remember when you were dating and he told you he loved spending Sunday mornings shopping at flea markets, then dropped them for football games as soon as you started having sex with him on a regular basis? Well, he's horny again like he hasn't been since then, so see if the concept still applies.

Your Spine

If you had 'back labour' (and you women know who you are), then I don't even have to begin to tell you about how sore your spine must be right about now. Some women had their babies pushing so hard against their backs that their tailbones were painfully bruised. These tailbone injuries can take months to fully heal, so don't be shocked if it is still annoying you by the time the baby is learning to crawl. IT WILL EVENTUALLY GO AWAY COMPLETELY. Other new mums feel a more general sense of backache after hours of the twisting and pulling on the connective tissue of their spine during labour. The Best Friends suggest that you visit an osteopath or a chiropractor sometime in the next few weeks. (Of course my Best Friend Mindy's brother, who also happens to be my Best Friend MaryAnn's husband, *is* a chiropractor, so we would recommend one for nearly any ailment, but I'm just giving full disclosure here.) In the meantime, any of the over-the-counter anti-inflammatories gives a lot of relief. Even better is stretching, and you can begin to do that right this very second, if you start slowly and gently.

Your Breasts

For the first several hours after giving birth, you will have the same large breasts you had at the end of pregnancy. You may notice a little colostrum leaking, but you might not. Either way, don't expect to see milk yet, because it isn't there. If you are giving breastfeeding a try, this is a nice time to get a compassionate nurse to show you proper 'latching on' techniques. Don't let her forget to tell you how to 'latch off' because pulling a sucking baby away from the breast results in a nipple that is stretched several freakish inches and then released with a snap. It will be a toss-up who will be more startled and cry louder, you or your baby. Practise and have fun now, before the baby is old enough to be really hungry and before the 'Milkman' comes and turns your breasts into unmanageable aliens.

On the second or third day after delivery, the 'Milkman' arrives, and he never comes unnoticed. First you may experience tingling in your breasts, almost like you need to scratch *inside* your skin. This sensation will be compounded by the feeling that your breasts are becoming progressively warmer and warmer until you are surprised they're not serving hot chocolate. While these symptoms may sound dramatic, they are small potatoes compared with the change in the size of your breasts. In as little time as a couple of hours, your breasts can and probably will nearly double in size. If you are fair skinned, you will clearly see the major vein networks and may be able to distinguish the milk ducts leading to your nipples. If you are brave enough to firmly run a finger down a milk duct, by the time you get to the nipple you'll probably have milk coming out. If you grew up on a dairy farm, you would recognize this technique as 'milking'. I remember finally falling into a deep sleep the day after one of my babies (who can remember which at this point?) was born. I awoke from a delicious nap to find two growths the size of regulation footballs on my chest, and they felt like they were alive! At the bottom of my old stationery drawer, hidden in a box with a key lock, are two photographs my husband took of me learning to breastfeed my older son (oh yeah, that's which baby it was!), and I swear to you my breast has a circumference at least three inches bigger than the poor little thing's head. I don't care how hungry I got; I would never have had the nerve to go eye to eye with that monster!

As shocking as that was, still greater was the discovery that breast milk doesn't come out of a hole at the tip of your nipple, like on a baby bottle. IT COMES OUT OF SEVERAL HOLES ALL AROUND THE NIPPLE, LIKE A RAINBIRD SPRINKLER! Now, how on earth did I live thirty-four years as a woman and not know this? Guess what else, no other first-time mother of my acquaintance knew either. I think the only person who was more freaked out than I was was my husband, who had had it up to here with the distortion of his favourite toys.

The 'Milkman's' arrival is referred to in the lingo as 'your milk coming in'. And while it is a good thing because your little baby is beginning to wake up and smell the milk shake, it can easily lead to too much of a good thing, which is called 'engorgement'. While this condition does not befall every new mother, it is common enough to deserve our attention. Engorgement happens when your breasts swell with both water retention and the sudden production of milk that is now trapped in all the ducts leading through your breasts to your nipples. This swelling can get so intense that the breasts feel more a part of Mount Rushmore than of your body. If you don't manage to get rid of some of that milk soon, you are going to become very uncomfortable. Chances are you and your baby don't have this breastfeeding business completely mastered yet, and the challenge will be to get the baby to rescue you from engorgement by sucking off as much as its tiny tummy will hold. This can be difficult, but we have some tips and tricks for you in the feeding chapter. If you are starting to fill up, call for a nurse or phone a lactation consultant because you need specific guidance AND YOU NEED IT NOW!

Your Belly

I know, I know. Your belly looks like a big lump of risen bread dough. It's still fat, but you might think it looks worse than when you were pregnant because at least then it was pulled taut and smooth, and now it's all lumpy and folded over. Don't cry, Best Friend, because this will improve with every day. (At least until that last ten pounds, when you must do crunches and sit-ups like a madwoman to ever even *think* about trying on a pair of hip-hugging trousers.)

If you had a C-section, your belly will have this lumpy consistency *and* an incision along the top of your pubic hair. You might notice that the skin looks yellowish underneath the dressings, but don't be alarmed because this is simply the stain from the Betadine solution they used before making the incision. C-sections can be closed with stitches, clamps or staples. I myself had staples, and I can tell you that as Gothic as they looked, they were removed a day or two later and that part didn't hurt a bit. It's probably safe to bet that the other closures are about the same.

Not only does your belly look pretty bad, but it might be tender, too. Since you have absolutely no muscle tone in your abdomen, your tummy is at the complete mercy of gravity. If you roll onto one side, there goes your belly, falling onto the bed beside you like a beanbag. If you had a C-section, you really must keep this gravity thing in mind because it can hurt a lot to do anything that tugs at that incision. Just lay a pillow over your tummy and remember to press the pillow against you gently whenever you stand, roll to your side or, most critically, when you cough or sneeze. The counterpressure helps tremendously, especially if you *believe* it will. Besides, there is little else you can do until it's time for your pain medication.

Your 'Privates'

The ordeal of passing a baby out of your body by way of your vagina takes an astonishing toll on those fragile parts. For years, we have protected that area: kept it out of the sun, dressed it in fresh underwear every day, powdered it after a bath, refused to let it be touched by anyone we didn't love (speak for yourself!), and then along comes this little baby who rips the whole thing to shreds. If his head wasn't enough to cause some stretching and tearing, his shoulders were right behind to complete the damage. It is common for doctors to make a cut in your perineum (that skin between your vagina and anus) to make more room for the baby to come out – the theory being that the incision can be easily stitched back up after delivery while a tear in another part of the labia or vagina is harder to repair. This cut, as you probably know by now, is called an episiotomy. There are two things you should know about it for now: first, it will be pretty sore after the epidural or local medication wears off. Second, don't look at or touch anything down there because it will put you off sex for the rest of your life. Trust us, things down there go back to normal, at least to the naked eye.

No matter how you delivered your baby, vaginally or by C-section, you will have a 'discharge'. This is a euphemism for the torrential flow of blood and God knows what else that pours out of you for several days. You will probably want to wear two maxi pads at a time for the first two or three days, and even then you will bleed on everything you come in contact with. I don't think I ever made it to the bathroom for a pad change in time. I was so embarrassed that I spent a lot of my supposed recovery time in the hospital cleaning 'discharge' off the floor so that my room didn't look like the site of some grisly murder. If you had a C-section or an epidural that has left you a little wobbly on your feet (primarily because you can't feel your legs), a nurse will boldly march into your room and lift your blanket to check the pads for herself. Under normal circumstances, this would be humiliating, I suppose, but after seemingly everyone in the hospital except the gift shop staff has given you an internal exam during labour, you won't care a whit. In fact, you'll be grateful to have someone take charge of the situation. This is a good time to remind you, yet again, of one of the *Best Friends' Guides* rules for pregnancy and recovery: never wear your own lovely nighties in the hospital. Mess up their gowns and sheets; that's what they are there for.

The episiotomy, and its close proximity to your anus (I hate that word so much!), might have tipped you off to the fact that your vagina isn't the only part of your 'privates' that is affected by pregnancy, particularly by vaginal delivery. This may be your introduction to nature's idea of a practical joke: haemorrhoids. Haemorrhoids are the result of herniated tissue in and around the anus (there it is again). They look and feel to the touch like tiny grapes, but they can hurt enough to make you weep when you sit down. While haemorrhoids are often caused by all the pressure of the baby squeezing through in a vaginal delivery, many lucky mummies get their little grape clusters even earlier, like when the baby is heavy in their belly and getting in the way of blood circulating from the legs back to the heart. (Think of this phenomenon as akin to what happens when you drive the car over a garden hose.) You can also thank pregnancy constipation for playing a significant role here because all that bearing down during a movement can push a grape out here and there, too. We just wanted to familiarize you with them so that you don't think, as I swear to God I did after my first daughter was born, that they were cancerous tumors. Sitz-baths, which are the same as regular baths except with less and hotter water, along with creams and a donut pillow will provide some relief until they shrink away.

Your uterus is the big hero in this birthing business, and it is probably exhausted right about now. It has grown from the size of your fist to the size of a beach ball, it has contracted and spasmed for countless hours trying to push out a baby who seemed wisely reluctant to leave and now it is expected to tighten right back up as if nothing had happened. And, if you had a C-section, it is expected to do all this after having been cut open and stitched back up. The first reminder you get that you even have a uterus might come with breastfeeding. As the baby sucks, your body releases a chemical that helps shrink your uterus. It feels like period pain, and after labour you are probably not too excited to be having flashbacks like this. I know it sounds like hogwash when people say there is a difference between 'good' pain and 'bad' pain, especially after what you've just been through, but this cramping *is* good. As my Best Friend Joyce remarked after the birth of her first daughter, your uterus feels 'heavy enough to be holding the island of Manhattan' for the first few days after delivery, and encouraging your uterus to contract means you'll feel like it's holding nothing heavier than a compact car before you know it. Besides, we Best Friends have a delicious little secret to share with you: that sensation of cramping while breastfeeding quite often evolves into those lovely uterine quakes that occur during and after orgasm. Swear! My husband tells me it was the pain medication, but I distinctly remember feeding my son about three days after he was born and being so overcome by the sensation of relaxation and 'after-shocks' that I nearly fell out of the bed, baby and all. No one has ever been so fervently grateful for hospital bed rails as I was at that moment.

Your Legs and Feet

Moving down your sorry body, we come to your legs. Good news here: aside from some residual numbness from any epidural you might have had, your legs and feet will have sustained little or no damage. Sure, there is always the chance that you will bloat with fluid like Monique, but you will pee that away within a day or so.

The most noticeable effect of childbirth on your legs and feet will probably be that they are stained with smudges of blood and Betadine solution from delivery. In fact, the first thing you can do to improve matters is put on a clean pair of socks. Then ask for a warm flannel to wipe away any other debris. What you really need is a nice warm shower, but we'll be having none of that until your nurse is certain that you can stand up without fainting or tripping. When you do get it, it will be one of the most exquisite metamorphoses of your entire life. I can still feel that warm spray of water (well, maybe it was a trickle; you know hospital plumbing) on my neck and back; it was bliss, in spite of my swollen vagina and tumbling tummy.

Keep in mind that the spinal pain medication given for C-sections and, for those of us who elect to use it, for vaginal births numbs you from your tummy down to your toes. That means that you must slowly regain the use of your legs, not leap right out of bed and fall flat on your face. Start by wiggling your feet and bending and straightening your legs. If that takes some real concentration on your part, you are definitely not ready to go the next step. For the time being, if you need to urinate, ask the nurse for a bedpan. They're used to it and won't think that you are just being demanding. They'd rather come in and help you now than to have you fall down on the bathroom floor on their shift.

If you have an exceptionally keen eye, you might have noticed that your feet haven't yet gone back to their prepregnancy daintiness. Guess what; they won't. Feet that are bigger by a half or whole size are one of the legacies of pregnancy that you take with you to your grave. In my book, that means it's time to go shoe shopping just as soon as you figure out how to put your pram together!

Your Skin

The first few hours after delivery, spend time admiring the baby, but don't bother finding a mirror to check yourself out. Wait until some of the swelling has gone down and the bruising has faded a bit. You think

I'm exaggerating, right? Maybe I am and maybe I'm not; it all depends on how hard delivery hit you. Broken capillaries on your cheeks, chest, upper arms, even in your eyes (remember my horror story?) are quite common. Some women actually get dark circles under their eyes. Those eyes with those dumpling cheeks can make a new mum look just like a panda.

You will be happy to hear that all of this water retention I keep mentioning will remedy itself within the next few days. You will remember how to urinate within the next four or five hours, and lots of water will be released that way. More shocking, however, is nature's most drastic measure for curing bloat: night sweats. One night soon, you will awaken to find that you not only have sweated enough to turn your nightie into a dishrag but enough to have soaked right through your sheets. These sweats will happen several times in the weeks after delivery, so you might as well expect them and prepare for them. If you put a mattress protector on your bed during the third trimester of pregnancy to save it should your waters have broken, leave it on. Otherwise, sleep on a beach towel every night. It's much easier to change towels in the middle of the night than to change an entire bed. I also gave up all silky/satiny nightgowns and pyjamas because when they got wet they felt cold and clammy. I stuck to 100 percent cotton anything, whether it was my husband's old T-shirt or my old flannel nightgowns; fashion be damned!

The Appraisal

Quick, take another look at that baby of yours! Isn't it just so stunning that you grew that little angel inside of you and it turned out just perfectly? Sure you have some recovering to do. But you do recover (almost completely). In fact, most of you recover so well that you'll be willing to do this all over again in a couple of years. Just don't expect to feel whole, healed, energetic and erotic for quite a while still. We don't care what other books or even your doctor might say in this regard: IT'S NINE (TEN) MONTHS UP AND NINE (TEN) MONTHS DOWN IN THE PREGNANCY CYCLE. Don't get frustrated if you think you're not healing quickly enough; a lot of women exaggerate about their rapid recovery in some misdirected need to maintain their Earth Mother status. Keep in mind that there is nothing less 'Best Friend' than competitive mothering. You live on this earth and you're a mother; you're automatically an Earth Mother. Case closed.

4

BABY EUPHORIA

'Everybody told me that I was going to love my baby, but they could never have prepared me for how MUCH I was going to love him!' I have never met a parent, mother or father, who didn't say something to this effect within a year of their baby's birth. It's true, there is no feeling more compelling, distracting, fulfilling, euphoric, miraculous and terrifying all at the same time. For some mums, the infatuation begins even before they lay eyes on the little creature; for other, equally wonderful, mums, the emotion embraces them gradually (think boa constrictor), but no one resists for too long. I know I mention Mother Nature an awful lot, but She really *is* amazing in how She makes sure that we are so preoccupied with the survival of our offspring that they become our lifelong obsessions. After your baby is born, you will frequently wonder what in the world you used to do to fill your time and consciousness. (Later, you will have moments of pining for that relatively carefree time, but let's get back to the spell you're under now.)

BABY EUPHORIA

Do I even need to tell you how beautiful your baby's mouth looks when he is sleeping? You know, the way it makes a perfect bow, and how it suckles as if something delicious were in there? Of course not! You play with his fingers when you feed him, you smell the fold in his neck every time you burp him, you rub his bottom every chance you get as if it were Buddha's belly bringing you blessings. But this doesn't really begin to describe how delirious we new mums really are. My Best friend Catherine swears that she was unreachable by phone or fax for over a week when her little baby was about three months old. Evidently, the angel decided to perform the miracle of growing dark, curling, luxurious eyelashes at that time, and Catherine was bent over her, watching each little lash unfurl. Nothing else on the planet was more compelling than this vision, not work, not friends, certainly not fitness, and often not food. People without children might think that this is a creative excuse to be lazy at best and kind of feebleminded at worst, but we mothers nod knowingly because we, too, have seen the way those lashes rest on those cheeks. God, we could cry right now just thinking of it.

All babies are beautiful, just to varying degrees, and in any contest, yours is the most beautiful of all. Right? Even if a tough delivery has left her with a slightly pointed head, even if she has a case of baby zits and even if her eyes still look crossed, she is without question the most exceptional baby that was ever born. If your baby is small, then all big roly-poly babies look ungainly and cartoonlike to you. If your baby is big, then all small babies look sick and scrawny to you. My babies were all quite bald for the first several months of their lives, and I was convinced that the Uncle Fester look was neater and cleaner looking, and therefore superior, to other, hairier babies who looked like Seinfeld's neighbor Kramer, at least to my biased eye. Whatever your baby looks like is what God intended all babies to look like. Everybody else's baby is just a runner-up. When your babies are grown and you find yourself moved by the beauty of someones else's baby, I bet you a million dollars that baby looks like yours did at that age.

Not only is your own baby a thing of beauty, it has undeniable charisma, too. You want to gaze upon her and be in her presence even more than her physical beauty can explain. She is just so darned adorable, in all senses of the word. She feels good in your arms, she smells heavenly, she looks at you as if she sees into your soul . . . Okay, maybe I'm going a bit far here, but I bet I'm not the only one. There is something so moving about the experience of knowing and watching your baby that you can become her very own groupie. You could envision a life of sitting backstage and watching your baby out in the world, performing her life.

One really good trick for keeping our attention is a baby's ability to change with every passing day. Even those of us with incredibly short attention spans can be riveted, noting the transformations that tiny babies go through. At two weeks of age, the baby you hold in your arms will have no resemblance to the newborn that the hospital photo service memorialized. And the round and dimpled baby you hold at four months is yet another baby. New babies are born with one head of hair (or, like my babies, bald as Kojak), then lose all that hair and grow in an entirely new colour and texture! Caucasian babies keep you guessing about their eye colour for as long as nine months! And we mums don't even know whose smiles our angels' resemble for more than a year because they toy with us so: first, making us wait for them to learn to smile, and then making us wait for some teeth to grow in to give some form to the loopy grin. One day you see your partner's charming smile in the way the baby crinkles his nose, and the next day you look at the baby's face to see old Aunt Maudie, without her dentures, staring back at you. Even as they grow out of babyhood, they keep up this morphing. My nine-year-old son is still messing with me by changing into a completely new person every six months or so. I'll see him out of the corner of my eye, and I will see a grown person standing there, and my breath will fail me for a minute as I drown in pride and heartbreak.

By comparison, we mummies, even those of us who change our hair colour every three weeks and can't decide if we are really Audrey Hepburn or Mary Tyler Moore at heart (no names, please), are achingly boring. Day in and day out, we have the same number of teeth (barring any disasters), our eye colour is the same (no fair counting contacts), and our general appearance is making one long, slow journey toward looking much more like our mothers than we'd ever wanted to.

POOS That Smell Like ROSES

An adjunct of this baby infatuation is a mother's miraculous immunity from being disgusted by anything that emanates from her precious child. I, who gag if anyone even swallows pills in front of me, have caught enough of my kids' projectile vomit in my hands to qualify as a special effects technician for any horror film. It has never made me sick or offended me, and believe me, I am very easily offended. I have been peed on often enough to think that a soggy lap is my natural condition as a mother. My sons, bless their little penises, have both given me a good squirt in the eye when I failed to take defensive nappy changing measures. Did I go running to a doctor, frantic that I had been exposed to bacteria and was certain to go blind? Of course not. As I recall, I just grabbed a spit-up cloth and dabbed up all the excess.

Not only are the vast majority of mums tolerant of their babies' emissions, my Best Friends and I are actually fond of several of them. Few things are more rewarding to us than getting a big bogie out of our sniffling sweetie's nose with one of those rubber bulb things. We can go into rapture over ear wax (even though we all know that nothing smaller than your elbow should ever go into a baby's ear), and burps and farts send us into some kind of gas-intoxicated bliss because we think they are such a relief for our darlings.

There are, however, two exceptions to this emission tolerance:

1. It Never Extends Beyond Your Own Nuclear Family.

No matter how many times you change your own child's dirty nappies, you will not be immune to the offensiveness of someone else's baby's poo. Even if you don't faint when your best friend's baby barfs on your sleeve, you won't wear the shirt one moment longer than necessary, whereas you can spend a whole day in a shirt your own baby has used several times as a handkerchief. Walk into a room where someone else's baby has just dirtied a nappy, and you will go running for the nearest exit. Still, while you may not be charmed by another baby's spits and spews, you will force yourself to transcend your discomfort long enough to help the baby and its mother. This is, after all, part of the Best Friends' Creed:

A Best Friend never lets ANYONE'S baby walk around in a terribly soiled nappy or with a runny nose if she has the tools to remedy the situation.

2. Its Potency Diminishes in Direct Relation to the Child's Growth.

I will never forget the day my Best Friend Linda confided something that just stunned me, the mother of two tiny boys. She said that she was well past wanting to coo at and kiss her twelve-year-old son any more: not just because he wouldn't stand for it, but also because he had smelly gym feet and B.O.! I couldn't imagine that the day would come when my babies' bodily functions would become just about as offensive to me as a stranger's, so I called my Best Friend Lori for a confirmation. She, the mother of a sixteen-year-old boy, in addition to her little boy and her new baby girl, quickly assured me that this was a universal truth. My brain felt the strain of trying to wrap itself around the unthinkable concept that my darling babies, whose entire bodies were delicious to me, would someday be adolescents and just as gross as all other teenage boys. Think about it: facial hair and zits on our little cherubs! I guess it's safe to assume that when our big boys throw up after drinking beer at a party we will be so grossed out that we will just throw them the phone and tell them to call an industrial cleaning service. But enough about that! Put it out of your mind right now. You have several more years of Eden ahead of you before that serpent raises his ugly head.

'If Your Baby and Your Partner were Drowning, who would You save?'

No man with any judgement whatsoever would dare ask his partner, the mother of his new baby, the question 'Who do you love more, me or the baby?' No matter how emotionally stable he is and how devoted he is to the baby, he is not ready for the answer that he'll get: new babies win hands down. If you don't think this can be a conflict for new parents, then you haven't come up for a breath yet since you delivered that baby of yours. In the *Best Friends' Guide to Pregnancy*, I shared the story of the night I told my husband I was unexpectedly pregnant with our fourth child. He explained the Partner-Child Hierarchy in this succinct way:

> 'Vicki, you are like a pie. Every time we have another baby, the other babies' pieces don't get smaller; mine does. I want a bigger piece of pie.'

Let's start with reassurance, as we Best Friends always try to do. This usurping of the role of 'The Person Who Rocks Your World' (the position traditionally held by your partner) by the new little enchanter is as normal as ants at a picnic. But here is a special message you should share with your poor, dejected partner mate right now (since he needs reassuring, too, from time to time):

> ★ *I am under a spell right now. It will not last forever (unless you're a pig or I have problems only Freud could understand).*

That's right, Mummy. It is understandable and acceptable for you to focus exclusively on the baby right now while she is so deeply dependent on you for survival and nurturing. Your partner may be as, or even more, infatuated than you are. Let's call this kind of love 'adoration'. To receive your love, your baby doesn't have to adhere to any standards of honourable behaviour, love you back, respect you for who you really are or promise not to sleep with your best friend. Those crucibles are reserved for your partner. To be loved, your baby only has to be.

For now and for the rest of your life, your job as a mother is to love your baby simply for being. (Trust us, this will become more difficult when they actually turn into human beings.)

Here is the other, equally important part of the equation: *Your baby will not always love you back, and you still must continue to love him anyway.* We Best Friends never cease to be amazed at how mothers are taken for granted. No child will ever grow up and genuinely thank you for the way you stayed awake all night to make sure the playgroup chicken eggs hatched safely, or for yelling at the football coach who called him a 'daisy picker on the right wing'. It's as though the children's credo goes something like this:

'You are mine. I lived in you, I drank from you, I wiped my nose on you and I barged right in while you were going to the bathroom. Your job is to love me, protect me, teach me and then prepare me to leave you, only to come back when my girlfriend dumps me or I flunk out of college. I will call you when I feel like it. If I am a boy, I will spend all major holidays at my partner's house, and, if I am a girl, I will finally begin to appreciate you after I get pregnant and become a mother myself.'

Keep this in mind when your partner wants a little TLC. I suspect that we would be wise to trust our mothers when they sing in unison: 'Don't neglect your partner for your children because your children will leave you in the end.' (Of course, a lot of men leave you in the end, too, but play along here.) Go ahead with your adoration (as if we could interfere with that!), but nurture your life partner, too. Remember, your *romantic love*, unlike your adoring love, is based on partnership, commitment and physical intimacy (yes, you will want sex again someday, I promise). Your *adoring love* is based on your acceptance of your role as a mother to ensure that this little baby gets well launched into the world. There is plenty of room for both kinds of love; after all, you're a Best Friend and you have a heart bigger than all outdoors.

My Baby: Centre of the Universe

Another universal effect on new mummies of Baby Euphoria is a radical skewing of perspective. It begins in pregnancy but comes into full bloom after delivery. No events, local or global, are witnessed and evaluated with any intellectual distance. Everything is appraised for its ability to touch your baby's life. My Best Friend Alison calls a similar phenomenon 'What Does This Mean to the Jews?' In both obsessions, everything from John Kennedy Jr.'s marriage to the availability of Vamp nail polish is viewed as a possible agent of change, good or bad, in the protected group's life. For example, if a new mother reads (no, make that, sees on TV news, since everyone knows new mothers don't have time to read) that the airlines are having another fare war, she doesn't digest this information as a traveller but rather as a mother who might, under just the right bizarre circumstances, need to airlift her baby to the Mayo Clinic for surgery or to her grandparents to baby-sit while she acts as mediator for the crisis in Palestine. If petrol prices go up, a mother will extrapolate that her child may fall down, need stitches, the car won't have a full tank of petrol, and she will have to wait in a two-hour line at the garage with her baby bleeding in her car seat. You can imagine what we do when we hear that a child in our Mummy and Me group has just come down with chickenpox. We spend no time at all being concerned about the child but immediately become concerned about incubation periods and whether our child touched anything that was touched by that germy kid.

I can see some very positive aspects to this narrow view of life. For one thing, it helps ensure that we otherwise-distracted mums don't miss information that really could pertain to us, such as the news about the danger of putting children in car seats equipped with air bags or the lead content of miniblinds. But our frantic efforts to stay on top of all pertinent news can also make us lunatics. For five years I heard and believed that organic juices were better for my babies than the sugar-water counterparts made by the big, bad manufacturers. Then three months ago, the baby daughter of a Friend of a Friend got deathly ill from organic apple juice that, because it had no preservatives, contained botulism. For several weeks, I was praying at the altar of synthetic foods again, and I'm only now finding some sort of balance in my choices. I still won't let my kids order hamburgers at fast-food restaurants, not because I would prefer that they not eat red meat, but because I am irrationally terrified of E. coli bacteria. Of course, they can eat chicken nuggets from those same fast-food places until they grow feathers, so, as you can see, my careful parenting is a tad inconsistent. I guess we respond to the big fires and try to step over the little sparks.

Mother of One, Mother of All

Not only is all news and information digested in the skewed Mummy Prism just described, but it is also filtered through a colander of emotional and maternal reactions. For example, once a woman becomes a mother, she identifies with all mothers. She may brush past a homeless woman alone on the street, but if that woman has a child in her arms, she may end up at the Best Friend's home for dinner and a bath and a warm wardrobe for the child. Identifying with other mothers, *not small-mindedness or even high-minded loyalty*, also turns us into the kind of women who gather together at parties to discuss the new young beauty on the arm of one of our fellow Mother/Best Friend's former husbands. Once we have babies, we are horrified by the thought that our partners could actually walk out and leave us. We vent and judge all over the place every time we read about someone who divorces his wife and sees his child every other weekend. No matter what the reality in the relationship was, if the woman is a decent mother, she can do no wrong and her chickenshit partner can do no right.

New mothers love all babies (well, not as much as they love their own, but they are no longer indifferent to them) even if they are strangers. News broadcasts that describe cruelties to children are unwatchable by new mothers. On Sunday afternoons I refuse to turn on the TV because all of the programming is for childrens' relief funds of one denomination or another, and I am devastated by the films of hungry babies. If one of those news magazine shows does a story on hidden video cameras revealing baby-sitter cruelty to infants, I have to take to my bed, so shot are my nerves.

I am certain that there are still thousands of mothers who have not recovered from the saga of Susan Smith, how she rolled the car her children were in into a lake. We were so heartbroken for her those first few days. Even I, who live over two thousand miles away from the Smith home, found myself looking around public areas like grocery stores and malls more carefully, just in case I could help spot the boys and their kidnappers. We all just ached for that mother who'd lost those precious babies. Then, to find it was she who killed them was the ultimate betrayal to the rest of us mothers. The Mothers' Criminal Code is this: all people who intentionally hurt or disappoint children must serve time in prison. All people who commit sexual crimes or worse against children must be executed, preferably within five minutes after they have been apprehended. (Can you believe I am saying this? I am an attorney and, intellectually, an ardent defender of the Constitution – but once babies are involved, I become a fascist.) And ANYONE, even another child, who gives my baby the hairy eyeball had better run fast because I come out slugging.

The Droning Phenomenon

The arrival of a baby into your life is more extraordinary than being invited aboard an alien spaceship, and, in many ways, it *is* like a close encounter with an extraterrestrial. It is only understandable, then, that new parents, particularly mothers, are eager to share their observations and discoveries regarding this little E.T. who is living in their home. At the risk of sounding harsh, we Best Friends feel it is our duty to tell you in no uncertain terms that NO ONE ELSE ON THIS PLANET IS AS INTERESTED IN YOUR BABY AS YOU ARE. I'm so sorry to have to be the one to tell you, but it's true. As miraculous as the birth of your own child is, you didn't exactly invent childbirth and people will not be eagerly seeking you out to hear the latest story of how Junior's runny stools are improving or how Miss Junior rolled over, left to right AND right to left, weeks before the books said she would.

You probably think that childbirth and child development, particularly yours, are the most compelling topics imaginable. I know we did. You just can't get over the fact that you, the same person who flunked Domestic Science in school because you couldn't sew an A-line skirt, created this complex, perfect and charismatic creature. Every little thing about him, from the way he has 'stork bite' marks at the nape of his neck (a temporary birthmark, for you novices) to the way he gazes into your eyes with his tentative focus and wobbly head, is just short of miraculous.

Not only do you notice every single thing, but you delight in relating it in great detail. Other people's news, such as your Best Friend's most recent blind date or your partner's career opportunities (except, of course, when viewed through the Mummy Prism), are piffle compared with the miracles you are witnessing on a daily basis. My Best Friends and I all confess to dumping our dementia at one time or another on one of our unsuspecting, childless friends:

'I just can't talk to you about your wedding, Emily, because the baby is getting his DPT shot tomorrow and his gums are inflamed and I don't know if he's teething or getting a cold and if he's getting a cold then maybe he shouldn't get the shot tomorrow because maybe it will make him sicker or maybe he will have a reaction that could lead to brain damage like I read about a few years ago, and I'm not really sure I trust what the doctor has to say about this anyway because Kate says that he told her that he didn't even give his own daughter the P part of the DPT . . .' By this point, poor Emily has either hung up on you or you then cut her off completely by the universal ending to all mothers' telephone conversations:

'Oh, I think I hear the baby crying! I have to hang up now!'

Just getting this information will not save you from the Droning Phenomenon. We all still do it; in fact, my husband is nearly as bad about it as I am, now that the boys are into sports. Still, keep in mind that other people, especially people who haven't got children of their own to drone on about in response, will greatly appreciate brief and superficial answers to the question 'So, how is the baby?' 'Fine, thanks. She's walking now,' is sufficient for nearly everyone who inquires. If you *really* want to be considerate, you can even refrain from showing the latest snapshots to anyone who happens to be standing still in your vicinity. Besides, you will discover soon enough that every time you put on a photo display of your beautiful baby, the other person has the reciprocal right to show you pictures of his or her funny-looking one. I know I'm being rough with you, and I don't mean to take away all your fun, but try for some moderation; it will get you invited back a second time.

Even if your partner is nearly as obsessed with your baby as you are, our advice is to try to avoid starting every conversation with him by saying, 'You'll never believe what the baby did today!' Artificial as it might feel, at least feign an interest in him and his life (remember the 'Vicki, You're a Pie' story?) and ask about his day first. Not only does this make him feel good (as it does you when he forces himself to ask about your day), but it helps keep you from being seen as one of those women who have checked out of the real world and moved into Mummyville. There is no upside for either of you to have your partner think he has June Cleaver for a roommate. I always found that my husband would wipe that glazed expression off his face if I sprinkled the conversation with some sordid, sexy gossip about someone he knew. The details of nappy rash put him into a coma, but the details of a Best Friend having an affair with her yoga teacher had him hanging on my every word.

Has Anybody Seen my Keys?

Absentmindedness begins in pregnancy, but it reaches its full and glorious bloom after the baby is born. Sure, even non-mothers occasionally lose their keys, but I bet they don't lose their cars as often as we do. You know those nightmares you've been having about leaving the baby in the dressing room at Gap? Well, they are the offspring of your recognition that you have no memory whatsoever. So many times I have found myself in church or baby group or the doctor's surgery, with the baby squeaky clean and dressed like royalty, and suddenly realized that my tongue felt like it was wearing a sweater. I HAD FORGOTTEN TO BRUSH MY TEETH! I would frantically dig in the changing bag for something to mask the morning mouth and usually came up with nothing more than a sticky bottle of Calpol.

Forgetfulness is not the only kind of absentmindedness we mums experience. We also lose our ability to understand logical relationships among people, places and things. For example, you can open the door to the refrigerator and actually wonder what is kept in such an appliance. I could just stare at all the milk, yogurt, peanut butter and leftovers and wonder what all that stuff was and what I was supposed to do with it. Department stores were my Armageddon. I would forget how to get to the lift (remember, mothers with buggies are banished from the convenient escalators near the middle of the store and relegated to the dark hidden corners near the freight dock where the lifts are kept), I couldn't figure out how to find the infant clothes or what their sizes meant. Then, of course, I would get lost in the carpark.

It's quite common for new mummies to have trouble completing simple tasks because they forget what they intended to do long before they have taken two or three steps in any direction. I would notice, for example, that the bin in the baby's room needed a new plastic liner. If I could keep that thought in my mind all the way through the nappy change, it was a miracle. Then I would wander into the laundry room, which is where I keep such stuff, look at the dirty towels, realize how much I didn't want to wash them right now, walk into the kitchen, look in the refrigerator, notice I needed more eggs, head to the pad of paper near the phone to write it down, pick up the phone rather than the pad and pencil, begin dialling, only to discover that I'd forgotten who I was going to call. The bin liners? Never thought of them again, at least not until the next nappy change.

You will come out of this fog, Best Friend, but I'm afraid I must be the one to tell you that you will never recover your razor-sharp, prepregnancy brain. Later, when the hormones have lifted and the baby is older, you will find that your brain damage is directly attributable to your lack of sleep. After that, you can blame it on the sheer quantity of information and concerns that a mother must keep in mind, like car-pool schedules, parent-teacher conferences, Little League opening-day parades and when the dogs have an appointment to be flea dipped. I am absolutely certain that I cannot take in one more piece of information without having to lose one that was already in my head; there just isn't any more room left in that part of the brain that keeps lists, schedules and nursery rhymes.

There is only one effective way to deal with your new affliction of absentmindedness, and that is to become a creature of habit. Remember how your mother used to tell you 'a place for everything and everything in its place'? Well, she clearly suffered from the same affliction, and it was the only way she could find anything. Immediately begin training yourself to find 'homes' for everything you use on a regular basis. Your car keys ALWAYS go in the bowl on the entry table, the changing bag ALWAYS hangs on the doorknob of the baby's room, your handbag ALWAYS sits by the door to the garage. No matter how rushed you are when you come into the house, no matter how thirsty you may be or how badly you have to go to the toilet, don't just set your stuff down anywhere; it's as good as lost.

Another trick I use is the 'If It Was A Snake, It Would Have Bit Me' Technique. In other words, place reminders where you literally must trip over them (but not where they present a risk for a mother carrying a baby). For example, if I run out of shampoo, I am certain to forget that fact before I finish my shower and long before I am dry enough to write it on the shopping list. So, I put the empty container on the shower door ledge where I must kick it to get out. Then, while I am towelling off, I throw the container into my sink so that I am unable to wash my hands or brush my teeth without looking at it. Sure, I may spend half the day with an empty shampoo bottle in my hand or pocket, but at least I stand a chance of remembering to get some more.

The last weapon against absentmindedness is to write everything down and make lists. I even carry a cheap dictating recorder in my car so that I can memorialize my thoughts in that instant before they vaporize. Of course, no list (no recording tape, for that matter) is worth a thing if you can't find it. The list needs a 'home', too. See, Best Friend, we've come full circle and you're catching on!

Staking Out Our Territory

Ask any new mother whether she wants her partner to help in caring for the baby, and she will enthusiastically say yes. But when it comes down actually to sharing the job, an amazing number of women all of a sudden become very stingy. They are the ones who say, 'Never mind, I'll change the nappy, since it fell right off when you did it last time,' or 'The baby seems to digest better when I feed her because you jiggle her around too much.' A partner doesn't have to be Pavlov's dog to learn quickly that he should stay away from the baby business if he doesn't want to get shocked.

Perhaps we new mums are secretly terrified that Daddy is going to be at least as skilful at childcare as we are. Where does that leave us? Especially if we have quit our jobs to devote all our attention to the baby? So many of us already secretly suspect that we are really amateurish at this mothering business, and if a *man*, someone whom God did not see fit to bless with a uterus, can do the job proficiently, then our self-esteem and identity lie in shattered little pieces on the bedroom floor. Trust us when we tell you in the kindest possible way: you need to get a grip on yourself, Best Friend. The big goal is to teach your child to get by in the world without you, not to guarantee that all her needs must be met by Mummy. Besides, I promise you will soon learn that there is no such thing as too much help when it comes to childcare.

5

BLUE, BABY, BLUE

There are three types of new mothers:

1. The type who give birth and resume their lives with confidence, clear thinking and enthusiasm;
2. The kind who give birth and wish that a fairy godmother would make the baby disappear and restore them to their former life; and
3. The rest of us.

Traditional wisdom (meaning 'male') has long held that the first example is 'normal' and what all new mothers should aspire to, and the second is classic postnatal depression, which is somewhat naughty and to be overcome or hidden at all cost, and that the third group doesn't exist.

Here's what the Best Friends and I think: the first group of new mothers, the kind who breeze effortlessly through the transition from human to mother, are either incredibly lucky or incredibly unobservant. I mean, how can you experience a metamorphosis from personhood to motherhood without some ambivalence, apprehension or anxiety? More revolutionary is our belief that the second and third categories are really one group, just with varying degrees of intensity. That's right, the *Best Friends' Guide to Surviving the First Year of Motherhood* is taking a stand that may blow a lot of people's minds and that is:

NEARLY EVERY WOMAN WHO GIVES BIRTH TO A BABY (AND EVEN MANY WHO BECOME MOTHERS BY ADOPTION) GETS POSTNATAL DEPRESSION.

You may read this and respond indignantly that I can't be talking about you because you are completely fine, thank you very much. If this is your reaction, then all I have to say is, do me the courtesy of reading this section again after the baby's first birthday and *then* tell me whether what I say is true. You see, it is stunningly common for mothers of one-year-olds to look back on their first few months of motherhood and wonder, 'Who was that crazy lady?' even though they would have stabbed with a nappy pin anyone who suggested they were a little 'postnatalish' while they actually were. I never recognized my symptoms of postnatal depression while I was experiencing them, and yet I am now certain, with the clarity of hindsight, that I had it in varying degrees with each of my four babies. My Best Friends Lori, Karen and May all had it; at least that was the unanimous vote by us, their 'sane' Friends, but they all denied it when we informed them of our diagnoses. After a while, we just factored their altered states into all our relations with them. We'd say things like, 'Don't ask May where we should have Cheri's birthday party because she's *postnatalish* right now.' Or, 'Well, Lori said she'd be here, but you know how she is right now . . .' And, 'We can go to Karen's house, but she probably still won't let us see the baby because she thinks we are carrying more germs than Typhoid Mary.'

Just the other night, Shirley, Mindy, Lori and Lori's sister and I got together for dinner and we started reminiscing about Lori's postnatal depression. Would you believe that nearly a year later, she still can't quite grasp what happened to her? She acknowledged that she was pretty freaked out after delivering her baby (how could she deny it with so many of us witnesses in the room?), but she had total amnesia about certain particularly comical (in hindsight, and only to us) events of the last year. I guess it's safe to say that postnatal depression is a little like being drunk, in that both conditions can lead to blackouts.

Shirley and I took tremendous delight in describing Lori's mood at Cheri's Christmas party a year ago. Let's start with the outfit – she had to have been wearing dungarees since that was her official postnatal uniform, regardless of the occasion. She sat in a corner with some of us Best Friends hovering around her and tried to articulate how unlike herself she felt, and how frightened she was that she would never be 'normal' again. We all clucked sympathetically and offered advice ranging from taking a week at a spa to just waiting out this depression. This wasn't the first time we had heard about her unhappiness, and I must admit, we were starting to find it a tad tedious, in that selfish impatience we all have regarding other people's crises. Finally, in a whisper, I suggested that Lori ask her doctor about antidepressants. Well, *that* got her mind off her depression for a while; she spent the next week calling every single friend she had to say that Vicki thought she needed Prozac, and did they, too, think she was crazy? To this day,

Lori maintains she wasn't even at that Christmas party. Meanwhile, she and her gorgeous daughter are so in love with each other that I think we Best Friends are slipping way down on the totem pole of her affection; they're already best friends and shopping buddies.

Postnatal depression is like PMT, just on a grander scale. If you are like me, the worst thing your partner can do is interrupt your ranting to ask whether your period is about to start. In my case, I am usually holding a bag of peanut M&M's in one hand, massaging my aching lower back with the other and screeching that my period has nothing to do with my moods so shut up about it! This lack of self-awareness is similar to postnatal depression. While you're in its throes, it seems like completely rational behaviour to make your partner change his clothes in the garage and disinfect with Phisohex before seeing the baby after a day at work. Your friends can suggest that your hormones are toying with you, but you feel persecuted and misunderstood by *your friends*, not betrayed by your *oestrogen levels*. I don't know if we have such a hard time diagnosing this completely normal condition because we *don't want* to see it or because we *can't* see it.

Then again, you may read our broad assertion about all women getting postnatal depression to one degree or another, and you may start to weep with relief that you are normal and you are not alone in your feelings. So many new mothers are completely unprepared for any feelings other than jubilation after the birth of their baby. Everybody is so full of congratulations, they expect you to glow with maternal satisfaction, and, truthfully, they don't really want you to tell them otherwise. People love life when it matches the sentiment of Hallmark cards and think you're a downer if you suggest that your emotional life might be a tad more complex than that.

Not that we *would* tell them about our fears that we can't take care of a baby properly, that we feel like we live in a vacuum with the rest of the world carrying on without us, that we have lost all interest in sex or even in our own appearance, that we would rather sleep than talk to anyone, that we cry several times a day, that we resent the toll the baby is taking on us. Heaven forbid that a new mother should speak the truth about how she is, or is not, adjusting! There are several reasons why it remains one of womanhood's deepest, darkest secrets:

The Shame of It All

First, there is a lot of shame attached to feeling less than perpetually elated by becoming a mummy. Mention postnatal depression, and the first thing people think about is a woman who doesn't want or love her baby. People unfamiliar with this condition usually fail to understand that loving your baby and loathing your life can be done simultaneously by new mums. She is considered an aberration of nature, someone disconnected from the normal instincts that a 'good' mother feels. We've all seen paintings of Mary and Jesus, and *that's* what a good mother looks like, by God! There's some story about a distraught woman running over her baby with her car because of postnatal depression. I don't know if it's true or just another bit of our cultural mythology, but it has caused many of us mums huge anxiety. 'Do these feelings of ambivalence mean that I might just wake up some morning and throw the baby out with the bathwater? Should I be kept under twenty-four-hour supervision?' Or worse, our maternal superstition takes over and we become certain that something unspeakable will happen to our baby if we are not grateful and appreciative enough. Never forget the power of superstition over mothers; it is MOTHERS who knock on wood, spit on the ground and whisper 'godblessem' when a child's name is mentioned. Ultimately, not only are we ashamed to talk to other people about our feelings, we are also ashamed to think about them!

Don't think for a minute that partners, mothers or mothers-in-law are any more enlightened about postnatal depression than the rest of society. Just try telling the father of your precious child that you aren't completely sure that you want to be a mummy after all. He may speak to you with understanding and reassurance, but if he is like all the men I know, he will freak out and threaten to report you to social services. Mention it to your mother, and be prepared to have her suggest that she take the baby to her house for the next couple of years. It's no wonder most of us in crisis learn to keep our mouths shut and suffer in silence.

Unfortunately, not talking about how we feel makes most of us Best Friends just feel worse. It would be such a relief to purge ourselves of our less acceptable thoughts because at least 50 percent of them would disappear into the ozone as soon as they were uttered. About half, according to my unabashedly unscientific calculations, of our negative thoughts are just that, thoughts. They are not opinions or beliefs. But they get scary when we hold them inside of us for too long because then we can't tell the difference between what we really feel and what we can imagine feeling.

Am I saying that all new mothers feel miserable, depressed and disappointed after giving birth? Absolutely not. What I am saying is that it's very rare for any thinking woman to accept and adjust to her new role and responsibilities without some hiccups in her emotional life. Mixed feelings about motherhood are not a sign of not loving your baby enough; they are a sign of anything from intellectual curiosity to exhaustion to a serious chemical imbalance.

The Fear of It All

Another reason that so many of us fail to recognize postnatal depression in ourselves is that we are afraid of it. We are afraid that if we have it, our behaviour is completely out of our control. In our own hysterical little way, we think 'postnatal depression' and we see *Cybill*. Since new mothers need to feel in control of the universe in order to protect their fragile babies, the worry that we, ourselves, may be the one un-controllable factor freaks us out.

Calm down, mummies. I can say with great confidence that your baby is absolutely safe in your loving care. You will devote your life to ensuring his happiness and well-being. I just wish I felt as confident that you would take such good care of yourselves! Postnatal depression, except in those very rare cases that you hear about on TV, is a piece of cake for the baby, but it can really be tough on the mummy. Our babies, not just our newborns but even our teenagers, are delightfully unconcerned most of the time about our emotional lives. Remember Nora Ephron's opinion in *My Life* when she said that most children, if they had to choose between having you in the next room being miserable and unfulfilled and having you in Hawaii finding your inner bliss, would choose having you crying in the next room. Sure, it might be a bit of an exaggeration, but I bring it up to reassure you that if you are caring for your baby, loving him and giving him attention, he will probably escape unaffected by your guilt about eventually going back to work or how resentful you are that you haven't slept in a lying-down position without a baby in your arms for more than three weeks. In other words, relax as you go through your changes. You'll soon become the person you recognize as you, and the baby won't have noticed a thing.

How Long Has This Been Going On?

Almost as terrifying as the worry that we will lose our ability to parent if we feel any of the symptoms of postnatal depression is the fear it might be a kind of insanity *that never goes away*. In fact, one of the most striking symptoms of postnatal depression is an utter lack of optimism. Some new mothers just can't imagine any time in the future when they will not be tired, or sad, or forgetful or anxious. The demands of caring for a child, usually alone in our society, are so repetitive and unrelenting that we measure our days in nappies changed and feeds. When it is our first baby, we are forced to make mothering decisions based on little more than gut instincts, and that, too, can make us feel like disaster is lurking around every corner. Sure, the books say that you will soon recognize a 'hungry' cry from a 'bored' or 'hurt' cry, and you probably will . . ., eventually. In the meantime, every cry gets your blood pressure into the triple digits and your adrenaline pumping like a locomotive. Then there's the baby's first illness; projectile vomiting alone has been known to make a mother lose her mind for good.

Trust your Best Friends; there is an end to this tunnel, and we are dedicated to helping you find it as quickly as possible. A lot of the improvement comes with the growth of the baby. Twenty-inch humans with big heads and no neck strength intimidate everyone except maternity nurses, who throw them around with the casualness of postal workers handling mail. But once they begin their journey toward hardiness and some form of independence, you can relax a bit (at least until they get their driving licence). As they grow, they learn to sleep, too, and this will work miracles on your mental health. Sleep deprivation, as we've said before, is one of the biggest bogeymen in a mummy's life. We have very little control over the baby's growth, however, and many aspects of postnatal depression actually have more to do with *your* growth so let's move matters along and give your growth a jumpstart. A good place to begin is by clearing all the misconceptions about postnatal depression out of the way. Here are the most common myths and the real truth about them.

MYTH No.1: 'NORMAL' POSTNATAL DEPRESSION, ALSO KNOWN AS THE BABY BLUES, OCCURS THREE OR FOUR DAYS AFTER GIVING BIRTH AND IS USUALLY LITTLE MORE THAN A ONE-DAY UNEXPLAINED CRYING FIT.

The Truth

Sure, you may get weepy shortly after giving birth, since that is when the most dramatic change in hormone levels occurs, but that is *not* postnatal depression, at least not the Best Friends' Kick-Ass Postnatal

Depression. Postnatal depression is when you haven't slept in two months, your baby is going through a growth spurt and you worry that you're not making enough milk (if you are, indeed, breastfeeding), you are not eating much of anything with nutrients, but you are still overweight, and then . . . the whole family comes down with the flu! If you don't find this overwhelming and debilitating, then Mother Teresa has found her successor. Look, I've been a mother for almost nine years now, and I think I still get postnatal depression, like three years ago when I was eight months pregnant and my three kids and I all got chickenpox. If you don't think I felt a lot of ambivalence about motherhood at that time, you have another thing coming.

MYTH No.2: POSTNATAL DEPRESSION CAN BE PRE-VENTED BY KEEPING A GOOD AND POSITIVE ATTITUDE DURING PREGNANCY.

The Truth

Talk about calling the travel agent and booking a guilt trip . . . This bit of misinformation implies that whether or not you experience any of the symptoms of postnatal depression is up to you. In other words, if you get it, it's your own damn fault. Not only is this not true, but it is also the kind of advice that sets you up for a fall. You can try, try, try all through pregnancy and maternity to be as positive as Pollyanna herself and still feel the effects of postnatal depression, except now you can add disappointment and self-doubt to the experience. Pregnancy and motherhood are incredible physical and emotional upheavals, no matter how thrilled you are to become a mother. Your relationship may be changing, your looks certainly are, and you don't really know what being someone's parent is going to involve. If you think that your job is to stay grateful, happy and content through the water retention, the vulnerability, the fear and the invasion of the body snatcher, it's no wonder you eventually end up depressed. This is not a matter of the power of positive thinking. The best and healthiest frame of mind is one that allows you to feel anything that comes along without over-whelming guilt. If the *Best Friends' Guides* do nothing more than help you give yourself permission to bitch and moan now and then without feeling like a traitor to maternity, then we have done our job. We have tremendous faith in your parenting and we're quite certain that you love your baby like crazy, so anything you do or think or say will be accepted in that context. In other words, you can't shock us!

MYTH No.3: POSTNATAL DEPRESSION IS A FIGMENT OF A WOMAN'S IMAGINATION; THERE ARE NO MEDICAL JUSTIFICATIONS FOR IT.

The Truth

They used to say this (and I even believed it!) about PMT and cramps, too. I guess it took more women insisting that people without uteruses might not know what they were talking about in this area. As a matter of fact, all of pregnancy and new motherhood are hugely affected by our biology. You don't think Mother Nature would just leave us to our own devices and expect the species to continue, do you? We are no longer in the driving seat when someone else's life is at stake, and considering how clueless we really are, we should be grateful to slip into the passenger's seat. As soon as we become pregnant, our hormones combine with our genetic programming to make us hopelessly devoted and fiercely protective of this new little life. Then, when the baby is born, add fatigue and inexperience to the equation and you have a form of torture the Marquis de Sade would delight in. Gosh, add a dash of mastitis and he would become positively giddy!

MYTH No.4: POSTNATAL DEPRESSION IS JUST THAT; FEELING DEPRESSED AFTER HAVING A BABY.

The Truth

Well, that's a very narrow view of the landscape here. Postnatal depression is a catch-all phrase for all sorts of emotions and behaviours that are new and unusual or more intense than before you had a baby. I developed headaches that lasered my brain from behind my eyeballs. My Best Friend Lori was forgetful and confused. She would walk purposefully into a room and have no idea why she went there in the first place. One time, she found her mobile phone in the refrigerator! Karen, as you know, was a tad phobic about germs. It was her darling husband who had to change his clothes and scrub before entering the baby's presence.

MYTH No.5: ONCE YOU GET POSTNATAL DEPRESSION, THERE IS NOTHING YOU CAN DO ABOUT IT EXCEPT WAIT IT OUT.

The Truth

If you feel like you are having trouble coping with motherhood, the first and simplest thing you can do for yourself is ASK FOR HELP. Do not feel ashamed about needing it; YOU WEREN'T INTENDED TO DO THIS ALONE. Remember, we humans are a tribal breed, and nature never intended for you and your baby to survive without the assistance of the other women in your tribe (Get it, Best Friends?). Whatever you do, do not take a passive approach to your unhappiness and do not pretend it doesn't exist. There are so many things that you can do to get back on track; it may be as simple as getting more sleep or exercising, it might be so stubborn as to require medication, but there is help out there. If you think that you and your baby are supposed to get through this first year isolated from the rest of the world, it's no wonder you're crazy.

If It Quacks Like a Duck and walks Like a Duck . . .

Still another reason why we may not recognize symptoms of postnatal depression is because of the name of the condition. You see, depression, meaning feeling sad and hopeless, is only one of the many ways this altered emotional state can manifest itself. If your feelings are strange and unsettling to you, even if you don't act like Richard Lewis, you still may have the TEMPORARY condition of postnatal depression. Here is a list of some of the symptoms:

1. *Feelings of Inadequacy.* This is bigger than the garden-variety feelings that you are a schlump because you can't seem to get the bed made before your partner comes home or because you still haven't lost your pregnancy weight. This refers to a belief that this job of being someone's mum is too big for you and that you'll fail. It also applies to comparing yourself with all the other new mothers you know and coming up less-than every time. (The first thing to do here is stop believing everything those mothers tell you.)

2. *Difficulty Making Decisions.* We aren't talking about the hard decisions, like when to wean the baby or what college to send her to, we mean not being able to decide to go out or stay in, to buy chicken or beef, to get dressed or stay in bed.

3. *Fear of Being Alone*. This symptom is much like the feeling of inadequacy listed as No.1. Lots of hormonally challenged new mums don't want to be left alone because that means they are alone with the baby that they aren't sure they can care for.

4. *Fantasies of Disasters or Bizarre Fears*. This was a biggie for me. I was forever imagining disasters that could befall the baby while she was in my care. I dreamed once that I put the baby in a car seat, put the car seat on the roof of the car and drove home without another thought. I also dreamed on a regular basis that I went somewhere with the baby and then left without her, completely forgetting that I'd given birth. My Friend Chrissie used to worry that she would stand too near a balcony or ledge while holding her newborn and inexplicably lose her grasp, sending the baby flying into space.

5. *No Interest in Previously Enjoyable Activities*. For quite some time after the baby is born, you won't have any time for any 'previously enjoyable activities', let alone any interest in them. This is completely normal, as far as we Best Friends are concerned. When we start to get a little worried is toward the end of the first year if you still feel a general lack of enthusiasm about everything, including your former pleasures, like getting out of bed, reading the paper and even sex still seems boring and not worth the effort.

6. *Breastfeeding Problems*. I almost hesitate to include this symptom in our list because I don't want every new mother who has a hard time mastering the art of breastfeeding to think that it is because she has postnatal depression. Ninety-nine percent of the time, breastfeeding problems are just that: normal responses to something that is very challenging (and often painful!) to learn. Some women, however, do have a difficult time relaxing enough to allow their 'letdown' mechanism to work so that the breasts can release milk, and this can be a sign of way too much postnatal anxiety.

7. *Headaches, Stomach Aches, Nausea, Muscle Aches*. You're reading a book by a woman who stocks Ibuprofen in her car, her bag and her kitchen, so I think that motherhood naturally involves a certain number of aches and pains. And we all know that there is sure to be lots and lots of discomfort during the period shortly after a woman has produced a baby from her innards. What you should be suspicious of are recurring aches and pains that seem to be unrelated to any known illness or injury. My Best Friend Terry had a lot of muscle soreness for

several months, and I had headaches so piercing that I thought I was losing my eyesight. (We're both fine now, thanks.)

8. *Nervousness, Shaking or Trembling.* The combination of your frayed nerves, lack of sleep and the exotic hormone cocktail you're on can make you as jangly as too many visits to Coffee Republic. Don't be frightened, but do be careful around the baby; we don't want anything valuable to get dropped and broken. Also, don't compound the problem by drinking beverages with caffeine in them, no matter how much you think you need that boost. It is also a good idea to call your doctor if this starts happening to you so that he or she can rule out infection or haemorrhaging.

9. *Compulsive Behaviours, Checking and Rechecking Things.* Once again, there is a thin line here between ordinary neuroses and problematical ones. I don't think there is a mother among us who hasn't obsessed that the baby will stop breathing if we don't pay attention to it every minute. How much handwashing is too much when all the latest findings show that flus and colds are passed by those very fingers? And that checking and rechecking, well, given what we know about a new mother's absentmindedness, it can pay to double-check whether we really did lock the front door or turn the kettle off. If you don't notice that this behaviour has become a problem, but those who love you have noticed otherwise, believe them.

10. *Avoidance of the Baby.* I saved this one till last because it is one of the scariest manifestations of postnatal depression. This is the one that shames us, makes us feel like wicked mothers and the one that makes us fear that we will never be able to love the baby properly. While this may sound like the most terrible symptom, it isn't necessarily. I know several new mums who have gratefully turned their babies over to nannies, partners, grandmas or anyone they trust to care for them. The babies are often just fine, but the mothers are dangerously depressed. The longer they keep their emotional and physical distance from the baby, the harder it is to close the gap. This is not about how much you love the baby; this is about how much you doubt yourself.

Delivery Room Disappointments

Some of us are so delighted just to survive labour and delivery and emerge with a healthy baby that we don't care whether we pooed on the table or insulted the anaesthetist's mother. Others, however, are devastated by the failure of the birth of their baby to meet all their dreams and expectations. For the nine (ten) months of pregnancy, we create and polish a fantasy about what giving birth to a baby will be like. Some of us start with a scenario that begins with the mummy-to-be rolling over to her beloved partner in bed and saying, 'Honey, it's time!' Then they call the midwife together, put the already-packed suitcase in the car and drive to the hospital, grinning with excitement and anticipation. Their midwife is there waiting for them and examines Mummy to discover that she is already seven centimetres dilated. She rallies now, her partner at her side and her focus object in her hand, as she breathes through the discomfort, just as they taught her to do in childbirth class. Three pushes, and the baby is out. He is perfect and all agree he tops all Apgar scores. The mummy is flushed with pride and elation. She begins breastfeeding immediately, and they all go home. Right!

This precious little story is responsible for more postnatal depression than you can imagine. Best Friends in maternity wards across the country are crying right this minute because they feel that they 'failed' their delivery or got 'gypped' out of it by some insensitive doctor because the births of their babies went nothing like this story. They may have tried so hard to prepare, endured so much pain without begging for an epidural, and then, after fifteen hours of agony, were told that the baby was in distress and had to be taken by C-section immediately. How quickly the atmosphere in a labour room can change from a sort of boring calmness to crisis mode when the labour doesn't progress.

Now that you have actually had a baby, it can be really funny to go back over this little story and mark with red all the passages that are outright bullshit. Where should we start? With the grinning ride to the hospital? Then there are those seven pain-free centimetres of dilation! Who writes this stuff, anyway?

Depending on where you live and what hospital you deliver in, you have about a 20 to 40 percent chance of delivering your baby by C-section.* That simple fact means that for between 5 and 10 per cent of us, this little fairy tale birth story is dust. Some of us labour for what feels like weeks, and we're so exhausted by the time we're supposed to push, that a nurse has to sit on our stomach to help get the baby out! Several of us fall apart and start accusing our partners of creating this

* Less in the UK.

torture for us in the first place. And where is the part about whining
and weeping in fear and pain? Giving birth is painful, messy, hard and
unpredictable, but the stories we treasure during pregnancy include
none of that.

I can't count the number of Best Friends who said to me, 'I know I
could have delivered naturally if they had given me just a little more
time,' or 'I wouldn't have needed the epidural if I hadn't had such
terrible back labour. I thought my spine was breaking!' or 'I should
have stopped working two weeks ago, then the baby wouldn't have
come prematurely.' Woulda, coulda, shouldas can imprison a new
mother and rob her of all joy and pride at becoming a mother. Talk
about being depressed; this is the major leagues for some mums.

SO NOW WHAT DO YOU DO?

Help is as close as a phone call. Start with the nonprofessionals first,
since we save the big guns like personal trainers and psychiatrists for
bigger jobs. Hire a sitter. If you can't afford that, beg a grandma or
Friend or perhaps even a partner (novel suggestion, don't you think?)
to take care of the baby for at least a couple of hours. My recommendation for those precious hours is to nap, but if you feel that a drive
in the car or a soak in the bath would make you feel better, then knock
yourself out. Whatever you do, however, do not waste this chance at
recapturing your sanity by doing the dishes or running errands. And,
even more important, don't feel guilty about taking a break from the
baby; if you've left enough bottles with the babysitter, the baby may
not even notice you're gone.

As great as a short reprieve can be, it probably won't be the solution
to all your postnatal depression symptoms. For me, getting some sleep
helped a lot, but my brain felt like there was some kind of limiter on it;
like something was squashing my ability to feel happy and optimistic.
This time I turned to my Best Friends for a different kind of help; I
begged them to call me every day and force me to go out and walk with
them. No, I didn't have the discipline to go every day, but I did get out
about three times a week at first. We would walk up and down the
streets, through the neighbouring foothills and hiking trails, even
through shopping arcades. And we would go fast, as fast as we could
move without getting so breathless that we couldn't talk. The walking
and the talking combined to provide the perfect therapy. I was losing
weight, too, and that didn't hurt my spirits any. As I got stronger, and as

the baby got better at holding its head upright, I occasionally brought him or her along for the ride in a backpack. The more the baby grew, the harder I had to work and the more fit I became.

There's no doubt that fresh air, a change of scene and dropping unsightly fat all contributed to an improvement in my emotional state, but I think the real magic was effected by the chemicals called endorphins that exercise released in my body. 'Hello, my name is Vicki and I am an endorphin addict.' If you get moving for no other reason than the 'high', then that's a good-enough reason. As you well know, I am not a doctor, nor do I know anything about biology that you can't learn on a good BBC special, but I do believe that postnatal depression can be related to a chemical imbalance as a result of pregnancy, childbirth and new motherhood. If you can add a little bliss to your life through the natural release of chemicals in your brain, you may be well on your way to finding your way back to well-being. If not, move on to stage three of our recovery programme.

Find some other mummies to hang with as soon as possible. No matter how shy you think you are, you can make more mummy friends than you'll know what to do with if you want to. If you belong to a church (or just live near one), find out if there is a Mother and Baby class there. Also check with your GP's office, the local community centre, the hospital where you delivered and the place where you rented your electric breast pump. If all that fails, you can start your own. Just invite any friendly-looking woman with a baby in tow to come by for some coffee. Trust me, they will be as eager for the companionship, empathy and reassurance as you are. You know how I feel about my Best Friends; I don't make a move without consulting them. I don't believe that any woman should have to face motherhood without a mummy Best Friend or two of her own to share her obsession. Only a woman going through what you're going through will be able to know the pride you feel when your baby smiles, the fear you feel when she won't stop crying, and the frustration you feel when you can't find one non-maternity article of clothing that fits yet.

Here is one word of caution: if you find that you have accidently acquired a mummy friend who makes you feel like you're in a parenting contest with her, DUMP HER AND HER PERFECT BABY IMMEDIATELY. Any woman who seems to have everything under control at all times is lying to you and to herself. You need a friend who knows that real acceptance and friendship are only possible between two living, feeling, honest human beings. Competitive mothering goes against all *Best Friends' Guide* rules and regulations and constitutes grounds for decertification. You know what that means: you no longer have the right to use the capital B when referring to yourself or your friends.

CALL YOUR GP!!! Guess what? You won't be her or his first patient to complain of feeling out of sorts after having a baby. Lay it all out for the doctor; no hiding the scariest parts or being embarrassed. They have heard it all before, and if you have a good and compassionate doctor, you will be gently guided into the right treatment. On the other hand, if your doctor fails to see the seriousness of your condition or if you are patronized by being told just to hold on until the blues pass, GET A NEW DOCTOR IMMEDIATELY. You can find an GP who specializes in postnatal depression by calling the hospital where you delivered and asking for details of a support group for mothers with postnatal depression. That group can refer you to doctors as well as provide you with lots of other people who know what you are going through.

Ultimately, the solution may include a prescription for one of the new antidepressant drugs like Prozac and Zoloft. This prospect may intimidate you or even offend you because of opinions about these drugs that you made before you understood how debilitating lasting depression could be, but if you are suffering, you may make a shrine to your chosen pharmaceutical company. I'm no doctor, but I do believe in cramps, PMI, postnatal depression and menopausal depression; they are not figments of feeble women's imaginations. If there is some relief that can be gained from any of these things that doesn't require a trip to Times Square, and that can safely see me through a bumpy part, I'm first in line. All I can tell you is, it's like plastic surgery; more people are doing it than you'll ever know.

Throughout this entire experience, one of the most important things you can do is to avoid isolation. Whether you just stay in touch with your old Best Friends, make new ones in a Mother and Baby class or get involved in a postnatal depression support group, you will need to connect with the womenfolk on a regular basis. Remember what we said about the tribal thing: Oprah and Rosie are great, but you need flesh-and-blood Friends, particularly in this uproarious time of your life. Remember, YOU ARE NOT ALONE IN THIS!

6

And Baby Makes Three

The arrival of a first baby changes *relationships* into *families*. Yes, I know that many couples without children consider themselves families, and I don't mean any disrespect to them. For most people of childbearing age, however, the birth of their baby is the event that moves them into a full-tilt, grown-up relationship. They suddenly care more about the baby's welfare than their own, they feel responsible for the baby's physical, educational and moral development, and now, more than ever, they wish there really were a Santa Claus. Heaven knows, the job of raising a child is so large that it is best shared by several people, maybe even a whole village, but this chapter discusses the more-usual child-rearing team of a mummy and a daddy.

All my Best Friends recall a moment shortly after the birth of their child when they looked from their baby to their partner and back to their baby and were amazed at the magic triangle they formed. It's an astonishing discovery when you realize that, through your baby, you and your partner are related. Even if that relation is not biological, it is deep and powerful in the way it unifies two people in the protection and love of the third (and fourth, fifth, sixth, etc.) and, one hopes, brings a new level of commitment. To put it more vividly, after I had children, I began to have a new respect for the Mafia. I can admire any group that says, 'You hurt my family, you hurt me!' because that's how my husband and I feel about our kids and each other. Most mothers I know are completely capable of physical violence where their kids are concerned, and I know that I could go all the way to a capital offence with no second thought. It's tribal and primitive and wonderful to feel so connected to something bigger than just you alone. It can also be frightening, frustrating and fatiguing, so don't be surprised if your transformation from relationship to family doesn't take place smoothly and instantly.

Short-Term Changes

Change of any kind is upsetting to most people, and the changes you undergo during pregnancy and parenthood are nothing if not startling. All you have to do is pull out a picture of you at nine (ten) months pregnant to remind yourself of one of the most obvious changes. I am much too superficial a person to try to pretend that morphing into a hippo didn't present a self-esteem crisis for me during my pregnancies, and I am still dreaming of a tummy tuck, but we deal with all that stuff in chapter 8, 'I Want My Old Body Back!' In this chapter, we are focusing on the *emotional* impact the arrival of a baby has on a partnership or reasonable facsimile thereof. If you think that having a baby doesn't change your relationship, you're still a little delusional, Best Friend. What follows is a list of some of the most immediate, and usually short-term, changes. Later on, we will talk about the changes that are here to stay.

1. *The Magic Spell.* When a couple have gone through a delivery together, the ideal result, aside from a perfect baby, is a deeper appreciation of the parents for each other. It doesn't always happen, and you shouldn't think you've been seriously gypped if you don't think you felt it, but it goes something like this: The mother is in love with and grateful to everyone in the delivery room who didn't let her die when she was certain she was going to, and for presenting her with the most precious baby in creation. That usually includes her partner. If morphine was involved, that blanket of love will extend to all of humanity, until, of course, the medication starts wearing off. If Daddy was particularly compassionate during that time, or if she is as senti-mental as most new mothers I know, then she will feel a love for him greater than she has ever known. The father, in turn, is usually thunderstruck by having seen his partner go to battle against unseen demons and emerge with his precious baby. This euphoria doesn't last forever; that's why I recommend you suggest an expensive gift while you are still lying on the delivery table. For the day or two that you live in the suspended reality and security of the hospital, you may feel like the three of you have left this earth and moved to your own private planet. Usually, by the time you leave the hospital, charged with the task of raising this tiny baby with only your partner to help, fear and panic will have broken the magic spell into little shards.

2. *Mutual Mistrust.* At some point soon after you have brought your new baby home, it will occur to you that maybe, just maybe, your mate isn't up to the job of parenting your child. After all, do real daddies still go play ice hockey with the guys in the middle of the night (because, they tell you, it's the only time the ice is free)? Do real daddies still secretly believe that they are going to grow up to be Bruce Springsteen? Do real daddies manage to stay sound asleep when their baby has been crying for fifteen minutes?

Don't think that your partner isn't having worries of his own. He is bound to wonder how a woman who loses her bag seven times a day can keep track of his child. He will wonder how a woman who hates to cook can provide for an infant. He will worry that you didn't mean it when you said that having a baby wouldn't lead to automatic poverty and that you would go back to work by the baby's first birthday. And he will feel almost certain that, given your present fragile emotional state, you will be unable to deal with any emergency involving the baby.

You have to keep two important things in mind when you are having these little lapses of faith. First, they almost always stem from your own gigantic self-doubt. We new mums can be so intimidated by our awesome responsibilities that we want to know that someone bigger, smarter, calmer and better than us is ready when we drop the ball. The logical person, next to Superman, is our mate, and any deviation from our picture of the ideal daddy is a threat to our emotional stability. Here's the news: you are up to this job! You will make it up as you go along just as the rest of us have been doing for years. You don't need Superman, because you are already big enough and strong enough in ways that you can't even see yet. Let your partner be who he is, too. His love for you and your baby are his greatest qualifications for parenting your baby.

The second thing to keep in mind is that most of these doubts will fade with the passage of time, partly because you both will calm down a lot over the next year, and partly because you will have demonstrated to each other that you really do have a knack for this parenthood business. After you have managed not to lose your baby for two or three months, your partner will begin to get over his fear. And, after seeing you and the baby through three months of colic, even a pretend Bruce Springsteen deserves the big respect as a real dad.

3. *Baby Obsession.* Mothers and fathers are known to succumb to the charms of their baby, often to the exclusion of everyone else. We

mothers are most susceptible to this private love affair, probably because of all sorts of biological reasons, but fathers, too, can fall head over heels. Two of the most common manifestations of baby obsession are the lack of interest in sex and the tendency to view the world as merely a stage for the use of your child. This *Guide* discusses both at length in chapters 9 and 4, respectively. We bring it up again now because, whatever form it takes, it usually results in one of the parents feeling left out. In the old days, before the baby was born, the love moved directly in a straight line between you and your mate. Now the relationship is triangular. The baby takes up so much of our emotional time and attention that often the only way we express our love for each other as parents is through the baby. It's like saying 'You know I love you, sweetheart, because I am caring for our child so lovingly.' This is all well and good up to a point, but it's important to remind ourselves that our relationship is more than just being the other parent to our child. You know distinctions are getting murky when you and your partner start calling each other 'Mummy' and 'Daddy.'

4. *Fear of Abandonment*. A surprising number of Best Friends report that they went through a very vulnerable time after giving birth when they obsessed about being left alone with the baby. Either they had gruesome thoughts of their mate dying or they worried that he would leave them for another, more *fun*, relationship. My Friend Erin had utmost faith in her husband's physical well-being, but she occasionally worried that his travels to Europe would provide wonderfully attractive alternatives to married-with-three-children. After all, she wondered, would *she* want to stay married to someone like *her*? The more I worried about my husband introducing me to the life of a single-parent family, the more crippled I became. I would look at myself in the mirror and decide not to bother with makeup or combed hair since my butt would still be huge and dimpled anyway. I can never remember if humans are animals that mate for life or not, but I think that we mothers have an instinctual fear of being abandoned before we have regained our strength and mental health after having a baby. If you are feeling particularly vulnerable right now, let us remind you that by the end of this year you will be back to your pushy, demanding, self-righteous old self, or at least I was.

5. *Trapped!* Having a baby raises the stakes in the relationship game. We tend to stay longer and try harder to work troubles out to provide a stable family for our baby. Let's face it: even though we all get married

(or make some other serious commitment) with the intention of it lasting forever, statistics show that lots of us change our minds later on. While it is always painful when a relationship goes sour, we all know that we do have that escape hatch of leaving. That hatch gets much tinier and harder to open when a baby is born into your relationship. No matter what happens in your love life with your mate, you will always be connected by this child that you share. Just look at Billy Joel; I mean, how many weddings of his former wife, Christie Brinkley, is the man expected to attend? In our healthier states of mind, we understand that this willingness to commit to another person for life, especially now that there is a child, is one of the bravest acts we will ever make. In the dark little corners of our psyches, however, is the annoying little question, 'You mean I'll never have sex with anyone else for the rest of my life?'

In-Laws and Outlaws

The birth of a baby not only expands your family by one, but it stretches it out to include all sorts of people who had marginal influence before. Get ready for the mixed blessing of having grandparents, aunts, uncles, and cousins more involved in your life. Your innocent little baby creates a biological relationship between people who might have had only a passing acquaintance, like your parents and your partner's parents. Your brother-in-law and his wife, whom you never much cared for, are now critically important to you as your baby's uncle and aunt. You want the baby to know them, to be friends with their children, to feel loved and protected by them. And they all have their two cents to add about how your parenting affects *them*.

Now that you are officially part of the clan, by virtue of birthing one of its kin, more attention is paid to you. You are taken more seriously as a member of your partner's family and viewed with more respect by members of your own (or at least one should hope so). This part of belonging to the family created by your child is great. Some of the other parts can be more problematic. All of a sudden, everyone seems to care where the three of you are planning to have Christmas dinner or which grandmother you plan to honour with your time on Mother's Day. There will be times when you will swear that it isn't the pleasure of your company they seek, but rather your contribution of the baby to the festivities. All this familial love is exactly why people like the Hatfields and McCoys have been feuding all these years. How you allocate your baby's time and attention among the various members of the family will be one of life's greatest challenges.

Our immediate advice is to stand up for yourself and your family from the start. There is no need to be petulant about what you want; it just makes you seem silly and spoiled. Keep in mind that you are not the only ones who love this baby, and it's only fair to share. Still, now is the time to begin defining how *your* family 'does things' like observing holidays and celebrating birthdays. Remember, all the other parents have had years of calling the shots, and it may be painful for them to let go or compromise, but you must help them to learn to share nicely with others. There is a legend in my husband's family that his sister and her husband used to eat dinner every night with her parents. Even though they were married, they didn't yet have children, so they were still the children themselves, as far as the parents were concerned. One night, she decided that she was going to cook dinner for her husband in her home. It took my father-in-law days of high-level negotiating to get his wife and daughter speaking again. But they have now been speaking for the twenty-five years since the debacle with no signs of stopping, so I think they got over it. It may be the same with your own relatives; they will think that unless you are all gathered at their house for a reading of *The Night Before Christmas* on Christmas Eve, the holiday will be ruined. Trust us; it won't. Traditions are great; everybody should have a chance to make them.

One of the many joys I wish for you, Best Friend, is that your children grow up knowing their grandparents. Sometimes the fates prevent this, but if your parents are alive and around, pull them into your life. Grandparents love your babies in a free and relaxed way that is impossible for us parents. They also offer a sense of belonging and heritage to children, and they are more than willing to tell embarrassing stories about you. As a mother, I have loved watching my kids through their grandparents' eyes. It's like rediscovering their magic by seeing it reflected in someone else's face. Until I had my first baby, I didn't know that I could love a person for the simple fact that she or he loved my child. The babies gave me a chance to appreciate my family just for being my family and loving us. Don't forget, grandparents are the only people who will listen to your endless baby stories because they are interested, not just polite. Who knows? They may even babysit now and then.

This love fest doesn't come baggage-free, however. These relatives of your baby don't love her in a vacuum. What she eats, where she sleeps, when she's potty trained and HOW YOU MOTHER HER all become legitimate subjects for their concern. Bless their hearts; they may try not to intrude, but all they succeed in doing is making little passive-aggressive statements that send you running into oncoming traffic. After your mother has asked you for the fiftieth time, 'Are you sure he doesn't need a hat?' it starts to sound like she has an opinion about the need for a hat, don't you think? And you can be damn sure it's not the same as yours. Even if there isn't a grandparent in sight, their presence is felt every time you or your partner makes a parenting decision because 'that's how my mum always did it.' We already know how fragile a new mother's confidence is, and there are few things that can threaten it more than the judgement of her own mother or mother-in-law.

Religion

Many of us are 'lapsed something or others' when we are shopping for our partners. We might not have been in a church or temple in years and the subject of religion gets discussed only as an intellectual matter, if at all, with potential life partners. Then, when the baby is born, out of left field comes running everybody's newly awakened faith. If the parents share the same faith, which generally only happens after lots of negotiating and one party changing religions, then there isn't much of a problem. The rest of the time, there is. I don't know what it is about Jews and Catholics, but I think about half the couples of my generation are Jewish/Catholic blends. Episcopalian/Catholic I could see, at least the songs sound the same, but no, Jewish/Catholic seems to be all the rage these days. And if you don't think this leads to some great and mighty clashes after a baby is born, you need to wake up and smell the coffee. Just bring this topic up with some of your mummy Best Friends and their mates; it's more fun than *The Newlywed Game*.

My Friend Mindy is Jewish and her husband is Catholic. I suppose that their baby girl would be considered Jewish, too, since, by Judaic law, the religion is passed down through the mothers. (Good choice, God.) But it wasn't too long after the baby was born that the Catholic grandma started lobbying for a baptism. This wasn't just a whim as far as she was concerned because her religion says that babies who haven't been baptized can't go to heaven. The Jewish grandmother was no more prepared to enter a Catholic church and commit her grandchild to the care of Christ than she was to deny the Holocaust. All of a sudden, Mindy, whose religion is Let's Just All Love One Another, was caught in the holy wars.

This particular crisis was averted when the Catholic grandma and her sister were allowed to take the baby to church for a very low-key baptism. Mindy and her side of the family just stayed out of it. Just like President Clinton's policy for gays in the military, they adopted a 'don't ask, don't tell' policy regarding that religious episode.

This wasn't the last time, however, that this kind of détente has had to be achieved in Mindy's family, and this is important to note because religion is an area where compromise will be required for the rest of your parenting life. Once they got past the baptism, it wasn't too long before the decision about the child taking First Communion took place. Then there's speculation about a Bar Mitzvah and where in the world she will eventually get married. What's really funny, at least to me, is that Mindy's daughter attends parochial school: a fundamentalist Christian parochial school! They even teach creationism there! But, it's a wonderful school, and her daughter is thriving, so Mindy just enacts her own 'don't ask, don't tell' policy; she is in charge of all the academic homework and projects, and her husband intercedes on her behalf when it's time to memorize all the Books of the Bible, in order.

I was raised a Presbyterian (if Sunday School every Easter counts as 'raising'), and my husband is from an Italian Catholic family. I maintained after our children were born that since I cared more about their religious instruction (and more important, since I was the only one who went to church at all), I should get to choose the church. After all, what did I know about Catholic services, with all that standing, sitting, kneeling stuff? My husband was fine about it, but I do remember the look on his face when he came to my Presbyterian church for our first baby's baptism. His whole family had flown in from New York for the event and we took up nearly three rows of pews. It was wonderful, with a church member singing and playing guitar, everybody coming up to see the baby and vowing to care for its spiritual upbringing in their congregation. My husband, on the other hand, whispered to me at the end of the little reception on the church terrace, 'Get me out of here. I feel like I've walked in on an episode of *Hee Haw*.' I guess all that goodness-and-light stuff really can depress a Catholic.

The Best Friends' advice regarding conflicts between parents about religion is this: you will find yourselves completely at odds with each other several times during the next couple of decades over issues that seem nearly as important to you as life and death. This is one time when winning by bullying really is a bad idea. The two of you must start with the question 'What decision can I live with?' If you look deeply enough, you will be surprised to discover that you can live with almost anything that doesn't threaten your child in any way. Work forward from there to your compromise. Negotiate. Feel free to bargain by saying things like 'I can handle the bris, but I still reserve the right in thirteen years to reconsider the Bar Mitzvah.' Remember, children aren't as doctrinaire as we adults. You can editorialize on their religious training as they grow up, explaining, for example, that the Sunday School's view of Jesus might not be the only view. Or you can expose them to the teachings of several religions that you believe have valuable wisdom to share. Remember, ultimately, you are your child's most important teacher of ethics, morals and spiritual development. Whether it's in partnership with some organized religion or in the privacy of your home, you and your mate will be wise to start talking about it now. You may surprise yourself with what you learn about your own faith.

Holidays

Aside from Thanksgiving, most of the really good holidays are direct creations of one religious philosophy or another. That means that even if you aren't very religious in a sort of church-or temple-going way, you won't be spared the holy wars entirely. You may not be able to name three apostles, but you know you would perish without a Christmas tree and presents on December 25. You may have to read the prayers for Passover since you have forgotten them from last year, but you know that those potato latkes are not to be missed under any circumstances. If you think about it, holidays are often more emotionally charged than discussions about personal religious beliefs. I think that this is because the big religious holidays involve more than that magic triangle created by you, your partner and your baby. Holidays are when all the relatives come out of the woodwork, carrying their traditions and customs with them. You know that any decision you make about the holidays pulls the pin from the grenade known as 'In-laws or Outlaws'. Once that happens, you can sit back and just wait for the eggnog to fly. Unless you are altogether without relatives of your own, you are guaranteed to feel like a wishbone at the holidays. As the daughter of your parents, you may feel particularly pulled in their direction. I don't know what it is, but there often seems to be more pressure on a woman to integrate her baby and husband into her parents' holiday world. I remember when my first daughter was born, I was secretly gleeful that, after the kids were grown and married, I would have at least one child who would come to *my* house for Christmas dinner. How does that old saying go? 'A mother loses her son to his bride, but a daughter is her daughter forever.' On the off chance that this is true, I'd better start kissing up to my girls right now. Why am I already hating my future daughters-in-law?

Most new little families are still pretty mobile and able to travel among the grandparents, stepgrandparents and all others who want to celebrate with them. During this time, most of my Best Friends took a mathematical approach; they added up all the forseeable holidays and divided them by the number of families vying for their presence. This is the path of least resistance, because you can point out your lack of bias in choosing one family over another. It isn't your choice; it just isn't their turn yet.

With the addition of a second baby, which, coincidentally, is when your first baby is old enough to know where he is and have an opinion about it, you will want to change the approach to allocating holidays. You will be good and tired of sofa beds and plane flights with a crying baby and trying to get a toddler to sleep in a travel cot. This is usually the time when you crave a holiday at home. If you haven't started some holiday traditions of your own, now is the time. The grandparents will simply have to come to you or understand that you may not take your show on the road with the advent of every major holiday.

When my husband and I had our first Christmas as just our little family, we both got anxious and unsure of what we were supposed to do. First of all, as long as grandparents were around, we always knew that there were responsible adults to make sure we had a lovely meal and toys that came in boxes saying 'some assembly needed' might actually get put together. Assuming those grown-up roles was intimidating (and tiring, I might add). Neither of us seemed to know whether we wanted the Christmas gifts to be opened in the living room or the family room or if any gifts should be opened the night before. Should we insist on having breakfast before opening the gifts? Are the kids allowed to open anything before the sleepy parents have gotten up and turned on the video camera? It took us a few years before we worked it all out, but now it runs pretty smoothly. In fact, once we decided the basics for each holiday, like the need to see snow at least once during Christmas, or the need for a big egg hunt for Easter, we got confident enough to ad lib a little bit. Now, once a few basic requirements are met, we can make our holidays great and personally ours nearly anywhere. It will help you stay lighter on your feet if you look at each holiday as something to be done again next year. Most of us get caught in what I call the 'Last Supper' obsession, where we focus so much on the need for a perfect holiday that you'd think it was the last one we'd ever have. Only Martha Stewart can take that kind of pressure, Best Friend. The rest of us are grateful that we get lots of tries to get it right. Relax and know that what didn't work for you this year can be fixed next time.

Discipline

As you look at your tiny new baby, you must think I'm some kind of ogre to even think of mentioning discipline in his presence. Calm down, Best Friend. I, too, cannot imagine a single baby behaviour that requires discipline. In fact, I might err too much that way, but we won't know for several more years, will we? As your baby starts crawling and then walking, he will begin doing some things that will inspire you to respond with an excited 'NO!' Who knows, you might already have made that exclamation during a relaxing breastfeeding session when your baby bit your nipple with his brand-new teeth. Aside from this primitive kind of setting of limits, it's silly to spend much time disciplining a baby during his first year; first, because he's still too young to play with matches or call you a nasty name, and second, because he doesn't understand your point anyway.

We mention discipline now because it's time for you and your partner to start *talking* about it. We don't just mean that you need to know each other's feelings about such things as spankings or time-outs. You should discuss how you feel about such things as food or toys as rewards for good behaviour. My Best Friend Jackie is constantly reminding her partner that a trip down to the ice cream parlour is not the inevitable ending to a nice day. And I, who constantly beg my mother-in-law not to send gifts and sweets to my kids for every occasion from Groundhog Day to their half birthdays, was so desperate to potty-train my first child that I gave him an M&M every time he would sit on the potty for me. I must really have been out of my mind because who in the world would want food and poo connected in such an intimate way?

Some people think that boys should be disciplined differently from girls. I know a wonderful man who teaches little kids baseball and other life lessons. He tells me that little boys should be spanked by their parents, but little girls don't need such a firm hand (no pun intended). If you ask me, this is an important discussion not just for the discipline ramifications but for the broader issue of gender equality. For example, it might be interesting to know now if your partner thinks little boys who play with dolls will become gay, or if little girls fixated on Barbie will become show-girls in Las Vegas.

The most important decision you and your partner can make this year is to stand united in whatever discipline and rules you set. You can bet that a child as smart as yours will learn early on to shop from parent to parent for the permission or indulgence he seeks, and your only hope for prevailing even occasionally is to present a united front. Kids need to learn not to manipulate you this blatantly. Besides, if you and your partner get dragged into arguments about behaviour while the child is standing there in front of you, then you blow the myth of the Omniscient Parent that we all depend on to maintain the upper hand. If you blow it for you, you blow it for the rest of us.

This solidarity is hard enough when you are in a happy relationship, but it gets harder than chin-ups when couples separate. First of all, divorced people don't usually have much interest in having long conversations with each other about anything, even their kids. If they could stand each other for that, they probably could have stayed together. This situation affects discipline because you both need to know all the circumstances surrounding any decision and what the long-term plans might be. If you think that Junior should have his video games taken away for a week and your ex is going to have Junior at his house within that week, you two have some information down-loading to do. Second, there are now two households and two different lifestyles. It's tempting for a parent who feels insecure (or guilty) to give in to all the child's demands, even if it means undermining the other parent. In fact, this undermining seems to be a favourite enterprise when the divorce wounds are still fresh.

The bottom line here is that you and your partner will not always agree whether your baby can taste a hot fudge sundae at nine months, or drink soda at nine years, but you need to discuss the party line in private and present it as a joint decision.

Job Assignments

Pretty early on in the parenting partnership, each partner will assume certain roles in relation to their baby/child. Especially if the mother does not return to a job outside the home, the tasks associated with primary care will for the most part be hers. It's pretty straight-ahead for the first year, with most attention being paid to eating, sleeping and the cleanup in between. Even in the first year, however, you might find job assignments occurring, either because you consciously divided the tasks or because you and your partner unconsciously drifted into preprogrammed roles. In our house, all areas of Health, Education and Welfare are mine. I am also in charge of Lost and Found. My husband is in charge of Defence, Fitness and, when the children were babies, he was Prime Minister of Burping. He could get a burp out of any baby, any time. It was a marvel to behold. He has a subspeciality in joke telling and teasing, both of which tend to make me nervous. We share Discipline, but I think I am the bad guy far more often than he is. Oh well, there's one in every family.

If you are unhappy with your job assignments or if they must change to accommodate a change in circumstances, like your return to work, the two of you must sit down and divvy up the jobs all over again. If you don't, you will succumb to the Superwoman mythology that says that you not only bring home the bacon, you fry it, too, along with doing the laundry, selling Girl Guide cookies with your daughter, being snack mum for your son's Sunday League team and staying a perfect size six. Trust your Best Friends, there is no such thing! My husband recently started leaving work to go to our seven-year-old's tap class. That job has NEVER come within his purview, and I was shocked when he took it on so that I could write this book. It just goes to prove, this family stuff works better when all your horses are pulling in the same direction. (And you can't beat a great daddy.)

The Tough Stuff

No matter how long you were together before you had your first baby, the odds are pretty good that you didn't spend too many evenings discussing what you would do if one of you were to die. Even going to a karaoke pub is far more enjoyable than talking about that. When you have a baby to provide for, however, this talk becomes inevitable. As painful and scary as this may be, you have to realize that any decision you *don't* make is a decision the government may make for you. The scenario that is usually most upsetting but most critical to address is what should happen to your children and your estate if something happened to both of you. You will have to discuss certain things like guardianship of your children, how any money or assets you leave will be paid (like whether they get your millions on their eighteenth or their twenty-first birthday), and how to protect what assets you have from unnecessary taxation. (Is there any other kind?)

There are several 'form' wills available, but we Best Friends advise a visit to a good lawyer so that you can be certain that you are accurately appraising your situation. This is a difficult time for you to be objective. A good lawyer can *gently* (lawyers, please note) inform you of your options and explain what your concerns should be, thereby starting a conversation that you and your partner may find difficult to begin on your own. Once the ice is broken, however, the task doesn't get easier until it's done and forgotten about. My Best Friend Patricia got so upset imagining her baby's future in all its possibilities and without her in it that they quickly adjourned when she ran out of the office crying. I kept up a brave front when our turn came, but my husband kept making the sign of the horns (an Italian thing with your fingers) to keep the evil eye from noticing the catastrophe we invited by talking of such things.

Be prepared to discuss the relative child-rearing merits of your sister versus your partner's mother. Be prepared to have your partner tell you and the lawyer, a total stranger, what he intends to do with the property he had before he married you. Be prepared to allocate pounds and pennies for every year of support for your child until he is eighteen or graduates from college. Be prepared to realize you don't have nearly enough life insurance. There are several excruciating things that you will have to do as a parent, like holding your child while he has blood drawn or a stitch taken in her forehead, and this is just another one.

There; you've taken this all very well. Now let's talk about something else.

I'm soooo tired, I haven't slept a wink

If you don't think getting enough sleep is important, talk to the guy who was piloting the *Exxon Valdez* when it ran aground and spilled its oil all over the Alaskan coastline. His excuse was that he hadn't been to sleep in forty-eight hours. If it worked for him, there's no limit to what we mothers should be able to get away with.

Sure, you've been tired before. You've been to all-nighters in college or maybe even been to a rave (can you imagine?). Even the last stages of pregnancy often led to insomnia, what with all that worrying and sharing a body with a full-grown baby. Still, no one is ever prepared for how deeply tiring it is to be a new mother. Of all the adjustments that are required of new parents, sleep deprivation is the universal killer. Every new mother I've ever met has just rolled her bleary eyes hopelessly when asked if she is getting enough sleep.

For the first few weeks after bringing the new baby home, energy reserves and adrenaline can protect us from the full effects of sleep deprivation. We may not be sleeping for more than two hours at a stretch, but we're so busy getting to know this new little human, and so concerned that something terrible might happen to it when we're sleeping anyway, that we don't panic at first. We also might be getting more help and encouragement from friends, relatives and the health visitor during those first few weeks. Then, as the baby approaches her first-month birthday, and you have been deserted by your mother and your partner, it occurs to you that this lack of sleep thing may not be ending any time soon. You have just entered the Endless Night, a place right around the corner from the Twilight Zone. A sense of panic starts climbing up your spine and over the top of your skull. From that moment on, sleep will be the major preoccupation of your existence. Don't jump! The worst will probably be over within the first three months, give or take a year or two. No, just kidding. Actually the baby's sleep patterns will change, often dramatically, with each developmental stage, so just when you've had it up to here with the 4:00 A.M. reveille, your early riser will be taking enough food at 11:00 P.M. to make her sleep satisfied until 6:30. Of course, now that she is so rested, she may want to skip her morning nap or to stay up with you and your partner to see *Newsnight*, so you will still be tired, just in a new and different way. Isn't motherhood exciting! The kindest thing you can do for yourself is to erase from your mind all expectations about how babies are 'supposed' to sleep because each baby has its own unique style and, even more important, because there will be many things that happen in her early life that will affect her sleep patterns. Getting your child to learn to sleep through the night at three months has absolutely no effect on how she will be sleeping nine months from now, when she's walking and finds her cot more like a holding pen. My Best Friend Lori's daughter is seventeen months old and she is already swinging herself up and over the cot bars to escape. She lands with a thud on the floor every time, but if she feels pain, she sure doesn't show it. In my own home, I currently have a three-year-old who is in a big-girl bed that she can climb out of at will. She often roams the house at night in search of a sibling or parent to cuddle up to, but she is equally happy to go into the pantry and steal all the sweets she was denied during the day. My seven-year-old has reached the age when the sounds of trees against the house or creaking floors can only mean that there are kidnappers afoot. Chalk that up to watching too much television news. These sleep issues are as much a part of parenting as Toys 'R' Us.

How Much Sleep Do You Need?

It turns out that we really do seem to need about eight hours of sleep a night, just as your mother told you. If you are sick, under unusual stress or recovering from injury or surgery, you may need even more sleep. Isn't that just the funniest cosmic joke you've heard all day? Brand-new mothers are almost always a little sick, they are definitely stressed out and recovering from anything from a fierce episiotomy to a C-section, and they are lucky if they get two stretches of two hours of sleep and one hour of 'quasi sleep' (when the baby is in your arms and you are sitting up, but you are in a coma) per day.

To add insult to injury, studies indicate that you need to get eight *consecutive* hours of sleep a day, not a one-hour catnap every three hours. It seems that our brains don't really wind down as soon as we lose consciousness but do so gradually, culminating in a phase known as REM sleep. For those of you who missed the programme about sleep, REM stands for Rapid Eye Movement. Take a look at your own sleeping baby if you want to see REM sleep in action. Newborns often appear to open their eyes or to look up into their foreheads, their little eyelids fluttering when they're sound asleep. They are REMing, those lucky angels. Apparently this is the time when we release our subconscious thoughts, synthesize the day's input and allow our brainwaves to calm down. We need REM sleep to keep from running to the top of a motorway bridge with guns and taking potshots at oncoming traffic.

Guess what? New mothers almost never get REM sleep! Those mini-comas we call naps don't give our beleaguered brains enough time to stop making to-do lists, let alone settle into rapid eye movement. Scientists (and masters of torture) know that waking a sleeping person several times a night and preventing him or her from drifting into REM sleep is a very effective form of inducing psychosis. That, my tired Friend, is exactly what our babies do to us. Isn't it amazing that anything so utterly adorable could be so sadistic, too?

We depend more than you know on going to bed at night and getting out of bed in the morning to offer structure to our lives. Even the simplest things become mysterious and confusing when you lose that daily punctuation. During the first week or so after bringing the new baby home, for example, the utter lack of normality confuses us so much that we never know when it's time to get dressed. Are we supposed to put on presentable clothes after the 5:00 A.M. feeding, or do we just stay in our sweatpants and partner's stained T-shirt until after the baby's bath and feeding at 10:00 A.M.? Then again, since most babies take a good long nap after a bath and a meal, maybe we should go to bed, too, and not bother to get dressed until after lunch. Before we know it, our partner is home from work and putting the Chinese takeaway on the table and we still haven't even put on clean underwear. I was so delirious in those early months of motherhood that I compromised and wore 'street clothes' that could be slept in. My theory was, since I never knew if I was resting or rising, I might as well be prepared for either. Loose leggings or thermals under a T-shirt and a long sweater or sweatshirt can work for nearly any occasion; just look at the most recent Timberland catalogue. If you feel an emotional need to differentiate between the presentable you and the private you, consider substituting real shoes for slippers when you think you might go out or receive visitors.

WHOSE FAULT IS THIS?

We are generally so unprepared for the utter chaos that a baby brings that we react as though something has gone terribly wrong. This frantic state must surely be a strange convergence of the planets, an event that couldn't be predicted and will never repeat itself. If we are not sleeping, if we can't seem to get a shower in, if we feel cranky and overwhelmed, somebody must have done this to us. Normal, garden-variety mothering couldn't possibly be this hard. Our plan for motherhood entailed a graceful transition in which we redirected our organizational and management skills from our jobs outside the home to the relatively simple tasks of taking care of a baby inside the home. It did not include feeling out of control, unprepared and overwhelmed by how unrelenting and endless the job would be. No one ever really explained to us that motherhood is like a caucus race; there is no start, no finish and you keep racing around in circles. The first thing our panicky minds start yammering is 'Everybody else manages to have children and not die. Why can't I?' Clearly, someone in this picture isn't living up to the challenge . . .

Is it you? Should you have paid attention when your cousin offered to teach you how to change her baby's nappy? Should you have skipped university and ten years of earning a partnership in the firm and had your baby when you were still young and energetic? Are you such a sucker of a mother that you are letting the baby call all the shots? Should you be exerting some authority over this tiny tyrant? Maybe you just don't have the deep maternal instinct that was supposed to be your birthright as a girl, and therefore can't calmly rise above the commotion. No, no, *you* know what you are; you're a wimp and not fit to be the mother of a guppy, let alone a human.

But wait a minute, you're working twenty-four hours a day here! This blame can't just be laid on your doorstep. If it isn't you, then it must be your partner. Yeah, *that's* whose fault this is! Only your blind devotion prevented you from seeing it earlier. If only *he* would hold up his end. After all, it was *he* who got you in this predicament in the first place. Sure, the baby books advise you to pump an extra bottle of milk so that he can feed the baby while you rest, but you haven't managed to squeeze out one extra ounce, let alone a full bottle. If Mother Nature is so smart, then why didn't She put working nipples on dads? And why does he get to escape to work every day and leave you alone to face this eight-pound bottomless pit of needs? He doesn't even always take your calls right away anymore! And what's with his always asking you, 'What should we do about dinner tonight?' He's a grown man – can't he focus that big, manly brain of his on this one simple task and just handle it? Is it too much to ask to enter the dining room and find a cooked meal already there, just once? And if *he* doesn't handle it, why doesn't he earn a better living so that you could afford to hire someone who will?

Then again, the poor guy looks as haunted and tired as you do. Sure, he isn't a wizard with baby wipes, but he is working awfully hard. So if it isn't his fault, there is only one possible culprit left . . . that's right; it's the baby's fault. Sure she's absolutely gorgeous and perfect in every way, but she really doesn't play fair. She sleeps all day, she cries all night, she is only happy if you are walking around with her in your arms and she screams when you sit down on your haemorrhoid donut to rest your aching back. She feeds until you think your breasts will fall off, and then proceeds to spit up what must be half of the meal. Then she wants to feed again and gets mad at you if the well has run dry. She hates her cot but loves your bed. You try to let her cry for a few minutes to let her learn to comfort herself, but she refuses to learn. You try crying yourself. She's right; it doesn't make you feel much better. The babies on TV and in books sleep all night, take two naps a day and never cry unless they have a dirty nappy or are hungry. Your baby, however, cries at phantoms, loves to party all night and naps un-predictably. Clearly motherhood would be a snap, if only your *baby* cooperated.

HERE'S THE TRUTH: THE BIRTH OF A BABY IS SUPPOSED TO BLOW YOUR SCHEDULE TO BITS, EVEN IF IT NEARLY KILLS YOU AND YOUR PARTNER. THIS IS NATURE'S WAY OF MAKING SURE THAT WE GET OUR NEW PRIORITIES STRAIGHT. THE THREE MOST IMPORTANT THINGS BE-COME, IN THIS ORDER:

1. THE BABY'S HEALTH
2. THE BABY'S COMFORT
3. THE BABY'S PARENTS' SURVIVAL (THIS IS A VERY DISTANT THIRD).

The Symptoms of Sleep Deprivation

Fatigue

Stop any woman pushing a pram and ask her how she is feeling at that very moment, and she will invariably answer, 'Tired'. It doesn't matter if the baby in that pram is three weeks or three years old. She might be tired, for example, from last night's battle with a colicky baby and the previous six weeks of all-night feeding. This is called Cumulative Tiredness. It makes you feel like you are wearing chain mail for clothing, or Eddie Murphy's fat body in *The Nutty Professor*. You move gracelessly, either herky-jerky (too much caffeine, Friend) or like you're living in jelly. If you lie down for a minute, you will gulp sleep the way a drowning person gulps air. Then again, this mother may be exhausted by the sleep disorder called Sick Baby Fatigue. In the first two years of life, little ones are often prone to colds, the flu or episodes of teething that all seem to come to a crescendo in massive ear infections. No mother worth her salt can go to sleep when her baby is miserable; the baby's howling will see to that. Then, for the parent of the older child, there is the sleep disorder called There's a Monster under My Bed, or a child's need for frequent nocturnal reassurance called I Need a Drink of Water, Again.

Nonparents may dream of going to Rome or attending the Academy Awards as a nominee, but your dreams are all about beds, hammocks and chaises. You want to crawl into one and not have to get out again for a month. By the time I had my fourth child, I was so fatigued that I would look longingly at hospitals. My idea of a great holiday would have been to be checked into a private room, hooked up to an IV full of nonfattening liquids and given a mild sedative. Doctor's orders would be for my husband, baby-sitter and extended family to protect me from all news from home. I would wake up for *Rosie* and *Oprah*, then go back to sleep until *Entertainment Tonight* came on. Maybe I would make *The X-Files* once a week. Gee, that still sounds awfully good . . .

Brain Damage

The brain of an exhausted mother feels like it is wearing a sweater. Sounds may be muffled, thoughts are indistinct and our receptors are blanketed. Being asked a simple question like 'Would you like a tuna sandwich?' can make us screw up our faces in concentration as we try to remember what tuna is while simultaneously determining if we are hungry. So scrambled are the lines of communication between the nerves and the brain that we can nearly cut the tip of a finger off while making dinner and not notice until the trail of blood finally captures our attention. In addition to losing our sensory skills, we often lose our coordination when we haven't slept in weeks. It is pitifully common for new mothers to fall on stairs, stub their toes on furniture and pinch their fingers in doors. For the longest time, I couldn't open a box with a knife or a pair of scissors without causing myself serious bodily injury. (A big problem for someone who only shops mail order.) I remember interrupting a phone conversation to my Best Friend Mindy to calmly inform her that I would have to hang up since I had just driven a fork into my forearm. Naturally, I was trying to do two or three things at one time, and I was too sleep deprived even to attempt one. Clearly, I should not have been allowed to touch sharp objects, but there wasn't a responsible grown-up in the house to stop me.

Decision-making skills, too, are shot to hell. We tired mummies don't know if we should go to the supermarket, if we should remodel the house, if we should let the baby sleep in our bed or if we should shoot ourselves between the eyes. We don't necessarily trust our skills in this parenting business to begin with, and now that sleeplessness has robbed us of our brains, we are really clueless. Why else do you think we worship Miriam Stoppard? We are begging for someone to come along and tell us what to do. This is also a key window of opportunity for a mother or mother-in-law to come in and take charge, if she is so inclined. No matter how worried you may be about her becoming the authority figure in your life all over again, take our advice and LET HER! (at least until you have recovered somewhat). You can always reclaim the throne in a month or two when you have the strength.

Concentration and memory are also casualties of this addled state. Good luck beginning any project, no matter how simple, and staying with it until it is complete. If you are like the rest of us Best Friends, you will walk into your kitchen four or five times, intending to unload the dishes that have been sitting clean in the dishwasher for three days now, and you will never manage to accomplish this feat. You may make it to the dishwasher, and you may even open the thing up, but you will not get those dishes into the cabinets. (Our advice? Consider the dishwasher the dishes' new home. Set the table from there, and get clean glasses from there as you need them. When it is empty, move the accumulated dirty dishes from the sink into the dishwasher, turn it on, and let those dishes live there until you need them.) If you think household chores are challenging, wait until you start getting those calls from the office. Remember how you blithely told your assistant to feel free to call you any time after the first three weeks, since you would be working part-time from home? Not only will you not be able to provide the answer, you won't even understand the question. In fact, it will take you a moment or two to remember who this person is who is calling and intruding into your cocoon in such a brazen way.

The scariest place a tired mum can lose her concentration is in the car. Every single one of my Best Friends (and I) have at least one terrifying story about driving our precious babies somewhere when we haven't slept in days. Some study I heard on a recent morning news show (yes, everything I know I learned from television) reported that a person who has not slept in twenty-four hours has the same lack of concentration and slow reaction time as a person who is legally drunk. Add to that a screaming baby in the back-seat where you can't reach him (because we all know that car seats can't go in front seats anymore because of the air bags) and you most assuredly do not have the profile of the ideal driver. How can you anticipate what another driver is going to do when you are not even sure what *you* are going to do? The fact that your shopping bag, your extra-large coffee-to-go and your bag are still on the roof of the car means nothing.

Short Fuse

Sleep deprivation not only takes the spring out of your step; it also takes the bounce out of your temper. You just can't roll with the punches anymore. Ringing telephones, TV commercials showing thin women with blown-dry hair and computer-generated telephone solicitations make you want to pound the floor with both your fists. Practical jokes are a capital offence, and even mild teasing is loathsome. Both my Best Friends Terry and Betsy (and the rest of us, I'm sure, if only I could remember that far back) would glare at us 'old mummy' Friends whenever we *lovingly* mentioned how spaced out they were or the fact that they hadn't worn anything but leggings and big shirts in four months. There is no such thing as a good sense of humour in a new mother. (And there is nothing more fun for old mothers than taking advantage of this.)

As we discussed before, it's really easy to pick a fight with someone near and dear to you when you are this exhausted. The usual target is your mate, but your mother might be a candidate, too, especially if she is generous enough to stay around and take the abuse. Tread easy here, Best Friend; this is a potential babysitter you are ticking off. The particularly enchanting characteristic of this kind of outburst is that you can't turn it off. You may begin an argument about who left the headlights on in the car, and after twenty minutes of fighting about it, you can't stop, even after you've realized that you don't really give a damn about the car or the headlights. It's as if your throttle gets stuck in rage mode and you can't turn off the gas. There is only one way to put out this fire – DOUSE IT WITH TEARS, THEN SMOTHER IT IN ICE CREAM.

Hopelessness

You know that you could endure this bone-crunching fatigue of your baby's infancy if only you knew that it would end. Best Friend, I promise you that it will end. It's just that I'm not exactly sure when. I realize that's no consolation when you wake up even more tired than you were when you fell asleep (perhaps because the taste of sleep is too fresh in your mouth), you think about how many nappies you will change today and how many hours you will have your blouse open, how many towels won't get folded and how you will have to use Kleenex for toilet paper because you haven't been shopping for a while. How can you face another day of that never-ending succession of chores, demands and half-completed projects? Quick, pull the blanket up over your ears to drown out the baby's cries and go back to sleep before your partner notices you're awake! Perhaps he will leap out of bed and rescue the baby from its dirty nappy and its hunger. He may even start the coffee and squeeze some juice for you. Yeah, and he might bake a loaf of banana bread and shampoo the carpets! What drug are you taking? GET UP AND FACE THE SQUALOUR!

Colic

This section of the *Guide* seems like a good place to bring up colic, since it has inspired more hopelessness than the *Newsweek* article saying an unmarried woman has a better chance of getting shot by a sniper than of finding a husband. If you have a baby who could be described as colicky (as opposed to just 'inconsiderate' or 'demanding' like the rest of them), you in particular will face every morning wondering whether the day will bring another interminable afternoon and night of high-pitched crying and misery (for both you and the baby!). Let's just call a spade a spade here. We could split hairs trying to categorize babies as either 'hypersensitive', 'hard to soothe', 'mood impaired', or 'sadistic', but let's just stick with 'colicky' since we all know who they are.

There is no lab test to medically determine whether your baby has colic, but if this sounds familiar, he probably has it. Somewhere at about two to three weeks of age, your previously perfect angel baby starts crying inconsolably. Often the crying begins in the afternoon or at dinnertime and continues well into the night, but this is not a hard-and-fast rule. The crying is piercing, as though someone were sticking the wretched little thing with a pin. In the beginning, we frantically strip all his clothes off, searching for the source of the pain; maybe a drawing pin slipped into the nappy when we weren't looking or maybe something sharp is lurking in all those folds of skin on his thighs. Not finding anything, we change the nappy, even though it's still clean enough to polish furniture with. We add or subtract clothes, thinking that he is too hot or too cold. We offer to feed him, and he either ignores our big old nipples or he feeds and then resumes crying with the same painful intensity. All my Best Friends who had colicky babies deduced that the problem lies in the baby's tummy. The way they strain and pull their legs up, they seem to have a major bellyache. There is a popular theory that babies who cry and fuss like this have immature or sensitive digestive tracts and that they are in pain from the buildup of wind, but the medical jury is still out on this. We desperate mothers will try anything from carrying the baby on our forearms with their faces down (the Football Hold), to bicycling their tiny legs to stimulate their intestines, to cuddling, cajoling and caressing them. We beg our doctors for relief and are sometimes even placated with drops (ask the doctor what they are) or maybe the suggestion that we try giving the baby herbal teas steeped in warm water. Ultimately, we just want to kill somebody.

I remember evenings when I would practically lateral pass my screaming son to my husband the instant he walked in the door, I was so anxious to go hide alone in the bathroom. My Friends and I all had days when we were just barely holding on until dinnertime when our partners would arrive to relieve us, only to get a phone call from them saying that they would be late. They might as well have told us that our lungs were being removed or our eyes poked out.

Every day for the mother of a colicky baby is a crap shoot (no pun intended, or even really accomplished). Will you manage to stay sane for one more day, or will you finally succumb to the urge to take the baby to the Post Office and send her second class to your mother-in-law? Your reserves of strength were depleted weeks ago, and now you are getting by on little more than determination, duty and Mars Bars. If it weren't for that crooked little smile surprising you once every day or so, you would have quit this job a long time ago. Still, if you could be completely honest without worrying about being reported to Social Services, you would have to admit that tubal ligation sounds like a pretty good idea. If you have read chapter 5, 'Blue, Baby, Blue', you'll know that you might settle into this feeling of hopelessness for longer than is bearable or good for you. Now is a good time to take a look at that part of the *Guide* again for more specific advice and reassurance.

Even though this is a book about us mums, not really about baby care, I can't resist adding a couple more remarks about colic. I have no cures to offer except time, so don't hold your breath. But where we mothers are concerned, I have something almost as important to say.

1. *Your baby is not colicky because of anything you did during pregnancy or your insecurity about being a mother.* If anyone tries to imply that this agony is your fault, you have my permission to slug her. All a colicky mother needs to really send her around the bend is to add guilt to her misery cocktail.

2. *Your baby is not colicky because it doesn't like you or your milk.* Colic isn't personal. Your baby just may not be able to express his adoration of you while his tummy feels tied up in knots. And, conversely, you may not be whispering love songs into his little ear when you feel like running as far away from him as possible. On the brighter side, the colicky baby and his mother may end up having a particularly close relationship because of the trials they endured together. Think of them as two war veterans whom battle has bonded.

3. *Your baby is not colicky because you are indulgent and have spoiled her.* This little zinger invariably comes from people of a generation more likely to be concerned about Social Security than the morning-after pill. This appraisal of your mothering usually goes something like 'In my day, babies were allowed to cry a little and they turned out just fine.' Oh yeah, then why was Prozac invented?

This rough patch will last for approximately three months, or not. (Sorry, this isn't an exact science.) At about that time you will make the gratifying discovery that your baby really was uncomfortable, not just a grouch. While the siege is on, however, do whatever you have to do –

bribe your partner, hire a babysitter, start therapy – to keep the wear and tear on you bearable. Learn, too, that it is completely all right to set the baby in the cot or crib for a few minutes while trying to drown out the noise with the running water of a hot shower. Clearly, your presence alone is not his cure but rather his reassurance, and you can only fulfill that need day after day if you carve out some time to blow off steam yourself.

Most important, try not to let a colicky baby set the mood for your home. It's so easy to be cranky to callers, snappy with your mate, and pessimistic about parenting in general when there is so much dis-comfort and unhappiness emanating from one tiny baby. Remember, the baby is not 'sick' and you are not doomed to this existence for the rest of your life. Ask a grandmother to come over during a really colicky time to provide those loving arms so that you and your partner can go for a drive or walk together to put things in perspective. It's not the baby in particular or parenting in general that is making your life hell; it's just a little problem with her wiring, or whatever, that's messing with you. Once that bit clears up, you will be free to focus on the countless reasons why being blessed with *your* baby is the greatest gift you'll ever know.

Illness

If the nightmares described so far aren't enough to make you promise to nap whenever the baby does, then here's our last shot:

If you don't get some rest, you stand a very good chance of getting sick.

Even in the germ-free environment you have worked so hard to attain in your home, there lurk cooties just waiting for your resistance to be ground down like a cigarette under a boot heel. A common scenario goes something like this. The baby gets a cold. This event in itself would be traumatic enough, but it is made even more miserable when you catch it a couple of days later. Your partner, ever the stoic, moves to the couch to sleep or suggests you sleep in the baby's room so that he doesn't get sick, too. Within three or four days, the baby is just peachy, but you are now blowing green stuff into endless boxes of Kleenex. About this time, your partner, in spite of his precautionary measures, comes down with a similar infection. Of course his is *much* worse and more debilitating (read 'masculine') than the wimpy little bug that got you and the baby. He is in bed whining about how he needs some

Vicks rubbed on his chest and you start coughing hard enough to crack a rib. You ignore the fever you've developed, partly because you are hoping it will disappear and partly because of that sensory obliviousness that new motherhood brings. It just couldn't be more miserable but quickly deteriorates further when your GP can't hear the baby's heartbeat over your wheezing and diagnoses you with walking pneumonia. Walking, my behind! You have been crawling for weeks now!

Go ahead and call me a doom-merchant. I am just telling you what has happened to me. There are exceptions, however. You could be like May and get an incurable skin rash. Or you could be like Sondra and develop aching joints that no amount of Advil can relieve. How about that breastfeeding mother's favourite, mastitis (also known as Flu of the Breasts). Then there are your run-of-the-mill headaches, diarrhoea and acid reflux – all common to tired women with children.

If you get sick, even if you are not sure that it's anything serious, get yourself to a doctor as quickly as you can. The longer you deny or ignore your illness, the more run-down you become and the more prone you will be to secondary infection. It doesn't pay anymore to be sick; the days of lying on the sofa and watching soap operas all day are over, Best Friend. Not only is no one going to take care of you, but you have a baby who won't cut you slack just because you're dying. It's in your best interest to do whatever it takes to get well quickly, because your new responsibilities wouldn't let up, even if you had open-heart surgery.

I was always amazed at how long I would procrastinate about going to the doctor when I was clearly infected. I would feel like death for two or three weeks and then surrender to a doctor's visit. Like all mothers, I believed that my parenting duties made it impossible for me to carve out an hour of time for myself, even if it was for a chest X-ray rather than something as frivolous as a lunch with Best Friends. Invariably, the doctor would prescribe sleep and a good strong antibiotic. Having a medical person tell me I needed rest carried so much more authority than the mere realization that I was exhausted. I would be better miraculously in twenty-four hours. What a numbskull I'd been to deny myself that relief weeks earlier, before I had gone completely grey and lost the will to live.

The Key to surviving the sleep crisis

There are actually two parts to the solution to the problem of sleep deprivation. First, you must get the baby to sleep, then you must get the mother to sleep. Rarely is the second part achieved without the first, unless, of course, your baby is already away at boarding school.

Getting the Newborn to sleep

New babies are very tricky. For the first couple of days of your acquaintance, most babies sleep so much that it's almost frustrating. You want to play with them and show them off to people, and they just lie there, snoozing blissfully. You wonder to yourself, 'What's the big deal with getting a baby to sleep? Mine's a professional.'

THEN, THEY WAKE UP!!!

No, they don't usually stay awake twenty-four hours a day, but they often seem to have no schedule. They are awake for a couple of hours, then asleep for two or three, regardless of whether it's day or night. If some kind of sleep pattern eventually emerges, it changes with frustrating frequency. THIS IS IMPORTANT TO KEEP IN MIND. Babies develop so dramatically and rapidly during their first year of life that the only thing you can expect is the unexpected. Don't hold your breath and wait for the status quo to return, because it almost never does: not just with babies but with kids of all ages. It's time now to learn to roll with the punches. This is not a state of suspended animation; this is your new life. Relax! It will be fun! (And if it isn't, you'll be too brain damaged to notice.)

Most doctors reassure hollow-eyed mothers who worry that they have done something wrong that how long a baby sleeps is often determined by how much he weighs. The rule of thumb goes something like this: if the baby weighs in the seven-to-nine-pound range, his tummy is probably capable of holding enough food to let him sleep for three or four hours. When the baby is up in the ten-pound range, and his tank is full, he can probably sleep a good eight hours. I wish we could tell you that growth alone would provide the solution to your sleep problems, but, of course, it's much more complicated than that.

Let's take a minute to congratulate and acknowledge all you new mummies who have babies who sleep from 10:30 P.M. until 6:30 A.M.

without a peep. I know you're out there, and I know you are gloating right now. The Best Friends' advice for you is to enjoy it now because by about three months of age your baby will realize that sleep, and the refusal to do it, is a very big stick for manipulating a mother, and he will beat you with it. In the meantime, rest up and try not to brag. (It's so un-Best Friend.)

Babies need two things to sleep: a full belly and a clean nappy. Keep that in mind when you go through your little bedtime rituals. After that, it's a free-for-all. Your baby may like to be swaddled up tight in a blanket, or he may absolutely hate being restrained and want to kick his legs with abandon. Try anything and everything that you think might put your baby to sleep. Some babies like to be jiggled; others like you to stand up and bounce slightly while holding them in your arms (I call this universal and primitive mother's dance the Baby Bop). Many fall asleep feeding or sucking on a bottle. (Pay no attention to those parenting experts who tell you not to put your baby to bed when he's already asleep because you are missing a valuable opportunity to teach him to put himself to sleep. These people are men or women who have had their kids so long that they have forgotten a new mother's desperation.) When all else fails, there is always a rapid roll through the neighbourhood in the buggy or a drive in the car.

You should experiment with all sorts of tricks and routines to help your baby understand on a Pavlovian level, that it is time to sleep. Several of my Best Friends swear by establishing a bedtime routine. Any series of little rituals, such as a bath, then a story and then a minute or two of cuddling can be as effective as a tranquilliser. They don't have any magical powers the first few nights you use them, but if you use them every night (without altering the pattern in any way because babies and children get all worked up over 'different'), you will be on your way, a penny at a time, toward establishing a savings account in the Bank of Nod. A ritual like this can be just as soothing to the parents as it is to the baby. Keep in mind that there is so much ad-libbing in being a new parent that having your bedtimes scripted and choreo-graphed feels like shifting into cruise control. Just remember, anything you introduce must be something that you are willing and able to repeat every single time the baby is supposed to sleep. If you play lullaby tapes, when you take the baby on an overnight trip, don't go without the tapes and the cassette player or you'll be sorry. If the baby has a 'cuddly' or a dummy, guard it with the attention afforded the Hope Diamond.

Whatever you do, don't spend one moment of the baby's first three months worrying whether you are 'spoiling' her. She is still incapable of taking advantage of you and she hasn't learned the sophisticated strategies of manipulation yet. If she cries, it's because she feels bad enough to do so. Go to her and help her feel good enough to stop. Later on, you may want to slow your response time down a bit, but for the first three or four months, you are so essential to her well-being that you might as well be her Siamese twin.

Even at the youngest age, however, babies are capable of learning two problematical habits, and you should avoid teaching them at all costs. They are:

1. Only mum can put her to sleep; and
2. She can only sleep in a room that is dark and completely quiet.

If the baby thinks you hold the keys to the Slumberdome, either because you sing to her or feed her before she drifts off, it stands to reason that you will never be able to leave the baby to go out for more than a couple of hours. If a sitter, even a doting grandma, tries to fill in for you one night and religiously follows all your sleep routines, they will still be rewarded with a crying infant insomniac. If you don't think your baby can tell you apart from everybody else, you are seriously underestimating human biology. Besides, if the baby can only be readied for sleep by you, it means that Daddy will miss all the fun of getting up in the middle of the night for a feed. You certainly can't deny him that.

Even more dangerous than making yourself a human teddy bear is training your baby to require silence and darkness to sleep. It always makes me giggle when I hear about new mothers who disconnect doorbells and telephones, put 'QUIET' signs on doors and whisper when their little darlings are asleep. Sorry, but you just can't exert that much control over the universe, Best Friend. Even if the microwave timer, the smoke detector, or the neighbour's dog doesn't sabotage your attempts at silence, the eventual birth of a brother or sister for your little darling will.

The real irony of this obsession with silence is that babies usually sleep particularly well when there is some sort of droning noise. An old trick of frantic mothers with screaming babies is to turn on the vacuum cleaner or a hair dryer because the noise puts babies to sleep like magic. If you want to get some laundry done, put the baby in his infant seat and put it on the drier (turned on to 'cottons', none of those wimpy 'permanent press' cycles) while you sort and fold. To witness something even more amazing, take your infant to a bowling alley or McDonald's. As soon as she is surrounded by bells, crashes, lights and screaming kids, she acts as though she's been dredged in Mr. Sandman's sleepy dust. Doctors say that this is part of their 'shutdown' reflex. Evidently, when there is more stimulation than their brand-new brains can assimilate, they just ignore it in the most effective way they can; they go to sleep.

Getting the Newborn's Mother to Sleep

You must be getting the picture that there often isn't much you can do to make a newborn sleep when he's not in the mood to. He's too used to the twenty-four-hour womb service he had for the previous nine (ten) months to wait patiently for food or a clean nappy or for someone to take him for a ride. As we conceded earlier, how demanding a baby is varies greatly from baby to baby, and you may have a nice quiet one. If you do, you might still consider finishing this chapter because your next baby could be a real screamer.

Since so much of the newborn's ability to sleep for long periods is a function of time, you need to have a strategy for surviving this endurance test. Trust us when we tell you it is physically impossible for a new mother to stay awake for three straight months, no matter how devoted or demented you are. The most common advice given new mothers is to nap when the baby naps. This advice is well and good, but it doesn't go far enough. *You need to sleep even when the baby doesn't.*

If some dear person were to care for your baby for just ninety minutes every afternoon so that you could nap, this motherhood thing would be a viable option. Then, even if you still didn't sleep through the night, you might still keep your health and sanity. This helpful person should usually be someone other than your partner, unless he has taken paternity leave or is otherwise able to nap at some other time during the day. Since he is often awake much of the night listening to you and the baby cry, and then has to go to work the next morning, he's got sleep issues of his own to deal with.

A relative is usually a safe and economical choice for the pair of 'loving arms' that will comfort your baby while you rest, but don't limit yourself if you have no family in the area. Even a competent teenager can help if she has the Baby Bop dance mastered and is comfortable around a newborn. Remember, you're not going to Paris; you'll be right in the next room if you are needed (though it may be quite a challenge for the sitter to wake you). Older women are particularly wonderful at this job. They might not be up to chasing a screaming toddler, but they can rock a newborn like a pro.

If you are fortunate and resourceful enough to find some help, you must promise us all that you will use it to get some rest. Surrender, Dorothy. Smart mothers, not wimpy mothers, know that the quality of their mothering is directly related to their ability to back off and refresh themselves before the brain damage becomes permanent. The house is going to be a disaster, your hair is going to have a skunk stripe and you are not going to dance along to a Richard Simmons tape for three months; now get over it. After this critical passage into parenthood, if your help is still willing and able, you can consider endeavours that are not horizontal. For the first three months, however, getting sleep should be your Holy Grail.

The Next Nine Months

I really wish I could tell you that after the first three months, your household would be sleeping like, well, like babies, but it's not a slam dunk. Babies, in their delightfully disorienting way, can go for weeks, even months, sleeping the whole night through. Then some cataclysmic event may occur, something like teething, an earache or a fever that wakes the baby in the night and is treated by extra love and attention by the worried mummy. Even through its discomfort, a smart little baby (like yours and mine) is capable of transcending the pain to realize that there is something really groovy about all this hands-on treatment. Ultimately you are faced with having to teach and reteach your baby to go to sleep and STAY THERE. This will be your life's work, in one fashion or another, for the next ten years, so pace yourself. I don't want to add any unnecessary pressure here, but you may be forced to live with the fallout from your sleep training for the next decade.

Two huge developmental leaps occur in the older baby that will make this sleep issue particularly complex. First, the baby discovers that he can stay awake for a long time if he wants to. That may sound obvious, but it really is a function of his brain development. When they are newborns, they are really little eating/blinking/ pooing/sleeping machines. They don't consider their options, measure their whims on a particular day or get in moods. They just sort of carry out their biological destiny. Then, one day, the baby is lying there, focusing on that silly black-and-white educational mobile you have dangling over his cot, and he starts looking around the room.

'Hey, cute Pooh bears on the cot bumpers,' he thinks. 'I like what you did with those clouds and that sky you painted on my ceiling, too, Mum, but could you lose the big stuffed monkey over in the corner – way too scary.' There is a whole world out there to explore, and they begin to find life too stimulating to sleep through.

As attractive as life's adventures seem, however, this baby is equally sure that they would only be worth pursuing with a companion. Just look at it from your own perspective: would you rather see Europe alone or with someone you love? (Especially someone who loves you back without measure, provides your favourite food on demand, is only concerned about your comfort and will even carry you everywhere you want to go.) Remember, it is only dawning on your baby that he is not physically connected to you. For the first few months of his life, he thought he *was* you, and now here he is discovering that you are detachable. This can be scary and lonely, both for you and the baby. I swear, there are times every single day when I know for a fact that one or another of my kids would crawl back into my uterus if I would let him. Babies and children need to feel connected, often literally, to their mother, father or some other special adult whom they love and trust. When my daughter was about three, she used to cry at bedtime because she didn't have a 'live thing' to sleep with the way Mummy and Daddy did. I guess we spend our entire lives looking for the perfect 'live thing'.

Imagine how your own baby feels when you put him in his cot and you walk out of the room. He may not have noticed your absence before, but he is getting the picture now. This is when you will have to figure out the Sleep Game and how it will be played in your house.

In our society, there are roughly three play options.

No.1. The Family Bed Option
No.2. The Teach-the-Baby-to-Put-Itself-to-Sleep Option
No.3. The Chef's Surprise

No.1. The family bed concept is one in which new parents bring the baby into their bed and let her sleep there with them until it isn't fun anymore. This concept, which would have been considered obscene by my parents' generation, came along with that whole wave of returning to nature that included other such fun ideas as natural childbirth and keeping the placenta in your freezer for good luck. Actually, the family bed is the way most of the world lives. This whole concept of dividing homes into individual compartments and isolating a single person in each one is a result of more culture and more money. The rest of the world is more apt to sleep in a family heap like a bunch of puppies.

There are some great things to be said about the family bed approach. First, it's the cosiest cocoon on the planet. Few things are more moving, especially to a woman still buffeted by her hormones, than having your entire little family in the warmth and protection of your bed. It smells safe and good, it's just the right temperature and, best of all, you're reclining, which is always a good thing for a new mother. A second big plus about the family bed is the convenience, especially for the breastfeeding mother. My Best Friend Sondra used to be able to feed her babies while she was lying on her side and facing them. Best of all, she could do it while she was sleeping. Even if you are more of a klutz, the way I was, you can still sit up in bed, stack pillows behind your back and in your lap, and feed in the traditional posture. When the baby is full, she goes to sleep, you roll her back on to the mattress and you are both snoring within fifteen seconds. Babies love everything about the family bed, and they do tend to be much less fussy when they're there with you. Mothers and fathers both appreciate the twenty-four-hour-surveillance aspect of the family bed because we are all paranoid and feel that our children might perish or disappear if we can't see them.

So, what's not to like about the family bed? you ask. Well, the biggest complaint among my friends and family is that, while the baby is sleeping great, the parents might be a wreck. Out of any lineup of a hundred new dads, at least seventy will step forward when asked, 'Which of you is secretly afraid that you will roll over on to the baby in your sleep and smother him?' You can try to comfort these poor men by explaining that even a newborn will speak up loud and clear if you are squashing him, but your success rate will be low. So, what you end up with is one of the senior family bed regulars leaving to sleep on the couch or half sleeping on the edge of the bed, holding on by his fingernails, while the little seven-pounder is hogging the prime mattress position in the middle.

Even if the fear of rolling over on to the baby is not too extreme, parents often tend to sleep very lightly when the baby is in bed with them because they are always 'on call'. Babies may look silent when you watch them sleep, but share a bed with one for a night and you learn a different story. They sneeze, they startle, they make adorable mouth noises, and every time they do, one or both of the parents becomes wide awake and ready to jump into action. They are like firefighters on watch with a little pyromaniac in their bed. The babies usually settle right down into that good old REM sleep, but the parents usually reach for the remote control and watch some all-night television until their blood pressure gets closer to the safety range and they are no longer at risk for a stroke.

Another complaint about the family bed (which won't really apply to you for several months but will matter a lot to your partner so go ahead and pretend it matters to you, too) is the lack of intimacy. What are you supposed to do with the baby when you and your mate are in the mood for a party for two? You either get up and put the baby in her crib or cot or you cancel the sex because it's not worth the work involved. Yes, I know that there are some people who would suggest that the baby be free to stay for the show, but I don't want to hear from them and I don't want to think that they may be people I know.

Eventually, the time will come when you will want the baby (or child) to stop kneeing you in the head in her sleep and return to her very own bed. This is going to be difficult, whether you do it at seven months or at seven years; they just don't want to leave all the fun of the family bed. Keep this in mind when making your decisions about your family's rules for the Sleep Game:

IT DOES NOT GET EASIER TO TEACH CHILDREN TO SLEEP ALONE AS THEY GROW OLDER

With this in mind, I always tell my Best Friends that it is easier to teach someone to stay in bed *before* they are old enough to climb out and walk back to your room unassisted. Which leads us to option No.2:

No.2. The Teach-the-Baby-to-Put-Himself-to-Sleep option is taught in a variety of forms and methods, but they all distill down to one point: you must let the baby cry until he goes to sleep. When I was a baby, necessity and good sense dictated that mothers had better things to do than tote babies around all day, so we were allowed to cry in our cots for periods of time that would look like child abuse to us sensitive mothers of today. I know, I know, I sound like your mother, but think about it: how on earth was a woman supposed to starch and iron five shirts a week and make a stew and do her mending with a baby in her arms all day? Hey, come to think of it, my mother wasn't any busier than I am right this instant, and I never let my babies 'cry it out'. Which one of us is the stooge here?

Anyway, the popular method used today goes something like this: parents plan to devote about three nights to teaching their baby to sleep. They go through their little bedtime ritual, be it a bath or a song or whatever, put the baby to bed, say good night and leave. The baby will call out for you or cry for mercy, and you call your reassurances in through the door or go in and repeat, 'Mummy is here, but it's time for you to go to sleep now' or some other mantra-like thing. You can appear in the room every ten or fifteen minutes to show the baby that you haven't moved to Hawaii, but you cannot pick the baby up and take him out of his cot without setting the whole lesson back to the beginning.

My experience with this kind of approach is that it really does work. My other experience is that it led to the biggest fights my husband and I have ever had in our married life. I can recall so many nights (remember, I have a lot of kids) sitting on a chair in the hall outside the baby's room while she screamed and begged to be rescued from this hell. I would cry silently and feel like vomiting, but I would sit in that chair, clutching my baby-care manuals for dear life. My husband would lock himself in our bedroom where he tried not to hear the crying. Then, every half hour or so, just as I was about to collapse from the pressure and the grief, he would march into the hall and ask, 'Is all of this bullshit really necessary? How in the world can you just let her scream like that and not help her?'

We happened to have a housekeeper at the time, and she sat on her bed, directly in my line of view, silently weeping into a hanky and taking one Excedrin every twenty minutes for the psychic pain I was causing them all. I often caved in on the 'three nights to a better sleep' prescription by snatching the baby to my bosom on night number two (okay, number one) and making us all feel better, at least for the time being. But I did eventually manage to make it through the gauntlet four times, once with each child, and it did work pretty much as I was told it would. Of course, my husband now counsels new parents with great pride and authority about his belief in 'letting them cry a little'.

My Best Friend Catherine and I were chatting on the phone the other day about her thirteen-month-old daughter. Catherine and her partner and the baby have been sleeping in the same bed since the baby was born, and they have loved every minute of it. But now, maybe because they are trying to give the baby a little brother or sister to pick on, or because she is nearly as tall as Catherine and taking up more than her share of the bed, they are planning to move her to her cot. Darling Catherine, the world's most loving woman, explained to me that her baby would take to the cot voluntarily because she had gained so much confidence and independence from her time in the family bed. As a matter of fact, Catherine said, she could almost feel her baby telling her that she had been nourished with security and high self-esteem and she was eager to be alone in her bed (which, by the way, is in the parents' bedroom). I listened and made encouraging utterances, then I immediately called another, more experienced mum to giggle about what Catherine has in store for her. One of these nights, she and her partner will be standing in the darkened hall crying and fighting with each other about whether to go in and rescue the hysterical baby or gut it out in the hope of a bed of their own. It's a parent's rite of passage. (P.S. In the month since I wrote this entry, Catherine's baby has clearly made it known that she hates her cot so much that she will begin to twist and shout even if you only walk her by it. If she actually gets put in, which rarely happens now, she roars like a lion. So far, the baby is winning.)

You see, raising children is like a Rorschach test. You are given this baby to care for, and sooner or later she's going to want to do something you don't want her to do, have something you don't want her to have, or behave in a way you don't want her to behave. That part is a given – the inkblot, so to speak. How you deal with it is what makes us all so different as parents and some kids wackier than others. This is hard work. Hardest of all is the fact that you are ad-libbing most of the time. You read every book, watch every documentary, and you pray for some enlightenment and guidance, but ultimately you have to make it up as you go along. If it's any comfort to you, we're all bumbling along in the same fashion. This trial-and-error parenting is what leads most of us to option No.3.

No.3. The Chef's Surprise is the option that most of the Best Friends I know end up with, if only by default. Some nights we luck out and the baby sleeps where you want him to and when you want him to without protest. Other nights, we are just too tired to teach anyone anything and we sleepwalk to our crying baby to snuggle him until he goes back to sleep. I swear, there have even been nights when I crawled into the baby's cot with it to give it a 'live thing' to sleep with. (Desperation leads to risk-taking.) This is the pragmatist's approach to child rearing. No matter what great plans or methods or schemes we have philosophically committed ourselves to as parents, in the end, we spend most of our time reacting to things that have nothing to do with our best-laid plans. A good parent, in my humble opinion, is one who is courageous enough to back off from a rule or a lesson when it doesn't work for her unique little baby. I don't care how many children are sleeping alone in their cots; if you and your baby just aren't up to the separation, you have permission to give up the effort. You can always try again another time.

From my sage and experienced vantage point of nearly nine years of mothering and not one day spent in juvenile hall (so far), I think that the Chef's Surprise is the best option of all because it allows for change, it doesn't set you or your beloved baby up for failure and it reaffirms what you already should know deep down inside – you are the best mother that little baby could ever have.

8

I want my old Body Back!

where we went astray

By the last few weeks of pregnancy, most of us were so eager not to be pregnant anymore that we spent hours fantasizing about our former bodies (or at least our idealized recollections of them) and how it would feel to have them back. Our imaginations went wild: We'd wear belts! We'd knock around in our favourite old 501s. We'd go braless! We'd drink Long Island Iced Teas and then have drunken, passionate sex (maybe even with our partners)! Even the prospect of doing the little things, like painting our own toenails or lying on our stomach, took on the seductiveness of something exotic and exciting. This pregnancy thing had been beautiful, fulfilling, spiritually enlightening, etc., etc., but enough already!

You didn't go totally crazy during your pregnancy; you only put on thirty (well, okay, forty) pounds, and it seemed like it was almost all baby. You expected to be a little out of shape after the baby was born, but those cheerful women's magazines assured you that there wouldn't be any damage a little exercise and dieting couldn't repair well before your six-week checkup. It would feel so liberating not to be carrying another human being around inside you that it would be no time before you had your old energy back. Not only would you get your old figure back, but you'd take advantage of your maternity leave to exercise twice as much as before. The difficult part of being a mother, *pregnancy*, was nearly behind you (not just in your behind) and you would be getting your old self back. YOU WOULDN'T JUST BE AS GOOD AS BEFORE; YOU WOULD BE BETTER!

The Rude Awakening

Now, here you are, wondering, 'What in the world went wrong?'

Exercise? You've barely got the strength to pour yourself a bowl of cereal, let alone begin a calisthenics regime. Even if you had the stamina, you certainly don't have the time. Exercise fits somewhere on the to-do list right after 'take a shower' and 'open the post'. Besides, what would you wear? What would hold those huge, hot and tingly breasts? You would rather pull your fingernails out one by one than be seen in a gym in a leotard right about now.

Diet? If you are breastfeeding, you are probably eating constantly, probably even more than you ate when you were pregnant. Even if you aren't breastfeeding, you haven't been able to get it together to make yourself a salad or roast a chicken since you brought the baby home. It's so much easier to live on sandwiches or Chinese takeaways. Besides, with the little sleep you are getting, food is your only source of energy. If you don't have a doughnut every afternoon, you are certain to collapse before dinner.

Sooner or later you are going to realize that you are still pregnant, even though the baby is no longer in your body. Think of this as the Fourth Trimester of Pregnancy. Your body is still not yours, but rather for the use and enjoyment of the baby. Your hormones are still wacky, you're half out of your mind and you can tell already that it's going to take a lot longer than you hoped for that person in the mirror to look like anyone you even vaguely recognize.

The ways you will know you are still pregnant are vast, but here are some of the most common:

1. You have hot flushes and night sweats.
2. You're cranky and tired.
3. It's been months since the baby was born, and you are still wearing maternity underwear.
4. You wet yourself whenever you sneeze.
5. Your breasts are heavy and seem to be alive (if you are breastfeeding, that is. Otherwise, they look quite unalive).
6. You still can't wear any of your old shoes.
7. Your upper arms are bigger than your thighs used to be, and your thighs are bigger than, well, let's just not go there.
8. Your skin is breaking out more than it did when you were looking for a date for the Sixth Form Dance.

9. You still can't eat or drink whatever you want.
10. There is so much extra skin on your belly that when you bend over, you look like an accordion.
11. Sex still hurts and you couldn't be less interested anyway.
12. Everyone and everything pisses you off.

It's so depressing, I know, but it's normal. Why should we expect a condition that took us nine (ten) months to develop to disappear in a matter of weeks? Sure, everyone knows someone who knows someone who wore her tight prepregnancy jeans two days after delivery, but I know just as many people who know someone who has seen the Loch Ness Monster. The Best Friends' rule of thumb is: *nine (ten) months up, nine (ten) months down.* I don't care how many actresses you've seen on TV in size-four skintight dresses two weeks after they've birthed twins. Let's not start that Duelling Mothers song again; it's against the Best Friends Credo. Besides, it's rarely a good idea to compare yourself with another mother unless you are certain that you really are superior, otherwise you just get your feelings hurt. Besides, for every skinny actress mummy you can name, I can name a personal fitness trainer, a chef/nutritionist and a full-time nanny. I wish all mummies had such a support system. I also wish there were world peace and free liposuction on demand, but wishin' ain't gettin'.

What I am going to tell you now is a generalization, but the Best Friends and I have noticed it enough that it is taking on the ring of truth: you can diet and StairMaster yourself to death and be within ten or fifteen pounds of your prepregnancy weight in about six months. You can also just attend to mothering your baby and getting back into life's regular rhythm and get within ten or fifteen pounds of your fighting weight in just about the same amount of time. Really! You probably won't be one of those blessed few who completely recover with no apparent effort (just as you probably won't win the lottery), but you *will* get in shooting distance of the goal. At the end of the first five or six months after the birth, you will be left with that last ten or fifteen pounds that you will literally have to beat off your body.

This Old Grey Mare

As the mother of four children, I've tried all different approaches, and I've generally ended up the same. Let me begin by saying that I gained between thirty-six and forty pounds with each baby. That weight gain seemed to be biologically predetermined for me, whether I ate everything in sight and rested in bed for four months or whether I was so busy at my job and chasing toddlers around that I often forgot to eat altogether.

After the birth of my first baby, I gloried in my madonna status. My entire universe existed for my new baby; feeding him, bathing him, changing him, dressing him up several times a day to receive visitors or take him on tours of the grocery store or shopping centres, and, of course, those impromptu photo opportunities. I didn't just eat a lot, I made dining an adventure. My Best Friends and I put our babies in their infant seats and took them out for Mexican food one day, Thai another, and some other regional cuisine the next. No matter what we had for lunch, it was ritualistically followed by something chocolate for dessert. The babies weren't yet into foods that required chewing, but we mums ate enough for all of us. In spite of this, about nine months into this mega-mother existence, I noticed that I was starting to shrink. My face no longer looked like one of the Campbell's soup kids, my underwear didn't just cover the top of each cheek and I was tucking things in again. That was incentive enough for me to dig into exercise and dieting to get rid of the last ten (or fifteen, really) pounds. It was harder than I thought it would be, but I persevered. Then, one day my husband actually focused his eyes on me while I was stepping into the shower. I swear it was the first time he had braved a look since the end of my third trimester. 'Hey, it's you!' he rejoiced. The real me was back!

By my fourth baby, I confess that I was significantly less romantic about cocooning. I had been pregnant or feeding, it seemed, for six straight years, and I wanted to get out of the house, wear tight trousers and drive in a car without plastic seat protectors and sunshades with teddy bears on them. Heck, I would have gone disco dancing or taken tango lessons if I'd found the time. I breastfed for a much shorter period. *Much shorter*, as in about three weeks. I had also overcome my guilt about babysitters, so I was able to leave the baby with someone while I exercised. So, at about two and a half months after the birth, I began to exercise in earnest. And, yes, the weight did come off, but not significantly faster than it had with the previous pregnancies. At about seven months post birth, I was becoming a reasonable facsimile of the former, unpregnant, me. And, true to form, it was really then that the programme of exercise and diet were most effective.

You may be disagreeing with me right now. You may be looking at yourself only, say, three months after the birth and insist that you are already positively melting away. Let me remind you about perspective and how seductive it can be: after being as big as a house just three months ago, being just chubby looks like a huge improvement. Don't kid yourself; you still aren't anywhere near putting on your old tight jeans.

The Best Friends' Recovery Programme

After going from 112 pounds to 150 pounds and back four times, I am going to share with you the secrets of getting your old body back, or at least a reasonable facsimile thereof. Just in case mummies' brain damage has taken its toll on you, I will remind you once again that I am not a doctor, nutritionist or certified fitness trainer; I don't even play one on TV. Nothing I am going to say has been proven to be good or bad for you, and I encourage you to consult someone medically trained before taking one word of my advice. All I have is my own experience and that of scores of Best Friends. So, here are our commandments for getting your body back.

1. *Don't Even Think of Exercising or Dieting Until the Baby Is at Least Three Months Old.* Really, what is the big rush? This precious and fragile time of adjustment passes in the blink of an eye; you deserve to take it easy. You may still be bleeding for several weeks after the baby is born. You will be desperately searching for a way to get more sleep, and your various body parts will still be too feeble to force into a step aerobics routine. I actually think five or six months is an even better waiting period because pregnancy and delivery really take up to a year to recover from, but if you are feeling anxious and need to get moving again, try to relax for at least three months. Just make sure that you are not hurrying yourself because of some half-witted belief that this is what Perfect Mummies do. As we've reminded you before, this is not a race or a test. You will not receive a mark or win a medal in front of your adoring fans. Take it easy on yourself; no one's really looking at you right now, anyway, except that darling baby of yours, and he thinks you're gorgeous. By the way, while I am suggesting that you skip any real fitness training for the first three months or so, I am not advocating that you take up residence on the couch with a bag of taco-flavoured Doritos at your side. Get out and get fresh air every day if you can. It may have precious little effect on your figure, but it does wonders for your spirit.

2. *Do Not Lift Weights*. Do not lift one single weight or use one single resistance training machine until you are within *five pounds* of your target weight. Contrary to what most fitness trainers, gym membership commercials or even your own instincts will tell you, *lifting weights is a bad idea*. First of all, your ligaments and muscles are stretched and loose during pregnancy to allow your pelvis to open wide enough to let the baby out. What that means for someone considering weight training is that your hip joints, your knees, your shoulders and particularly your belly may not be sufficiently recovered to bear any more weight than yours and the baby's. Second, weight training, as practised by 99 percent of us, is not particularly effective at burning fat. It is designed to stimulate your muscles to get stronger. They get stronger by getting bigger, and this is where we have the problem. No woman who is carrying a thin layer of body upholstery known as 'baby fat' needs to exaggerate that fact by puffing it up with big muscles. It's like wearing thermal underwear under your jeans, and who needs THAT? After you are at or near your target weight, resistance training will be good for you to restore tone and strength. After the fat is gone, you will actually want bigger muscles to help keep it gone, since the bigger a muscle is, the more calories it burns for any activity.

Remember: FAT PLUS MUSCLES = GLADIATORS;
SLENDER PLUS MUSCLES = CINDY
CRAWFORD.

3. *Eat Only One Meal a Day*. Relax, I didn't say eat once a day. In fact, I think you should eat several times a day, but only once should you sit down and tuck into those three-coursers that were so much fun during pregnancy. According to popular wisdom, this meal should be breakfast or lunch, when your metabolism is burning calories more actively than it does at night. This one meal should provide lean meat, chicken or tofu, as many vegetables as you can eat (unless you consider corn and potatoes vegetables, then use some restraint). To avoid feeling cranky and deprived always include a food that my Scottish friends call 'fuller': you know, something that makes you feel full and satisfied. A light pasta, baked potatoes, rice or a piece of bread are all good 'fuller'.

One last bit of advice about your one 'real meal' of the day: make sure that you actually put your portions of food on a plate. No fair just eating out of containers or saucepans because you will invariably eat twice as much when you 'just pick'.

At least once a week, make a big pot of soup to eat at those other times when your body thinks it needs another meal. I always throw all the loose vegetables that have fallen to the bottom of my vegetable tray into a broth made from chicken or turkey parts. Sometimes I'll add cooked macaroni or rice to my bowl or mug, but never to the soup pot because by the fifth day you end up with something resembling homemade paste. Once or twice a day, when you have visions of chocolate cookies dancing in your head, run for the soup. Fill a cup and nuke it in the microwave before you even pass the drawer where the biscuits are hidden. Remember, you are now eating to avoid hunger rather than for recreation. If fingers that aren't constantly tossing tasty titbits into a mouth make you fidgety, take up needlepoint. You should see the collection of pillows and Christmas stockings I've amassed while trying to break the caramel popcorn or Cheetos habit. If all else fails, put the baby in the carriage and get the hell out of the house.

4. *Cut Out the Desserts.* Almost all of my Best Friends and I became quite devoted to dessert when we were pregnant. Ice cream, in particular, seemed our just reward for gagging down whatever proteins and vitamins our pregnancies required. My Friend Rosemary felt like crying if her partner took her out to dinner and didn't stop at the frozen yogurt place on the way home. After the baby is born and you are emotionally up to the challenge, you must begin weaning yourself from the dessert habit. Sure, I love biscuits as much as (if not more than) the next person, but we have to stop using them as punctuation for every meal. If you just can't live without something sugary and fatty (and who can all the time?) then cheat occasionally, but understand that you will have to cut something else out to allow for the indulgence. Unfortunately, that may mean that you have to compensate for those two (five) Snack-Well's by only eating an apple at lunchtime. You're a big girl (even bigger than usual), so I won't lecture you about needing nutritious food for your own recovery and for the baby, if you are breastfeeding. We Best Friends confess to occasionally indulging in 'compensatory dieting', meaning we skip a healthy meal in an attempt to compensate for the banana nut muffin we ate in the supermarket checkout queue, but we also feel appropriately guilty about it and mature enough (just barely) not to do it very often.

My husband, who has reached the age when his metabolism is no longer his friend, has introduced me to Häagen-Dazs non-fat sorbet for dessert, and it actually tastes decadent. Ultimately, however, you will have to go cold turkey on desserts. But if you still can't imagine getting up from a meal without something sweet crossing your palate, go for fresh fruit. If you're like me, fresh fruit for dessert will be so depressing that you'll just skip that course of your meal entirely.

5. *Stock the Refrigerator, Car and Nappy Bag with Low-Calorie Foods.* When you're home and feeling a hunger pang and can't bear the thought of another cup of soup, a cooked chicken breast, especially one that has been skinned and cut into bite-sized pieces, is just as convenient to reach for as a bag of crisps. The key is you must prepare it in advance and have it waiting for just this moment or else it's taco-flavoured Doritos every time. Tuna salad made with non-fat yogurt instead of mayonnaise is another great, low-calorie thing to keep stocked in the refrigerator. It tastes pretty good, too, especially if you're starving. When I failed to take my own advice about advance preparation, I used to snack on corn tortillas warmed in the microwave and flavored with the tiniest swipe of crunchy peanut butter. Remember, though, only ONE. Other snacks that I stashed in my car and nappy bag were flavoured rice cakes by the bushel and, of course, popcorn. I never could gag down the air-popped stuff, but I did learn not to crave the butter and salt. I'm still addicted to popcorn, and I will eat it for dinner when my kids and husband aren't around.

6. *Breastfeeding Will Not Give You Your Figure Back.* It is a myth or some insidious La Leche League propaganda that breastfeeding burns so many calories that it will make you lose all your baby fat. Perhaps this theory would be accurate if you fed your baby for two years or more, since I think by that time the baby would have sucked nearly every living thing out of you, but for those of us who don't breastfeed or intend to quit before the children are old enough to vote, it doesn't pan out. The concept of getting as much food as we want as often as we want it is largely a modern phenomenon limited to the very rich or very lucky. Think about it: you don't hear much from India, Africa or China about postnatal dieting, or dieting in general. I guess there is no better weight-loss programme than an insufficiency of food. Since the beginning of time, Nature has designed mothers to store extra fuel for those days when their men didn't bag a boar. That extra fuel is manifested on our bodies as round cheeks (front and back), fatter upper arms and big butts. As long as you are the sole provider of nutrition for your baby, Nature is going to do her best to keep those stores in place. I don't know how she does it – probably some work stoppage of the metabolism – but those extra ten pounds are nearly

impossible to budge while you are breastfeeding. Most of us would be fine about being victims of this miracle if we weren't regularly subjected to the *Sports Illustrated* swimsuit issue or Claudia Schiffer and her friends from the carwalk.

Whatever you do, don't let this weight thing depress you. Just put your cap-sleeved shirts away for a couple more months and leave your bathing suit in the back of the drawer. (We all know that sunbathing is ageing, and that's even worse than fattening!) Out of the big story that is your life, this short chapter of mothering an infant is a pretty quick read. The inconveniences or sacrifices you make now will seem like pretty small potatoes when you look back on them. Try to relax and enjoy this time and know that once it's over, it's over. Thin arms are available whenever you want them, and they're not all they're cracked up to be anyway because children like more softness in their hugs.

7. *Don't Believe in Fat-Free Foods.* Fat-free does not mean calorie-free. Just because your favourite bakery has come out with coffee cake that they call low fat or fat free does not mean we should declare a national holiday. They are still filled with calories. I don't care which Zone you live in, the more calories you eat, the fatter you get. When people ask me what I eat to stay slender, my answer is 'Nearly nothing,' and it's the pathetic truth.

8. *Don't Join a Gym.* Walking and jogging are the most effective, cheapest and safest ways to lose weight and gain mental health. All those celebrity mums that you've seen recover sufficiently from childbirth to pose naked on magazine covers ran that baby fat off. In the beginning, while you are still building up your strength and endurance, you can bundle the baby in a front pack and go for a long walk through your neighbourhood. As the baby gets heavier and you get more fit, you might want to leave him with a sitter while you strike up a faster pace and increase your distance. When the baby is about five months old or older and no longer a Mr. Bobble Head, try carrying him in a backpack for your excursions. If you can get a pack with a light aluminium frame and a wide hip belt to help distribute the weight, you're set. Before you invest in one, ask around to see if any Friends have one that they have outgrown. Ideally, these packs should just be passed around until you and your mummy friends have outgrown your childbearing years. We are willing to stake our Best Friends' status on this one deduction: the single most important factor in walking or

running is to devote at least forty-five minutes, but preferably an hour, to each session. None of this twenty-minutes-gets-the-heart-rate-up stuff. The success lies in the time spent. Naturally, if you're sprinting for an hour, you'll burn more calories than if you amble, but even an hour of ambling can be a pretty effective fat burner. You will automatically go faster as you get accustomed to this aerobics conditioning, *but you must still commit the hour*. It's rather like there is a threshold that is crossed after a certain amount of time, and only then does the good fat-burning mechanism kick in. You may prefer cycling or stair climbing or aerobics classes, and certainly anything you do that keeps you moving for an hour is great, but all the research shows that the treadmill or the Nordic Track-type machines are by far the best fat burners, even if only because they are harder to cheat at than the other equipment. Don't forget to carry water with you at all times because you will become dehydrated long before you feel thirsty: not a good thing for anyone, let alone a breastfeeding mother.

I have only one Friend who shed her substantial maternity weight within days of giving birth. Only after I got to know her better did I realize that she didn't breastfeed and, therefore, felt free to begin the Phen-Fen diet immediately. (See how insidious postnatal depression can be?) My other Best Friend Annie lost a lot of pregnancy weight earlier than might have been expected, but I think that had something to do with her hearing her partner had been having an affair during her entire pregnancy. Stress can do that to a person.

Why go to the trouble of losing the weight if you're just going to get pregnant again?

Don't succumb to the temptation to give up before losing those last few pounds. Any weight you still carry two years after giving birth or by the time you get pregnant with another child cannot technically be referred to as 'baby fat'. It's just plain fat, and you own it. It will be such a relief to get close to your goal after over a year of looking like something out of the Macy's Thanksgiving Day Parade that it would be a cinch to call it a day and wear one size larger for the rest of your life. Compared with right after the baby was born, you are a veritable twig! But this is not the time to let your guard down. There will be other babies, each threatening to add five pounds to your pre-baby weight. Then there will be the slower metabolism that plagues most of us after our fortieth birthdays; that's a guaranteed five to ten pounds lying in wait. And after all that, there is the famous middle-aged spread that comes with the menopause! I don't want to be an alarmist, but if you cave in now to the fat monster, he's going to know you are a pushover and plague you for the rest of your life! You may be wondering where the old, relaxed Best Friends of *The Best Friends' Guide to Pregnancy* have gone. It's still us, honest. We just want you to see the big picture, and that does not have to include a big you.

Internal Fitness

One area that needs a special fitness programme all its own, especially if you had a vaginal delivery, is your pelvic floor. I can't draw you a picture of your pelvic floor because I have no idea where it really is. I can, however, suggest a few sensations that I am certain involve your pelvic floor. It definitely involves the things that quake inside you during an orgasm. It also affects the suspension of your bladder, which you will recognize if you pee every time you laugh out loud or sneeze. It is this area, too, that contracts immediately when you step to the edge of a precipice and look down. Its most-fun manifestation is the squeezing sensation that you use to tantalize your partner after orgasm but before withdrawal. If you're still drawing a blank here, practise stopping the flow of urine a couple of times while you go to the toilet.

The special fitness programme is called Kegel exercises. You might have started them during pregnancy, but you can resume doing them within hours or days of delivery, depending on how sore you are. I can try to tell you how to do a proper Kegel, but a far better idea would be for you to take a minute during your first internal exam, at your six week check, to ask your doctor to teach you. Yeah, right, you are saying to yourself: I'm going to look like the world's biggest idiot. Look, Friend, I would never suggest anything to you that I hadn't done myself. What you need is for the doctor to feel inside you while you contract to tell if you're hitting the right muscles and holding hard and long enough. Come to think about it, maybe this is something your sex-starved partner might want to help you with. Hmmmmm . . .

Irreparable Damage

It will help you if you understand which parts of your body can go back to the way they were before and which things are forever changed. After all, why waste your time on things that are lost causes when you will need to focus so much attention on the things that can be fixed? In a nutshell, here are the things we Best Friends think you will be hard-pressed to restore to their previous glory:

1. *Your Breasts*. They may still be looking very Lollobrigida right now, particularly if you are breastfeeding, but this lushness is short-lived. Not only will your breasts not return to their pre-pregnancy size and shape; they will be smaller and skinnier. If you have ever wondered why the women in *Playboy* don't look like the women in *National Geographic*, there is one simple reason: childbirth. (That, and maybe a little surgery.) If you are considering not breastfeeding because you want to save your breasts, don't bother. It seems that it's the pregnancy, not the feeding, that takes the biggest toll. The French maintain that you can protect your breasts by wearing a well-fitting bra every minute of your life, especially while you sleep, but they also allow dogs and smoking in their restaurants, so their judgement is questionable.

2. *Your Feet*. Even though the swelling of pregnancy is gone or on its way out, your feet may still be half to a full size bigger than they were before you got pregnant. Perhaps it was all just too much for your poor little arches to carry all that weight and they just collapsed. All we know is that our feet get bigger and stay bigger. For those of us still labouring under the sexist delusion that small feet are somehow better than big ones, the sensation that we are traversing the earth on two canoes is upsetting. But look at it this way: you are probably due for some new shoes after a year of being out of the fashion swing. Besides, once your feet have collapsed beneath one pregnancy, they have nothing left to surrender if you get pregnant again. In other words, they won't grow with every pregnancy, so go ahead and get the expensive shoes and don't feel guilty.

3. *Your Belly Button*. I can tell you if a woman has had a baby simply by inspecting her belly button. Go ahead and scoff! I know my navels and I can recognize one that has been stretched nearly flat, or worse, popped inside out, and then relaxed again. No matter how firm your tummy gets, your belly button will look a little haggard. You can have a stomach that's hard enough to play backgammon on (go ahead and

dream), but you would have to have a plastic surgeon to restore your button to its former perfect circle. In case you're curious, here's what to look for: belly button traumas vary from mother to mother, but they usually involve some sort of 'hooding' of the top part of the circle or 'button'. It's a small thing, but almost all of us are left with about an eighth of an inch of skin that doesn't remember where to go.

4. *Your Belly*. I can stand a conversation's distance from you and hand you a fold of skin from my belly. Okay, so maybe I exaggerate, but there's easily an extra handful or two of fleshy stuff around my middle. Sure, I was a sitting duck for Mother Nature's cruel tricks. After all, I was thirty-four when I had my first baby and thirty-nine when I had my fourth, so any elasticity in my skin was getting tired anyway. I am also a freckled, fair-skinned Irish lass with skin that was meant to stay perpetually damp and in the dark. And while it soothes me to say that I lost all the poundage of my numerous pregnancies, I also lost the ability to bend over or sit without my belly pleating like a little dirndl. Would I trade a baby for a six-pack stomach? Well, it depends on the baby and the day . . . Naw, just kidding!!

All right, I admit it! I did go so far as to ask a plastic surgeon what he could do to set things right in my personal equator. I had studied liposuction in magazines and on television shows with keen interest. In fact, if the truth be told, I used to fantasize about it when I was driving the kids to school. But my bubble was burst when he told me that fat sucking was not the solution. Evidently that would just give me more lifeless skin. What I needed was a tummy tuck! What I *really* needed was to have my head examined because that procedure leaves a hip-to-hip scar that looks like your pelvis is smiling. Talk about your grim jokes! I've just surrendered and learned to make friends with lycra and all other fabrics with a memory.

5. *Your Stretch Marks*. I understand that you might be reluctant to claim these purply red abominations as *yours*, but if your genes determined that you would get stretch marks, they are, indeed, yours for the rest of your life. (Or until they perfect that laser treatment I keep hearing about.) While it might be true that they would have been less abundant if you hadn't gained so much weight during pregnancy, you shouldn't blame yourself; just the increase in size of your breasts would have given you stretch marks if they were your hereditary disposition. In other words, here is one more thing for which you can blame your mother!

Attitude

When I was pregnant, I was amazed by the curiosity people had about my weight gain. Right after they asked how the baby and I were feeling, they would ask, 'So, have you gained very much weight?' or 'How much have you gained so far?' I never could decide whether I was supposed to get tearful and tell them the truth that I had gained in two weeks what the books said I should gain by the end of the first trimester, or lie and act like I had this whole pregnancy thing under control. I usually opted for the latter because I believe deep down that they were hoping, in some perverse way, for the former. I know the national obsession with thin transcends pregnancy and recovery, but I want to address this time of your life in particular.

Becoming a mother is such an overwhelming transformation that we tend to try to break it up into bite-sized chunks, like those twelve-step programmes that advise recoverers to take it 'one day at a time'. Pregnancy is broken up into three trimesters, months or even weeks for easier digestibility. Motherhood is marked by a series of milestones or achievements, both yours and the baby's. We look forward to when the baby smiles, when he sleeps through the night, when he sits up, when we go back to work, when we actually want sex again, and when the baby walks. But one of the most universal finish lines that we mothers stretch toward is 'when we turn into our former selves'. After nine years of motherhood, what I can say, at least for myself, is that we are never going to be our former selves. You can buy a sports car, get as thin as a fashion model or become the CEO of your company, but you are not who you used to be. If you secretly believe that the sooner you get control of your weight, the sooner you will get control of your life, you are heading for a big disappointment. You have changed in the most profound way; you have discovered a love and devotion that places the happiness and well-being of your baby at the front and centre of your life's focus.

If you will take this one bit of advice, it could make this entire year a little calmer for you: THIS NEW YOU IS A DIFFERENT BUT BETTER YOU. Who would trade your compassion, your vulnerability, your strength, your commitment for the person you used to be? Relax and surrender to the evolution that has become your life. You were once a human being and now you are a mother. We all know which one is better.

9

sex? what sex?

No Best Friend worth her salt will deny that her sex life was knocked for a loop by the arrival of a new baby. You already know what all the physical changes and riotous hormones did to you during pregnancy, and there is no reason to think that this postnatal stage should be much different. We really must talk a lot about this for two reasons. First, you will not be prepared for the sheer variety of the assaults childbirth makes on your sexuality. Second, you will reach a point where you'll worry that your relations with your partner are so far gone that if he doesn't go off and have an affair soon, you just might have to suggest it to him, to alleviate some of the guilt.

You're still pregnant!

We are here to tell you that you aren't crazy or asexual. Your orgasm machine is not broken. You have not fallen out of love with your partner. Divorce Court is not just around the corner. Simply put, you are still pregnant; it's just that you've reached that 'fourth trimester' when the baby is NOW carried *outside* of your body. The Original Best Friend, Mother Nature, is using her entire arsenal of tricks, from hormones to humility, to keep you focused on your baby and not on getting pregnant again.

One of the *joys* of life is that everybody is unique, but one of the *comforts* of pregnancy and parenthood is that we're all more alike than we are different. With that in mind, we think you should be prepared for your sex life to be anywhere from unusual to downright crummy for up to a year. It probably won't take that long to get back in the saddle (ouch!), but the progress from dysfunctional to operational is usually made in baby steps. (See, those baby references pop up everywhere.) One bit of advice we can give you right now is to beg (or bribe with the promise of sexual favours) your partner to read this section of the book. And if he won't read it for himself, discuss it with him, because you both need to be reassured that the ardour will come back and what you are feeling now is common to nearly all new mothers. Don't let him delude himself into believing that all the other couples in your Lamaze class are enjoying Victoria's Secret (whatever that secret may be) while you guys are still in the T-shirt-and-sweatpants phase. Best of all, it doesn't last forever. Only people who are way too young to be parents in the first place are back at it sexually right after the baby's birth. You know what they say: 'No brain, no headache.'

The First Six weeks

You won't need any doctor to tell you to abstain from sex for the first six weeks after the baby is born (although they will). After the lurching, rolling, bucking, stretching, tearing and Lord knows what else you have endured to get this baby from up inside your body to a blanket in a crib beside you, you won't want to have anybody messing with your body, especially DOWN THERE, for several weeks (maybe as many as fifty-two, but I'm getting ahead of myself here). As far as most new-mum Best Friends are concerned, they don't want to see anything come near their dainty parts for several days if it isn't filled with crushed ice or spraying a local anaesthetic.

The good thing about the doctor's prohibition of sex for the first six weeks is that it lifts all responsibility from you, like the doctor's notes that got you out of gym class. It's not that you haven't been dying to 'do it' as much as your partner has. (Yeah, right!) It's not that you're unsympathetic about his needs. (Needs, schmeeds!) It's certainly not that you don't find him hunkier than ever. (Haven't really noticed lately.) Of course not! You'd be all over him like a duck on a june bug if you could. But, *damn it*, the doctor has forbidden it! (God bless the NHS!)

This is actually the easy part of postnatal sexuality. The rules are clear and no one's feelings are on the line. Besides, you are both still so busy and enraptured by this little being who has come to live with you that the first six weeks pass in the blink of a bloodshot eye. It gets tricky after this because popular wisdom dictates that couples should be ready to resume 'normal' sexual relations as soon as they are given the 'green light' by the GP at the six-week postnatal check. Don't panic yet! The

Best Friends weren't ready then, either, and we have all sorts of advice for you, but we'll get to that part in a couple of pages. In the meantime, our best advice for this first month and a half is: BE NICE!

During the first six weeks, the most important thing you can do to nourish your relationship is to be *courteous* to your partner. This will be harder than you imagine because fear, combined with sleep deprivation and wicked mood swings, tends to make even the sweetest among us lash out like vipers at our nearest and dearest. I remember my husband finally getting out of bed at around 4:00 A.M. to remind me that he needed to go to work in three hours and would appreciate it if I would take the crying baby into another room so he could get some sleep. I could have calmly explained that I had been walking with the crying baby since midnight, and I was about to fall to my knees with exhaustion. I could have taken the baby into the living room on the theory that it didn't make sense for both of us to stay awake all night. But, no, I chose to let loose with the most vitriolic stream of consciousness imaginable. I made *Who's Afraid of Virginia Woolf?* seem like a nursery rhyme.

Part of being nice includes occasionally acknowledging your partner's existence. It can be so tempting to fixate on the new baby that anything else needing your attention, from a ringing phone to a whining partner, can feel like a somewhat annoying interruption. As a general rule, this is not a good thing for relationships. Yes, simple courtesy may be a stretch during the first six weeks, but fake it if you have to. It's like smiling; you can start out forcing it, but it won't be long before you actually *feel* like smiling. In the long run, you will be grateful that you never said half the wicked things you thought (like snide comments about his ancestors or what you really think of his dancing). Take it from us Best Friends, a partner is a good thing *not* to lose during the first year of motherhood.

The Six-Week Checkup

About six weeks after the birth of your baby, you will visit your GP or midwife for a checkup. This usually involves a thorough internal and external exam. Assuming that your cervix is closed and healed and your uterus has shrunk satisfactorily, your doctor will probably tell you with a smile that you can have intercourse again. Oh, goody.

IF YOU ARE WITH US, BEST FRIEND, YOU WILL NOT SHARE THIS NEWS WITH YOUR PARTNER!

Our goal is to banish this infamous and inane measurement of time. The last thing you need in your condition is a partner who is eagerly ticking the days off on his calendar with a big red circle around day 42. There is no reason you should think that your sexual readiness can be as scientifically predicted as a NASA liftoff. Tight cervix or no tight cervix, forty-two days just might not be enough. I don't care what I said about the sanctity of the 'doctor's note' regarding the prohibition against sex for the first six weeks; the doctor's declaration of sexual readiness is absolutely meaningless unless YOU feel ready. We can all protect our partners from this senseless setup for disappointment if we join in solidarity in saying that A NEW MOTHER IS READY FOR INTERCOURSE WHEN SHE SAYS SHE'S READY FOR INTERCOURSE, whether it's in forty-two or one hundred and forty-two days.

Don't worry: You're Normal

Sure, you will hear stories about other new mums who slipped back into their former sexuality with the ease of Esther Williams entering a pool. You might even be Esther yourself, and if you are, all I can say to you at this point is, congratulations and don't forget your birth control. But if you feel about as sexy as Alice, the Bradys' housekeeper, we Best Friends are here to rescue you from all guilt and insecurity. Consider this:

Everybody lies about their sex life at some time, and the biggest liars of all, bigger even than teenage boys, are new parents. My Friend Karen recently leaned across the table during lunch, grabbed my arm with a little more strength than was absolutely necessary, and asked in desperation, 'Why isn't anyone honest about this? It's just like how no one really tells you the truth about how much it's going to hurt to have a baby! Postnatal sex is terrible!' If you believe what some Pollyannas say, all new parents, except your partner and you, are barely hanging on till the six-week checkup when the doctor gives them the okay for intercourse. They are so hot for each other that they are about to explode with sexual desire during that six-week waiting period.

I told Karen what I am going to tell you: these people are either *still* taking their pain medication, and I mean the good stuff with warning labels about not trying to drive while under its influence, or they are too embarrassed to tell the truth. Just to cover all my bases, I concede that there is an exception to every rule, like that friend of a friend who wore her old jeans home from the hospital after giving birth. However, that exception is more rare than mums in bikinis at Little Dolphins Swimming Classes. If you remember from the *Best Friends' Guide to Pregnancy*, even my Friend Pamela was tapped with morphine before she had oral sex with her husband just hours after a C-section. Five years later, she's not only not giving him that little gift, she's divorcing him! But don't get me started . . .

You may be wondering what gives me any authority to speak for the entire New Mummy population (besides my own belief that what is true for me is true for the universe), and that is an entirely reasonable question. I have consulted no psychologists or medical specialists (although I have taken the advice of a former Hollywood-producer-turned-sex-aids-therapist who discreetly gives dildo demonstrations to the very same women you read about in the tabloids). I pay little attention to scientific surveys because, as I said, most people are lying anyway, and I haven't conducted personal interviews based on a random cross-section of the new-mum population. What I *did* do was evaluate all the new mums who were established Best Friends or who earned Best Friend status by speaking candidly and courageously about their own weird postnatal sex lives. While I made sure to listen to any and all stories, I stacked the deck with a disproportionate number of women who could only be called 'HOT'. I'm talking about certain TV stars who were so sexy that they made cutoff jeans a fashion icon, I'm talking about Best Friends who actually keep a variety of sex toys (like things that require batteries) under their beds, I'm talking about a rock star who loves giving head even more than getting it. And (though I never thought I would bring this odd bit of my personal history out of the closet of Things I've Done That I Would Prefer Not to Tell My Children) even I, as a Playboy Playmate of the Month (oh, God, I've said it!) was once considered a hot tamale, and I turned into cold guacamole after the arrival of each child. And it's not just me; it happened to Playmates of the *Year*, the ultimate sex goddesses (if federal inmates and teenaged boys are any indication), too!

This was no random sampling. There were no finicky, inhibited or otherwise take-it-or-leave-it women in the group. And after a glass or two of champagne (except for those Best Friends in recovery, of course), all of my interview subjects felt that the arrival of their beloved babies had, at least temporarily, bruised the ripe fruit that was their sexuality. Hey, if it can happen to them, it seems reasonable to assume it can happen to anybody.

A Baby Love Affair

Cuddling, romancing, kissing. Sure, they are important in keeping the relationship intimate, but don't feel too bad if most of that action is directed by both you and your partner to your baby. As a matter of fact, my Best Friends and I have this theory that new mummies don't miss sex as much as they might because they get so much from their closeness with their baby. Think about it: you have someone to touch, hold, hug, kiss, smell, even feed. Your partner can join in if he wants to, but often new dads are unsure about their mothering skills and they might not feel as free to kiss every little part of the little one's body as you are. My Best Friend Kelly has a Friend who got so involved nuzzling every inch of her newborn son's skin (which, as we all know, is the most delicious substance heaven ever concocted) that she found herself eye to eye with his little penis. There she was, smack dab in the middle of her first real parenting crisis. Should she be free and liberated and kiss him all over, without discriminating among body parts? Or should she get all Freudian and decide to leave that particular sensation for him to discover sometime after he's old enough to drive? Or perhaps more accurately, till he was old enough to *park* with some curious teenage girl. She was a little sad to confess that she put his nappy on him and resumed kissing the more p.c. parts.

Breastfeeding Orgasms

This is a good time to speak candidly, again, about the pleasure many women get from breastfeeding, too. Not only do they feel the closeness and intimacy of feeding their babies from their bodies, but there's that fringe benefit lots of Best Friends experience which is uterine con-tractions that feel like the aftershocks of orgasm. Right after the birth of the baby, these contractions can hurt like period pains, but later, after the uterus has got over the trauma of pregnancy, they can feel great. As I mentioned before, I got such a thrill out of it that I almost fell out of my hospital bed. I really went as limp as a noodle, and the baby and I would have puddled on to the floor if we hadn't been corralled by the bed rails.

Let's be honest. If we are getting our kicks through motherhood, it makes sense that we aren't prowling around after our partners in the hope of getting lucky. They, however, are beginning to prowl and are preparing to pounce.

New Daddies

It's not just mums whose libidos have been rocked; dads, too, often have a significant postnatal sex droop. They may not have had to give birth to the baby, but chances are they had to *watch*, and that can be pretty hard at times, too. They, too, are exhausted and in a blended state of euphoria and shock: one minute weeping at the sight of the baby's fingers as they squeeze into tight little fists while she sleeps, the next minute sobbing over his realization that there is no way on this earth that you two can afford a child. Unless you live in Buckingham Palace, the crying baby that is keeping you awake all night is keeping your partner awake, too.

I have several Best Friends who say that their partners were turned off by the sight of them feeding the baby. My Best Friend Terry was so conflicted by this that she would hide while feeding. I guess this accommodated her wacky husband's maintaining the fantasy that God invented breasts to be big boys' toys, not little boys' sustenance. This subject is discussed again in the chapter on breastfeeding, but it doesn't hurt to mention again here that the decision to breastfeed should be somewhat mutual. Before the baby is born, you should allow your partner to share his feelings about your suckling someone other than him. Unless he is a schmuck, he will express his secret concerns, then ultimately leave the decision in your hands. And, unless you are a schmuck, you will listen to his concerns without threatening to report him to the La Leche League, then perhaps compromise on such things as pumping milk into bottles for him to feed the baby or promise to wean the child before she is old enough to open a jar of peanut butter unassisted. Sometimes a partner's requests are quite simple and don't require much sacrifice on your part. For example, he may be queasy about the prospect of you whipping out a giant nipple and feeding the baby in front of his parents or at theme parks. Yeah, yeah, we all know it's the most natural thing in the world, but now is not the time to get your partner in touch with his animal self.

Speaking of watching a birth, the experience of seeing a baby squeeze out of his sex kitten's vagina can wreak havoc on some men's libido. I don't know if they become afraid of their partner's vagina; maybe it has something to do with the fear that anything that can open its mouth that wide might have cannibalistic tendencies, or that they begin to see that dainty aperture as something more like one of the chutes at a water theme park. Simply speaking, it is a scary sight to some men, and they never quite think about their wives' sexuality the way they did before.

It's hard to predict which men will be affected by being right in the catcher's position during their partners' deliveries. Some find it a glimpse into the mysteries of heaven. To others, the word *Exorcist* comes to mind. You really can't know before the fact which category your partner will fall into. For that reason, it's a good idea for all men who don't have their heart set on being the first to see the top of the crowning baby's head to be assigned to a standing position up near the mother's head. This way, both the mother and the father get to meet the baby face-to-face at the same time. Besides, the presence of a partner up near her head, where he can whisper encouragement in her ear or pull her into a sitting position to push, is more valuable to a delivering mother than having him in a front-row seat announcing 'I can see its head!'

Ultimately, horniness and short-term memory loss will overcome any finickiness your partner may have about your reproductive organs. The only time I have ever heard about a man never getting over this disillusionment concerned a superstar musician who picked up the sexual slack by having sex with any groupie he wanted. Unfortunately for our partners, most of them are not Elvis, at least not in the literal sense, and they don't have such enviable options. Where most relationships are concerned, there's only one restaurant in town; if you're hungry, you eat there.

Another reason for a cooling of the sexual ardour in some men is a funny old psychological phenomenon called the 'Madonna/Whore Complex'. As I recall from college psychology classes and old issues of *Cosmopolitan*, some men divide women into two categories: the kind you want to have sex with and the kind who are mothers. In this Peter Pan world, sex is a naughty thing and it's wrong to have naughty feelings about your mother, who is pure and above all that sweating and pawing. The inescapable conclusion for these poor fellas is that, once their sexy wives become mothers, they aren't sexy anymore.

If you should find yourself saddled with a guy like this (and they wonder why we get postnatal depression!), it appears you have two choices. Either you can resign yourself to a life of abstinence and give your partner a subscription to *Psychology Today*, or you can shake some sense into him by actively demonstrating just how slutty we mothers can be. Go ahead, put on the garter belt, talk dirty, give him a blow job while he's driving the car. (God, remember that?!) My Best Friend Lori postponed her sexual reunion with her partner for several months after her little girl was born until she knew she was ready to rock her man's world. She took a hotel room and left a message with his secretary for him to meet her in the lobby bar. Lori, a brunette, sat there waiting in a blond wig and a scandalously revealing dress. His take on the matter? It was definitely worth the wait, and sex has been great ever since.

'Inebriate and Lubricate'

So, here it is: the moment we've all been waiting for. What do you do, just jump into bed and go at it? ABSOLUTELY NOT! Things have changed in the last couple of months, and your sex life is going to have to adjust to accommodate them. First of all, you need lots and lots of foreplay. Foreplay, ideally, should begin out of the house with a nice dinner and a good bottle of wine. If you decide to stay at home for your reunion dinner, then you should send the baby out or lock her in her room with your most trusted (and discreet) babysitter. It generally doesn't help move the romance along to have either of your parents sitting just a room away, so try to find someone less Oedipally involved to look after the baby for you.

So, here you are, just the two of you, staring across the table into each other's eyes, his reflecting desire and yours suggesting terror. As you sip your wine, do your best to keep the conversation away from all things baby. This will be nearly impossible, I know, but limit the gushing and rejoicing about every little goo goo and burp to the first ten or fifteen minutes. Then move on to more grown-up subject matter. I have always found that one way to ease into conversation about ourselves and our feelings is for my husband and me to gossip about other couples that we know. Nothing malicious (at least not usually), just the comforting distance of talking about a relationship *like* ours that *isn't* ours. After a few more sips of wine and this literal kind of oral sex (as in talking), it won't be long before you start feeling a little seductive, a little carefree, maybe even a little *childless*.

Now that you have his attention, you should take this glowing moment to explain a couple of things to your partner about how you'd like this sexual encounter to go. No need to be bossy here, just pique his arousal with your depiction of how nice and slowly you'd like him to proceed. Sure it's sexy, but it's also absolutely essential to approach your delicate little vagina gingerly after all it's been through. If you had a vaginal delivery, especially with an episiotomy and a little tearing and bruising, you probably feel about to lose your virginity all over again.

To spell it out for you, actual penetration should be gentle and eased into. It also should not go too deep in the beginning because the cervix, which connects to the end of the vagina (think of the end of a tunnel), might also be sore, having recently achieved the feat of opening to more than ten times its normal size.

No amount of easing and gentleness will be worth spit if you don't also use something much more lubricating than, well, spit. The postnatal hormones of new mothers, especially those who are breast-feeding, deprive them of all normal sexual lubrication. In other words, even if you are as aroused as a bunny, you will remain dry, dry, dry. If you don't use a gel of some kind, sex will feel like one really vicious rug burn. Just trust your Best Friends on this, and make sure to have lubrication on hand when the big moment comes. Otherwise you will have wasted a perfectly good bottle of wine. My Best Friend Donna was given a gel by her GP – I guess as a sort of congratulatory gift at her six-week check. She brought it over to show to some of her other mummy Best Friends, and we unanimously advised her to throw it in the bin. Not because we were trying to destroy any suggestions of imminent sex before her horny partner saw them, but because we all knew that this first sexual reunion was too big a job for amateurs. We mums had long ago followed the endorsements of our gay men friends and opted for a brand called KY, the smoothest mover on the market. It's widely available, even at the most 'hetero' drugstores.

where the Body Goes, the Head Follows

For a lot of us new mothers, the prospect of shifting gears at the end of the day from mummy mode to sex kitten seems impossible. Just the suggestion of it can make us feel edgy and pressured. Don't make it such a big deal. Before you try to hide in the closet to avoid the whole thing, consider taking it in baby steps. Once again, breaking it down into bite-sized chunks (bad metaphor) makes it less overwhelming. Start with kissing. Even if you don't feel kissable, kiss anyway. Chances are, you will begin to feel more and more kissable. If you don't, move on to something else that makes you feel good. It may start out feeling mechanical, but it generally gets real after a few minutes. By the time the whole thing has climaxed (if you know what I mean), you will probably turn to your partner and say, 'Hey, that was fun! Why don't we do it more often?'

The brain can be your biggest enemy in restoring your sex life. First of all, it gets stuck in 'Function' and is concentrating on everything going on in the house except in the bed. Is the baby crying? Is the phone ringing? Is there anything for dinner? The biggest sabotage, however, is a brain that asks 'Why would anyone want to have sex with someone like me?' Admit it, Best Friend, you have asked yourself that question at least once since pregnancy and childbirth. Here we go again with yet another form of the Myth of the Perfect Mother. If you are thinking that you are undesirable because you are not thin enough or energetic enough or happy enough, then you are buying into those 'standards' again. You are doing great and you'll continue to feel better and better as this year progresses. In the meantime, put some Tina Turner on the stereo and blast it. If she doesn't have you feeling sexy about yourself within two songs (remember, you *must* sing along), get out the Hitachi.

10

Food Glorious Food!

Pressure, Anyone?

When you have a newborn baby to feed, your options are limited and clearly delineated: either you breastfeed him or you feed him formula, or you fashion a combination of the two. Pretty simple, right? WRONG! The Food Issue is the most controversial decision you will make in your foreseeable future as a mother. Think about it; aside from deciding whether you wanted to have natural childbirth or go right for the drugs, this is your first serious judgement call as a mum. If you're lucky, it will be the trickiest question you'll have to face for several years. If you're really lucky, it will last you right up to the time your child asks you if you ever had sex with anyone besides Daddy or before you married. By that time, you will have been battered by so many hard decisions along your parenting path that you will, hopefully, be a little less terrified of making the wrong choice and ruining your child's life. Right now, however, you are still convinced that any mother worth her salt has the wisdom of Solomon regarding all things baby. You're still at that stage where you think there are right and wrong answers and that wrong answers are fatal. It's only later that you learn that most things are not really decisions for you to make, but rather realizations for you to discover. Put less philosophically: calm down because no matter what you decide for your child, you can always change your mind later. That's what's so fun about raising kids: they're more like sturdy and slow-cooking stews than fragile, on-the-brink-of-disaster soufflés. But I'm sounding more like your mother than your Best Friend, aren't I? . . . Sorry, won't happen again.

Let's Ask the Man on the Street for His Advice

One thing this Food Issue has in common with choosing whether or not to have a drug-free delivery is the fact that everyone you meet has an opinion about it. 'What business is it of theirs?' you might reasonably ask. Why, none, of course. But that doesn't dampen the enthusiasm of complete strangers who come up to your pregnant self to enquire about your plans for delivery, whether your midwife advises episiotomies as a rule and how much your insurance covers. Same way with feeding. The entire world finds it essential to know *what* your baby will be eating and *how* it will be administered. And if that's not intrusion enough, they ask how *your* mother fed *you*!

Don't think for a minute that I am cutting these people any slack by suggesting that they are just benignly curious, concerned about your well-being or simply taking a sort of unbiased survey of all the new mothers they meet. Not in a million years! These people have full-blown opinions and you are entitled to them, no matter how much you might protest to the contrary. If you are undecided about whether you will breastfeed or bottlefeed, these eager beavers will lobby for one side or the other, usually with ample and convincing testimony about their own perfectly miraculous mothering experiences. But you don't have to be a mother to have strong convictions on the Food Issue. This is a subject that seems to be fair game for anyone, even if they have only seen babies on TV. Men can advise you to do whatever their own partners did, which, it goes without saying, was the *best* choice. And if the advocate has never had a baby or partner, he can simply recommend that you do whatever Katie Couric and Jane Seymour did. After all, if it's good enough for Katie and Jane, it's damn well good enough for a nobody like you.

What really gets my knickers in a twist is when a pregnant woman or new mother has already made up her mind in favour of breast- or bottle-feeding, for her own presumably valid reasons, and some well-intentioned busybody (oxymoron?) tries to make her change her mind! You would think some of these people were getting a commission on each convert, they sell their point of view so enthusiastically. These folks really should consider getting a hobby, or maybe a LIFE! I think that new mothers or mothers-to-be should answer the question 'Are you going to breastfeed or bottlefeed?' by asking back, 'What would you prefer me to do, sir (or ma'am)?' After they make their recommendation, and you can be certain they will, just say with all the sincerity you can muster, 'Then that's precisely what I will do. Thank you so much for your guidance.' If they detect a little sarcasm in your answer, good; they deserve it. If they don't, you have still nipped a diatribe in the bud, and you should feel free to continue abusing them until they stop talking.

some common considerations

The Best Friends, as a group, do not sanction or endorse any feeding method. Several of those cherished friends are individually rebelling against this policy because my Best Friends will not be 'ssshhhed', but I'll explain to you what I explained to them: *this is* my *book and they are only living in it!* Sure, we all have our unique and wonderful opinions, but, for once, we are not going to force them down your throat. (You can thank yours truly for that.) The party line is simply that we are unanimous in our belief that a mother's job is to feed her baby good, healthy food whenever he wants it. The particulars are up to you, and your countless advisers.

You are already well aware of the many considerations that a mother must weigh in selecting one method over another. I think that one real big question is 'Did I give birth to this baby?' You would be amazed at how many adoptive mothers are willing to take hormones to induce their bodies to make milk. Look, as far as I'm concerned, anything that is good for your baby and good for you is wonderful, but this sounds a little bit like one of those breastfeeding evangelists got to them with the myth that better *bonding* (BIG buzzword) occurs when the baby actually drinks your liquids. Trust me; I know as many alienated children who were breastfed as who drank formula from a bottle. This kind of advice goes under the 'Why Buy Problems When They're Giving Them Away for Free?' category.

What follows is a list of some of the most common considerations that help a new mother decide how she is going to feed that little thing.

1. *Whether you feel comfortable with the notion of turning your lovely sex toys into udders for the next few months* and whether your partner feels at least a little comfortable with that idea, too. Remember, having a supportive partner when you are learning to breastfeed is critical because his disdain or impatience can be the straw that breaks the struggling feeder's back. I have already mentioned my Best Friend

Terry, who used to sneak up to the nursery to try to breastfeed whenever her husband wasn't around because he wanted his wife back, tits intact, as soon after her pregnancy as possible. As you might suspect, the whole thing was a disaster for feeding because the pressure of hiding, hurrying and not being able to rely on her partner for reassurance made Terry's letdown reflex go on strike. It seemed that the only time her breast milk flowed freely was during orgasm or when she was dressed in a couture gown and being introduced to presidential candidates. Her husband must have been horrified by the deluge, but I'm sure some of the politicians found it a welcome distraction from the endless chatting and handshaking.

2. *How soon after delivery you intend to return to work.* The fact that you are going back to work does not preclude breastfeeding, particularly now that those brilliant electric pumps can be rented so easily, but if you only get six weeks paid maternity leave, you might not have enough time to master the techniques and establish a good milk supply. This is not to say it cannot be done. The issue here is whether you are willing and able to return to the stresses of a career and spend every free minute feeding or pumping to stimulate more milk production. Remember, milk production works on the principle of supply and demand: your body will keep supplying milk as long as your baby wants it. It will even increase production in keeping with your baby's growth.

3. *Whether your baby was able to come home from hospital with you.* There's no use pretending that these things don't happen, even when nearly every time there's a happy ending, but there are a lot of reasons why newborns must spend extra time in hospital. Prematurity is a frequent reason for the extended stay. Since you will orbit around that hospital like the moon around the earth, proximity is not always the reason why breastfeeding may be hard to establish. In fact, premmies often are not yet strong enough to feed effectively, so a mother who intends to breastfeed may have to pump her milk out on a regular schedule to build up the milk supply and give it to the hospital for the baby's feeds. Mothers who are committed to breastfeeding for its nutritional value and to enabling the baby to have the protective antibodies that a mother passes on to her child through her milk are usually willing to put up with the difficulties and inconveniences that are often associated with all this pumping and delivering. But mothers whose greatest interest in feeding is the physical intimacy with the baby

might lose heart when that part of the mix is denied them in the beginning. Mothers with a toddler already at home may find that breastfeeding a new baby who's still in hospital feels like the Indy 500, with its marathon of endless driving and getting nowhere.

4. *The condition of Mummy's health after delivery.* Since nearly anything ingested by the mum gets passed on to the baby through breast milk, an important consideration is what she will be eating or taking in the way of medication. If you need to take antibiotics after delivery, chances are good that your doctor will prescribe one that can be tolerated by a breastfeeding baby, but not all medications are so well tolerated. Make sure you discuss these matters with your doctor.

Breastfeeding is never an option when the mother has HIV and the baby does not. I don't think I will ever get over the outrage, sadness and vulnerability I felt about the deaths of Elizabeth Glaser and her precious daughter, Ariel. Ms. Glaser contracted the virus from a blood transfusion and unknowingly passed it along to her baby girl by breastfeeding her.

Rather than leave you here in a puddle of tears, let's move on to say that most of these decisions are not so cut-and-dried. You will usually end up weighing whatever risks there may be against how serious you feel about breastfeeding and see which way the scales tip.

5. *Which type of food your baby tolerates better, formula or breast milk.* Just to show that even Mother Nature occasionally makes mistakes (like every other mother since Eve), in some *very* rare cases, babies cannot digest their mothers' milk. Sure, even a successfully feeding baby may get indigestion after Mum has wolfed down a large helping of broccoli cooked in olive oil and whole garlic cloves, but the milk itself is not the problem; Mum's food intake is. Babies who truly can't digest their mother's milk are thought to be lactose intolerant. Funny, I always assumed that only applied to cow's milk, but I've been told that it applies to all milk manufactured in a nursing mammal. Milk-based formula isn't an alternative, either, but soya-based formulas just might fill the bill. If you and your doctor discover that your baby is lactose intolerant, you will embrace the concept of formula as the most natural source of nutrition in the world, no matter how much you dreamed of breastfeeding.

6. *When the breasts are too small or the nipples are inverted.* Actually, breast size is a 'faux' consideration in the Food Issue. All breasts are the

perfect size for breastfeeding. My Best Friend May, whose breasts look like two chocolate chips (but pink) sitting on eggs sunny-side up, had enough milk in those things to sustain a day-care centre. If we were together more than ninety minutes and her baby wasn't around, she would have to go to the toilet and express some into the sink. I used to feel physically ill at that spectacle, not because it was shocking, but because I saved each drop of my breast milk and still never had more than two bottles in reserve. And good luck if I tried to get my milk out with anything less than a high-performance, fuel-injected, chrome-plated breast pump. I could be so engorged that I cried when wind hit my breasts, and I still couldn't get the milk out. May, however, daintily leaned over the sink a bit and pressed the flat of her hand against the top of her breast and out it poured.

If there is any truth in the myth that breast size has anything to do with breastfeeding, I can make a better case for small breasts than for large ones, even though your endowment is out of your control. Imagine that: for the first time since puberty, small-breasted women can be grateful that they never got near a B cup. (Just for the record, you'll probably find that small breasts are as dramatically deflated by motherhood as their more ample colleagues.) First of all, let's think about the weight of those breasts. My large-breasted Best Friends often suffered from backaches and sore shoulders, not to mention that it was nearly impossible to find a bra to fit. Then consider the newborn baby trying to latch on to a breast that is nearly twice the size of its head? It's a good thing their sight is still fuzzy, otherwise they would run screaming from the room. By the way, as much as suffocation would seem like a danger as that tiny face gets lost in those magnificent mammaries, babies have no trouble finding little air pockets and breathe just fine. The more immediate challenge presented by big boobs is that the new mother may have trouble seeing over them to tell whether she is getting the baby to latch on properly. Later, the sensation in her nipples will let a mother know if she has achieved docking position, but in the beginning, nothing is instinctive about breastfeeding.

This business of inverted nipples (which I never knew existed until I started reading pregnancy books) is your call, mums. If you feel that having nipples that don't get aroused to a point is an impediment to breastfeeding, that's fine with us. If, however, you are heartbroken about this state of affairs, we might be of some service by telling you they sell little silicone shell-things to help with this in most maternity stores. When worn, they apparently create suction that pulls your reluctant nipples to attention. Having breastfed four kids (for successively shorter times with each child, I should add), the most shocking thing to me about the whole experience is the way the baby takes all the pigmented part of your nipple into her mouth and halfway down her throat, rather than sipping daintily from a hole at the tip of the nipple's point. Inverted, extroverted, I can't really see how such small variances in breasts can matter when a baby is getting little streams of milk from all over your nipple, not just the tip. Besides, if the baby (or feeding machine, for that matter) is sucking with its usual force, there's no way your inverted nipples can stay hidden for long. We're lucky our nipples don't get sucked right off our bodies!

7. *How serious your need for sleep is.* All new mothers are sleep deprived, but breastfeeding ones are usually particularly so. Think about it: if no meal can be served to your baby without your active participation, it's safe to say that Dad has a pretty good gig. Yeah, yeah, yeah, we all know about the babies who sleep through the night as soon as they come home from the hospital, but is it *our* fault their doctors refused to induce labour even though they were two months past their due dates? The rest of us usually end up with little chicks who must eat with the frequency of hummingbirds. If you, too, have a baby who wants to feed all the time, consider this factoid; an African tribe was studied recently to determine why their babies cried an average of one-third as often as your basic Western baby, and the reason is simple – the African babies feed about every *thirteen minutes* and for up to *three or four years*. The point here, it seems to me, is that most babies want to cuddle and feed most of the time, and the compromise between your need to have a life and their need to be attached to you is usually worked out slowly over the first year of life. In the end, I always decided it was time to wean when I got to the point where I couldn't weigh fruit at the market and do the multiplication required to figure out how much six bananas were going to cost me. Lack of sleep made me stupid.

All the chirpy little books that root, root, root for the homemade stuff reassure us bleary-eyed zombies that you can sleep more if you express milk so that Daddy or some other loving person can feed the baby. That's only partly true, according to my unscientific survey. You see, since milk production is gauged by how much and how often the baby eats, a mother who is not drowning in an endless milk supply will still have to wake up and pump during this feeding. If she doesn't, she will soon stop having enough milk at that time. Then it's a matter of days before she uses up all her refrigerated breast milk and has a very hungry and ticked-off baby on her hands around 2:00 A.M. An obvious compromise would be to feed the baby formula for one or two feeds a day. Be warned, though: those two feeds that don't depend on you may be addictive. Once I got off my own high horse and agreed to supplementary soya formula once a day, I was on a giant slippery slope that could only end in the baby and I becoming formula junkies.

For every woman like me, who loved breastfeeding while it lasted but felt like it made me stay pregnant and restricted, there is another one like my Best Friend Karen who felt that feeding her baby and devoting her life to her were just this side of heaven. To assuage my guilt about my selfishness, I mutter under my breath, 'Sure she's having a great time! It's her FIRST baby! Get back to me when she's trying to pump while attempting to keep big sister from clobbering the new addition.' I swear, my heart is black!

8. *How confident you feel in your ability to breastfeed.* No one knows how good she will be at feeding a baby before she's tried it, but some of us approach the challenge with a lot more insecurity than others. The reason this matters is because, for nearly every new mother I've ever met, breastfeeding is harder to learn than an authentic tango, and a lot more painful. If you interpret these difficulties as indications that you are doing something wrong or are not properly equipped for the job, then you may be inclined to call the whole thing off. If, however, you just know that you were made to suckle babies, in spite of the nipple blisters and the constant worry about whether the baby is getting enough to eat, then chances are better that you will forge on ahead.

The most common reason that I have heard for women giving up breastfeeding almost immediately is 'I couldn't make enough milk to satisfy the baby's needs.' Trust me; I can see how any sane woman with a baby screaming for more milk every hour or two can start to think that the baby is starving to death. If I may stand on my soapbox for a moment, I would like to lay the blame for this 'insufficiency' at the feet of our health-care system, which sends brand-new mothers home with a baby they intend to feed before their milk has had a chance to come in yet! A mother who is rushed out of hospital must then figure out proper latching on, deal with engorgement and endure bleeding nipples all by herself. This usually leads her to feel that she had only two options: to quit breastfeeding altogether, or to carry on even if she thinks she may be doing it wrong. The decision to quit under these circumstances can be heartbreaking and humiliating. It's one thing to decide that breastfeeding doesn't suit you, and it's an entirely different thing to feel that the experience is being taken from you before you even get to try.

The decision to carry on without proper instruction and support can lead to a very sick baby. While it is a rare occurrence, you'll occasionally read stories about babies who were malnourished and jaundiced because their mothers didn't breastfeed them correctly. More specifically, they didn't know how to get their babies latched on. What's particularly pitiful about this situation is the fact that new mothers often are not just uninformed about proper breastfeeding technique; they know even less about what to look for in a baby to make sure that he is thriving. My bet is that those mums could have breastfed as successfully as Bessie the Cow if they had had firm and friendly nurses who took the time *while they were recovering in hospital* to jam their breasts into their tiny babies' mouths and get latched on properly. As my mother-in-law always says when people do anything unkind or irresponsible to children, 'It's a SIN.' Boy, is it ever. It is your job, Mum, to assertively seek the help you need in hospital and from your community midwife or health visitor. Don't assume that there is someone keeping track of your progress, because the hospital staff may let you be the one to fall between the cracks. In your most polite manner, insist that you will not leave the hospital until you feel sufficiently educated to take the baby with you.

For some of us, breastfeeding requires the sort of faith that you usually only hear about in church or temple. You must have faith that God will provide, on a very basic level. You see, the tricky thing about feeding is that you have no real tools for measuring intake. Your baby gets hungry, you put him to your breast, he sucks, you hope he's getting something, he finishes and usually goes to sleep without so much as a thank-you. You don't see the milk coming out, except in a few leaking drops, you don't see how full the baby's tummy is, you just trust and pray that it's all working as it's supposed to. Later on, you will rely on other indicators like the sensation of your breasts filling up between feeds and how quickly the baby goes from frantic sucking to longer, relaxed pulls on the breast and you will become as astute as a tea leaf reader at interpreting the contents of your baby's nappy. But in the beginning, you would give anything for all newborns to come equipped with a meter indicating how many ounces the tank was holding after each feed, or better still, for your breasts to have calibrated markings like a measuring cup.

Even after you have got this breastfeeding thing mastered, more tests of your faith await you. It happened to all my Best Friends, but I will use Karen as the example, since she is the most recent victim. In her desire to be all things to all people, Karen agreed to fly to Las Vegas with her partner, her mother and some of her partner's clients. Of course, as a breastfeeding mother, she took her five-month-old baby, too. She knew that she could join her partner and his clients in the casino or at dinner in between feeds because the baby had committed to a regular schedule of feeding about every four hours, with one longer span from midnight until about 5:00 A.M. Naturally, traumatized mother that I am, I vehemently advised against this trip. My experience has always been that the worst parenting experiences befell me when I was away from home, GP and therapist. But, I eventually curbed my pessimism because I didn't want to sound like some old crone hexing what would probably be a delightful experience for the whole family. To cut to the chase, Karen never once left the hotel room in three days, not even to see Julio Iglesias from front-row seats. Her baby ate and napped and fussed in such rapid succession that Karen was certain something had happened to rob her of plentiful milk. Clearly the baby was miserable and starving, and nothing Karen did seemed to be of much help. She called me one night (probably the night everyone had abandoned her and the baby to see Julio) to ask if I had ever experienced this kind of hell. Yes, about ten times, I told her. I prayed with her to the Goddess of Milk and reminded her of the importance of having faith in her abundance. In medical terms, this crisis is known as a 'growth spurt', where, in preparation for, well, for a growth spurt, the baby instinctively knows to suck, suck, suck, to help his breastfeeding mother increase her milk production. It doesn't usually take more than three or four days for one's mammaries to respond with more milk, but the fear and doubt, as well as the fatigue, have KO'ed countless new mums who saw no relief in sight.

9. *Your threshold for pain.* I just read an article in a mothering book that contained this line: 'It's not supposed to hurt to breastfeed.' Well, it may not be *supposed* to hurt, but, Friend, that first month can hurt so badly that you see stars and break out in a sweat whenever your baby looks at you hungrily. I recently went to lunch with eight of my mummy Best Friends, and after the champagne had flowed for about an hour, I started a game sort of like Truth or Dare. The single most shocking and guilt-lifting bit of truth shared by nearly all the mothers was that we hoarded our prescription pain medication, no matter how badly our 'privates' ached, and saved them up for the critical half hour before it was time to feed. Yes, I am confessing what you think I am

confessing: I took the drugs those first couple of weeks simply to endure the pain of breastfeeding. That's how much it hurt me (and several of my Best Friends). You're talking to a woman who endured childbirth and a nose job with very little complaining, so I can't be dismissed as a wuss.

Books on this subject say that women with fair skin, like freckly white me, are particularly susceptible to sore and cracked nipples, but my Afro-Caribbean Best Friends tell me that this delightful experience is transracial. I used to wonder in nauseous amazement how my babies would accept my cracked and bleeding nipples, but it never seemed to faze them in the least. I guess they pull the nipple so far back against their palates that their sensitive tongues are nowhere near the disfigured parts.

Sure, pain during breastfeeding can be a sign that you don't have the baby positioned properly or that she isn't latched on right, but it can also just mean that it hurts to have vice grips in baby costumes squeezing and pulling our delicate breasts. I got just as many cracks and scabs feeding my fourth child as I did my first, and I think it would be safe to say that I had the proper technique down pretty well by then. My Best Friend Lori said that even with her third baby, she would sit in her bed and start weeping silently when she heard the little darling start to stir and awaken in her crib. At the time, Lori had a nanny who used to chirp in an English accent, 'Get ready, Mummy, here we come!' as she brought the baby to her. The sound of that voice would induce terror since it was always followed by a pain that ran through her nipples, up her chest and neck and exploded in her brain.

If you are committed to breastfeeding your baby, your faith will be called into play once again. This time you have to believe with all your heart that this pain will soon disappear so completely that you will almost forget it ever happened (that is, until the next baby comes at you with hunger in his eye). If you can get through the first four to six weeks of hardship, you will be rewarded with breasts that are as tough as saltwater taffy and just as chewy. You will not only be able to get the baby latched on while seated upright with a pillow in your lap and your feet on a stool, you will be able to do it while walking through a shopping centre and pushing the empty pram with your free hand.

There are some new mothers who find the emotional adjustment to breastfeeding at least as painful as the physical, if not more. It makes a lot of sense to feel that the intimacy of a baby feeding from your breast is somehow odd or intrusive of your private space, especially if you have lived all this time without seeing anybody else doing it. Remember, we breastfeeding mothers have only come out of the closet in the last fifteen or twenty years, and there has been a lot of resistance to such 'public displays' as a woman putting a baby to her breast. Funny how there's not much outcry about teenagers heavily petting on the benches in most suburban shopping centres, but breastfeeding can really rev people up. (Breasts, in general, seem to have that effect on some people.) If you are having a hard time feeling comfortable about feeding, but don't want to give it up, create a universe in which you can feel safe and discreet whenever you breastfeed. If that means retreating to the privacy of your bedroom every time, so be it. Don't get pressured into more socializing or working than you can do and still be home to feed every couple of hours. You'll probably eventually turn into an exhibitionist, like several of my Best Friends, but if you are still uncomfortable about six or eight weeks into feeding, you may find tremendous relief with an electric breast pump. That way, the baby gets mother's milk and you get to keep your shirt on more often.

One last thing on this subject of breastfeeding pain: lots of pregnancy books advise the mother-to-be to begin preparing her nipples for feeding by rolling, pinching and rubbing them for the month before the baby is due. I cannot tell you whether this preparation works because I could never bring myself to try it. My hands would go numb at the prospect. My Best Friend Sara thought it was kind of fun, but she did it more to bring on labour than to toughen her nipples, since breast manipulation can release oxytocin into a woman's system. Besides, she had her partner doing all the rolling, pinching and rubbing for her, which I have to think added a little something to the sensation.

10. *Who your friends are.* As with many aspects of parenting, the regard in which breastfeeding is held varies slightly from generation to generation and from region to region. Sue me if I'm way off base here, but it seems to me that formula feeding is more common in areas where women still get perms. Maybe it's a shared belief in better living through chemistry, or maybe it's just coincidence. You'd have to ask an anthropologist. As far as generational diversity goes, all I can tell you is that when I announced to my mother and mother-in-law that I intended to breastfeed my baby, they both looked at me as though I were some kind of gypsy-wet-nurse-She-wolf-exhibitionist. It all smacked of Ellis Island to them.

No matter how committed this *Guide* is to supporting you in any choice you make regarding the Food Issue, it would be coy of us to suggest that, as we enter the new millennium, breastfeeding and formula feeding are equally p.c. All you have to do is consult any of the countless books on pregnancy and child care to know that nearly every single baby expert with a publishing deal thinks breast is best. And it's not just experts and hippies anymore who believe that women should breastfeed their babies. You are much more likely to bump into breastfeeding proponents than formula fans in most shopping arcades across the country. Even television commercials for formula give a tip of their hat to the homemade stuff by qualifying their claims of being the best thing since ambrosia by modestly adding 'next to mother's milk'.

Perfect Mothering

If you are leaning toward formula feeding, this national mood can be tremendously intimidating. Not only does nearly every mother I've ever met exaggerate about how long and how exclusively she fed her baby, but non breastfeeding mothers often feel obliged to fabricate some medical excuse for their failure to adhere to 'Nature's plan'. And if they just aren't in the postnatal mood to have this discussion, they feel forced to lie and say they are breastfeeding. Keep in mind that, as a new addition to the ranks of motherhood, you haven't had a chance to discover the fundamental tenet of motherhood:

MOTHERS DON'T HAVE TO BE PERFECT, JUST GOOD ENOUGH.

Being new at this job makes you particularly sensitive to the judgements and opinions of others. Any suggestion that you aren't 'giving' enough of yourself or 'sacrificing' enough for your baby is devastating. Our advice in such matters, should you choose to take it, is to turn a deaf ear to all motherhood advisers who look to a list of rigid and unbreakable rules for their guide to perfect parenting. So far, in my parenting experience, embracing rules for mothering has not been quite as useful as a good ad-lib and staying light on your mummy feet. Think 'float like a butterfly, sting like a bee,' and you will be ready for most jabs this mothering job lets fly.

Rules that imply that you are not quite staying in the top-ten percentile in your division for perfect mothering are most often pointed out to you by the least intuitive, most clueless and insecure mothers on your block. I will never forget when I was committed to

FOUR MONTHS of bed rest during my first pregnancy. I had a condition called *placenta praevia*, which usually involves haemorrhaging and keeps you on pins and needles, to say the least, and this friend of a friend called me frequently to warn me about such things as the hidden dangers of the high formaldehyde contents in cot mattresses or to fret about the high concentrations of pesticides in baby food. There I was, a virtual prisoner, having the you-know-what scared out of me by this woman who sounded as prepared, certain and committed to healthy, homegrown motherhood as anyone I'd ever met. It turns out that 'committed' was a word that *did* apply to her, but only in its other sense, if you catch my drift.

P.S. I kept the cot mattress and compromised on the baby food by buying jars of the kinds with names like 'Earth's Best – No Sodium, Organically Grown'.

Except for that rare wrinkle in time when most of us were babies, breastfeeding has pretty much dominated the field. Even Neanderthal mothers realized you couldn't sustain a baby by throwing it a pterodactyl bone every couple of days. Still, there is a tendency among today's mothers to view breastfeeding with the same pride and proprietorship as Marconi must have had for his wireless. I guess it's like falling in love; until it happens to you, it doesn't really exist. On the other hand, as our own mothers will quickly point out, our entire generation is a testament to the fact that formula-fed babies can survive and even prosper. The really good news here is that you do have options and you should feel free to deal with the Food Issue in whatever manner is best for you and your baby. All things being equal, you might want to give breastfeeding a try because you can switch to formula whenever you want to. On the other hand, after the first few days of motherhood, if you haven't breastfed or pumped out your milk, the supply will end and so will the chance to change your mind. No pressure here, Best Friend, just a little more information should you need it.

Bonding through Food

The subject of communicating your love for your baby through feeding is one of civilization's stickiest wickets. In the beginning, your intentions are as clear and pure as the baby itself. The baby relies on her mother for all her needs, and she would perish without you (or someone like you). She gets hungry; you feed her. And while you feed her, you hold her close, you sweet-talk her, you kiss her hands and gaze into her perfect face. The need for this closeness is almost as fundamental as the need for the food. Some people might suggest that breastfeeding attains this closeness, this bonding, more effectively than bottle feeding, but that feels like rules again and makes me suspicious. Any mother who holds her baby in her arms to feed her, as opposed to propping the bottle up on a pillow and letting the baby suck alone in a crib, will enter into that magic circle of connecting that fulfils them both. Speaking from my own personal experience, I do have one bit of wisdom to pass on. For people like me, who can't sit still and focus on one thing without worrying about calling the refrigerator repairman, signing up for Jenny Craig and feeling the urge to return the six calls collected by my voice mail, breastfeeding is a phenomenal invention. It forced me to sit down, relax and pay attention to the gift that was my baby. It even released chemicals in my brain that got me a little high, which only offered positive reinforcement. Even though I love and adore my babies so much that I could break from it, it would have been very tempting for me to hand the bottle to someone else and rush off to do some silly errand or chore. Mothering is daunting in that it asks you to connect intimately with someone else for endless periods of time. I always sensed that my babies and small children wanted more from me than I was sure I had, and it still scares me sometimes. But even with that knowledge, I find that I'm the one who stops the 'let's pretend we're kitty cats' game before my daughter wants to, even though we've been on our knees crawling around the floor for an hour. I'm the one who gets tired of reading stories long before the kids have gotten tired of listening to them, even if we have read four books already, and they've heard them so often we can all recite them by heart. It pains me to know that I will mourn the passing of this need for me that they feel now, but that pain doesn't ensure that I will always know when it's time to stop working or reading the paper or spacing out and devote myself entirely to them. At least when I was breastfeeding, a wisdom far more divine than mine ran the show.

Perhaps because feeding our infants was a very clear and direct way for us to focus on them, many of us mothers stay involved with our children and their food longer than we should. You can probably see it in your own mother; you rush into the house bursting with some bit of news that just must be shared immediately, and the first thing she says to you is, 'Sit down and I'll fix you something to eat first.' You feel as much like eating at that moment as you feel like smashing your finger in a door, and you think that only a person with serious brain damage could react so inappropriately. The point is, these moments of big emotion can be so complex and overwhelming to a mother that the only way she can face them is to feed you. We all will eventually yearn for the day when our children's needs could be met with a bottle or breast, and you can't really blame your mother for falling back on old techniques when your needs get more complex. If a bottle of milk was good then, a pastrami on rye couldn't hurt now, could it?

Even in this first year of motherhood, we mothers are sending out all sorts of signals about the Food Issue to our babies. Everyone knows that we women in this era are completely nuts about the Food Issue in our own lives. We are crazy about food or we are suspicious of food or associate love with food, and all the while we are checking the mirror or scale to see if our feelings about food are apparent to other people. I don't think I've ever been in a Mother and Baby group where one or another mummy didn't ask, 'Do you think my baby is too fat/thin?' Remarks like 'She eats so much that she must be building up extra fat cells' or 'I must be making cream instead of milk because Junior is getting so nice and chubby' are made all the time by women who don't recognize that they are already laying food judgements on their little babies. At one end of the spectrum are the mothers who try to limit their babies' consumption of milk or formula to help them avoid a certain future of obesity, and at the other end are the mothers who stick a bottle into the baby's mouth as the solution to everything from boredom to teething and take personal satisfaction in a fat baby as a sign of good mothering.

It's probably too late for any of us to re-educate ourselves about the Food Issue, but it would be a tremendous gift if we managed to pass on one simple lesson to our children: eat only when you are hungry, and eat until you aren't hungry anymore. It will blow your mind in the next few years how often you will use food as a bribe or a reward or as punishment, as anything but nutrition. Even those of us who consider ourselves quite conscientious in these matters get into all sorts of battles, large and small, over what food and how much of it our children are supposed to eat.

Your child will be eating the same foods as you (well, maybe not the sushi) by the end of this first year. Even before she is old enough to reach out and help herself to your plate, she will be watching you eat with tremendous interest. If you eat all day, if you eat sitting down at a table or leaning over the kitchen sink, or if you end a crying jag by eating, she will notice. This, you will learn, is why parents of ancient generations coined the phrase 'Do as I say, not as I do.' The problem is, it doesn't seem to work that way. And, as much as I hate to say it, the occasional appearance of fruit and vegetables on mum's plate might help justify all those little jars of puréed green and orange stuff that you feed the baby.

what a Difference a year makes

If you are a brand-new mother, it may be nearly incomprehensible to you that by the end of this year, your baby will actually *eat* some of his birthday cake! Here we all are, worrying about the battle between bottle and breast, and the whole issue will be a fading memory by the time this year ends. Sure, there are some other smaller debates awaiting you during this year, like when to introduce solid foods and whether to begin with cereal or fruit, but as the first birthday nears, your baby will be sampling from all the food groups. In fact, by that time you will be as busy keeping things out of his mouth as you are putting things in.

The Best Friends and I want to let you in on a little secret among mothers that isn't talked about as often as it should be: giving your baby a taste of fruit or cereal for the very first time is more fun than a Ferris wheel. Their look of surprise and shock is so sweet and funny, and the thrill of being the one to get to introduce them to one 'real food' is exhilarating. They are sure to spit out anything you feed them, but that part is great, too, because you are pretty certain that this is a skill they will eventually master. Have a camera ready for a real hoot.

As your baby moves from milk or formula to solid food, there are some great life lessons for us mums to learn. First, no matter how anguished you get over trying to make the right choices and decisions for your children, they will thrive and move on to another set of problems for you to obsess over. Keep in mind that if you blow your wad now on infant feeding, you might not have anything left for the crisis of potty training. Second, the Food Issue is complicated enough without adding competitive mothering to the mix. If a mother you know tells you that her precocious little darling is already eating with a fork and your child can't pick up a Cheerio and get it into his mouth, congratulate her and forget about it. What and when other children are eating has absolutely nothing to do with your baby. I guarantee, by nursery all the little kids will be able to sit at a table and have a meal, and even if they don't, who cares? As long as you and your GP are satisfied that your child is healthy, you are doing a great job.

11

Keeping Everybody Healthy

One of the most daunting aspects of becoming a mother is realizing that you are responsible for the health and well-being of your tiny baby. Your heart is more than willing to do whatever it takes to live up to this responsibility, whether it is to have the poor little thing chuck up on you or donate every single organ you own to her for a transplant. Your brain, however, gets a bit twisted over the prospect of a complete amateur getting the job of health-care provider for a helpless baby. What in the world, you wonder, do you know about fevers, teething pain, diarrhoea and stuffy noses no bigger than a 5p? Unless you are a paediatrician or a paediatric nurse, chances are you know nothing. (By the way, even my friends who *are* children's health-care professionals get just as freaked out by their own kids' illnesses and injuries as the rest of us. The only difference is, they usually have the *home* phone numbers of their other doctor friends, so they can get help on the line faster than you and I can. Plus, they are treated nicer at the hospital and not accused of being unnecessarily hysterical.)

Rather than sit here, paralysed by the overwhelming challenge of being the only thing that stands between your baby and disaster, let's break the task up into bite-sized bits. First of all, you are not alone in this job. If you spent your pregnancy right, you found a fabulous doctor to guide you and step in at times of emergency. If you haven't found the doctor of your dreams yet, fear not, for we can tell you what to look for and where to find it. Not only do you need your doctor in place, you will also need to have your own Motherhood Survival Kit for the mummy medic work you do in your own home. We will discuss the Best Friends' 'can't live withouts' in that section. Our grandmothers really were right when they said that an ounce of prevention was worth a pound of cure, so we will share our tips for how to keep your baby's environment safer than a mine field without turning your home into the Hot Zone.

There will be thousands of times in the next year (years) when you and your partner will stare at the baby with concern and ask each other, 'Is that normal?' Often one of the hardest jobs of being a mummy medic is distinguishing between completely normal stuff and stuff that needs professional attention. While we believe you can never go wrong by playing it safe, you will soon become a nuisance and annoyance to your GP if you call to report every little excretion your baby makes. We will give you a collection of 'Weird but Normal' things that we have all noticed about our perfect little babies.

Ultimately, in spite of your very best intentions and precautions to the contrary, your baby will most likely get sick sometime in this first year. You may be optimistic about the baby's ability to get well, but you will be certain that you will die from this illness. Fear not, your Best Friends will help get you through. Remember, it's happened to all of us and we all survived with minimal brain damage. Oh yeah, and our kids are fine, too.

The Doctor

It's generally a good idea (and a good way to pass the time) to start interviewing baby doctors while you're still pregnant. Knowing who your doctor is in advance means that he or she can be on call during delivery, in case there are any complications, and can come to the hospital after delivery to perform an examination on the baby and, God willing, declare him perfect and ready to go home with you.* Now, if you don't have a doctor of your own this early in the game, relax, because, as you probably have already discovered, the hospital has its own paediatricians to care for your baby with the same skill and concern. We Best Friends just happened to find this first trip through motherhood to be slightly less terrifying when we knew and liked the person who was calling the plays for our baby-care strategies.

There is also something rather nice about having a paediatrician* who has literally known your child since birth. If circumstances are such that the doctor who visited you and Junior in the hospital is the

* Most GPs in Britain do not do this. If you have your baby in a GP unit, your GP may be on hand but if all is normal, your midwife will handle your delivery.
* In the UK, most paediatricians are attached to hospitals, although increasing numbers work in community units. Or, you could find a GP with a special interest in child health.

same one to give Junior his pre-secondary school physical, terrific. But, if your child is in good health, with no special needs of his own, you shouldn't fear changing paediatricians throughout your child's life, according to *your* needs.

This freedom to change is an important point because first-time mothers tend to have what I call 'Tar Baby' syndrome about their infants. Remember the story about the Tar Baby? Everyone who touched it got forever stuck to it. New mums are the same way. We think that anyone who has come within the sphere of our baby's physical or emotional needs must promise never to leave us. That is why we cry if our nanny quits or if our paediatrician announces that she is taking a six-month maternity leave. What, leave our baby for some unborn, unknown baby of her own?! What kind of insensitivity is this?! Remember what your mother told you about boyfriends? Well, there are plenty of other paediatricians in the sea, too.

Choosing Your Baby's Doctor

I keep referring to this special doctor as a paediatrician, which is technically a medical doctor with a speciality in children's medicine, when I talk about the doctor you choose for your beloved baby. And, since I have always lived in cities large and dense enough to have air pollution problems and at least fifty Walmarts within the city limits, there are more medical specialists than you can shake a stethoscope at. But, if you live in a small town or are involved in a health practice that has doctors who specialize in family medicine, I'm sure you are in good hands, too. Unless your child has special needs, in which case both paediatricians and family medicine doctors would probably seek out a specialist for that particular need or condition, the day-to-day medical care of your baby (and the day-to-day hand-holding of you) can be done by any well-educated, experienced and COMPASSIONATE medical professional. I just continue to lump these doctors all under the heading of Paediatrician so that I distinguish them from the doctors who specifically deal with *your* health.

1. *Ask Your Best Friends to Recommend a Doctor.* Chances are, if they are your Best Friends, they are looking for much the same relationship with a baby doctor as you are. If you are wary of too many antibiotics and want a doctor who encourages breastfeeding, you probably have several Best Friends who are concerned about the same things. You know, it's that birds-of-a-feather kind of thing. For example, here in

Malibu, where I live, we have a lot of 'birds' who think healing crystals in a doctor's office are the sign of enlightenment and open-mindedness. Conversely, where my Best Friend Janet 'flocks' in Staten Island, a healing crystal is apt to end up in one of the doctor's orifices if he comes near the baby with it.

Friends are also great sources of information that you might be embarrassed to ask the doctor about yourself. Your friends will give you the real skinny on whether the doctor returns your calls quickly, whether the nurse is snotty to all the mothers or just hates you specifically, whether the doctor votes Labour, and all other pertinent but sensitive intelligence.

2. *Ask Your GP to Recommend a Colleague with a Special Interest in Child Health.* Now that you have this deep and trusting relationship with your GP, take a few minutes out of one of your exams to chat about baby doctors. If your doctor has kids of his or her own, you might even get him to divulge the identity of that select individual who takes care of them. For a lot of us, there is just no greater source of security and smugness than to know we go to 'the doctors' doctor'. Keep in mind, however, that 'doctors' doctors' are often held in such high esteem by their peers because of their extraordinary technical skills or their prestige in the academic world. Those qualities are well and good, but if that doctor isn't the kind who will hand you a tissue and pat your back while you recover from your infant's first vaccinations, then who needs 'em?

3. *Visit the Candidates.* Ultimately, chances are you will select your baby's doctor for visceral reasons. Once you have established that her medical credentials are impeccable, the most important characteristic you will look for in a baby doctor is trustworthiness. You will need to feel that this doctor *cares* for you and your baby on some level. You will want a doctor who listens to your questions without hurrying you along or looking bored, even though you are not asking anything she hasn't been asked ten thousand times. You will want someone who speaks to you as the intelligent person you are in all areas of your life but emergencies concerning your baby. Put yourself in your baby's place, too. Will he like this doctor five years from now when she is trying to remove a marble from his nose? Will he trust the doctor with his confidences, like, 'I just found a hair in my armpit,' or 'What is a wet dream?'

Perhaps the most important thing to look for in a prospective doctor is her faith in your mummy medic abilities. You know your baby better than anyone, and you certainly pay attention to his every hue and colour, and you need a doctor who will give credence to your insistence that something 'isn't right' even when it all looks fine to her. At about eighteen months of age, my son began to wheeze after running or when he laughed with particular gusto. I took him to the doctor to be checked for asthma. She heard nothing and saw nothing, but I was the one who heard him breathe, I was the one who saw how pronounced the dark circles under his eyes would get and my heart just told me it wasn't right. Cut to three years later during a soccer game when he can't breathe at all because the grassy field brought out his allergies with a vengeance. Who knows what would have happened if I hadn't begged everyone to 'indulge' me by teaching me to use a bronchial inhaler on a four-year-old and to rent for home use a machine that administered a medicinal mist to clear out the allergens and shrink the swelling in his chest?

We mummy medics are often the first ones to diagnose problems with our children. One of my Best Friends spent this entire school year being told that her child wasn't working to standard because he didn't pay attention and he wasn't reading well. *She* was the one who knew all along that he was smart and interested in school, but that something was standing in the way. Recently, she took him to an ophthalmologist and learned that his eyes didn't track together properly. That meant that he often sees double images of some written words and misses other words entirely. I guess that could interfere somewhat in one's schoolwork, don't you?

If you have a doctor who seems to minimize your role as diagnostician, or who you think resents it if you discover a problem he or she has missed, you need a new one. Your child's well-being is far more important than a doctor's need to maintain some notion of professional superiority.

In that same spirit, if your doctor does diagnose a problem and suggests a treatment that you question, you'd better be able to speak right up and state your concerns. Obviously, it doesn't help to speak your mind in an aggressive manner, which, face it, we nervous mothers and fathers tend to do under stress, but a fairly calm discussion of your uncertainties is well within the rules of play. Getting a second opinion is allowed, too, and nobody's nose should get out of joint about her authority and expertise being questioned. Ask your doctor NOW how she would feel about your consulting other doctors should a problem arise. Ninety-nine percent of them will give you the 'correct' answer about supporting and even encouraging you to seek other opinions in such events, but pay attention to their body language to get a feel for how enthusiastic they really are. Ask them for examples of when they have collaborated or deferred to another doctor. If they can't think of an instance, you may be in the wrong office.

As in real estate, one of the most important elements in choosing your doctor is location, location, location. Not only do you want the doctor to be reasonably nearby, but you want a hospital with which he is associated to be at least as close. In fact, having that hospital as close as possible is even more important than being near the doctor since visits to the former are usually emergencies and visits to the latter tend to be scheduled. Still, it is awfully nice to be able to bop on down to the doctor's office to have a look in your fussy baby's ears without having to make a day of it.

4. *Assess the Office during Your Interview.* There is much more to a baby doctor than the person, herself. You should like the environment, the staff and the way the practice is run. You may have already discovered the corollary to the secret pregnancy discovery: 'Your midwife is at least as critical to your survival as your doctor', and that is 'The practice nurse is at least as critical to your survival as a mother as the baby's doctor.' Meet this person, usually a woman, right away. She will usually be the one doing the measuring and weighing, asking the general health and development questions and attempting to solve any breastfeeding problems. Here are the two most important facts about the nurse:

1. It is SHE, not the doctor, who gives injections. Doctors like to be the 'good cops' in this relationship; and
2. It is far easier to get her on the phone during the day when you just want to ask a quick question, like what that white, milky scum on your infant's tongue signifies. (Thrush; look it up in Dr Spock.) My Best Friends and I all developed deep relationships with these wonderful people who were willing to talk us down when we thought orange poo meant colon cancer (it doesn't) or a baby sleeping with her eyes open was a sure sign of demonic possession (it isn't).

Your introductory visit is a good time to do the white-glove test on the office. Chances are, dust won't be of concern, but take a look at the toys in the waiting room. Do they all look like they have been slobbered on by excessively germy kids? How about the floors and carpets? We all know that's where your baby will end up as soon as she is old enough to squirm out of your arms. Most important of all, at least to us Best Friends, is an office that schedules different parts of the day for 'sick child' visits and 'well child' visits. There is no bigger drag than to bring your pristinely healthy baby into an office, only to be told to take a seat in the waiting room next to a four-year-old with what is obviously chicken pox. Some doctors even have two separate waiting rooms for sick and well children. Come to think of it, no matter how scrupulous the doctor's office is about not mixing healthy and infected children, bring your own toys and teach your child not to touch anything that isn't his. And remember, wash your hands as soon as you get home.

Community units and larger GP practices often offer other services besides medical treatment. There may be a lactation specialist on staff or available on referral who can visit you at home to help get that infernal breastfeeding mastered. You may see a bulletin board with listings of parent support groups or Mother and Baby classes or the cheapest place to rent a breast pump. Often the office staff will be familiar with the counsellors or group leaders or even merchants posted on their bulletin boards and can give you a personal appraisal of them. I have been to doctors' offices where someone on staff was an infant/child nutritionist. This kind of thing might be interesting to you. (Even though it just made me feel compelled to lie about how much of my baby's food was from organic fruit and vegetables grown in my own composted garden. As if!)

5. *How to Talk to a Doctor*. While the doctor you choose should speak your native language, or at least one in which you have fluency, there is still a skill to communicating properly with the doctor. Remember, doctors are basically people, and they respond to certain behaviour much the way the rest of us do. Here are a few Best Friends' hints for ensuring that your baby's doctor is listening to you and understanding you.

1. *Get to the Point Quickly*. Remember, these are not just incredibly busy people but incredibly smart people who just might have a very low boredom threshold. For example, if your cruising baby has fallen against the coffee table and cut his forehead, NEVER begin the conversation with the doctor or anyone in his office by apologizing for not having bought one of those rubber coffee

table bumpers to prevent this accident. You can beat yourself up later in the public square, but right now there is one thing to say: 'My eight-month-old has cut its forehead and it's bleeding everywhere!' This gives the doctor an opening to ask how long and deep the cut is and to tell you what to do about the bleeding. If you are lucky, the doctor will also take a moment to tell you what all new mothers need to know: children's head wounds bleed like a cattle slaughter, even when they are not even serious enough to require stitches. Think like a caveman when you feel like a blithering idiot: 'Baby, head, cut, blood, help!'

2. *Prioritise Your Consultations with the Doctor.* In the rational part of your brain, you know that not all concerns about your baby's health are equally pressing or urgent. I am well aware that our irrational brains take over at the slightest provocation where our babies are concerned, but you really must try to take a deep breath and assess the situation for a moment before acting on it. I remember when my Best Friend Beth's daughter was in nursery and was sent home with head lice. Understandably, as a first-time mum, Beth thought head lice were on the same scale as scabies or tuberculosis. She called the doctor's answering machine, since it was after office hours, and left a message for the doctor to call her immediately because she had a medical emergency. Imagine her hurt and humiliation when the doctor yelled at her over the telephone, 'If you think I want to interrupt my dinner to hear about your child's head lice, you had better think again!!!' Sure, the doctor was insensitive, but he is only human and I can see how, after a bad day, talk of nitpicking could ruin his appetite. All we are advising is that you give some thought to the appropriateness of your call or visit before just instinctively picking up the phone.

Obviously, fevers, bleeding, chills, repeated diarrhoea, listlessness and pain are all reasons to hightail it to the doctor, as are any other symptoms that you intuitively feel just can't be put off. But, if your question is of a more general nature, like 'Why does my baby look all around the room stretching my nipple in his mouth while I am trying to feed him?' save it for business hours and after the doctor has attended to his office appointments.

3. *Collect Several Questions for One Visit.* Rather than call or drop by the surgery every time you notice something new about the baby or want to discuss the relative merits of introducing fruit versus cereal as the first solid food, keep a list of the topics and make a

sort of agenda for each scheduled visit. Remember, even though this is a scheduled checkup for the baby and not an emergency, the charm of brevity still stands. Don't ramble on and on about every single breath the baby takes because even if your doctor were your baby's father, he would begin going out-of-body about halfway through.

4. *Kiss Everybody's Ass.* Doctors and nurses, while generally better paid, often receive the same lack of consideration that we give our children's teachers. Perhaps we parents are so wrapped up in our kids that we think the rest of the world exists simply to meet our darlings' needs, or maybe we get so distracted when our children's welfare is at stake that we forget the little niceties, like 'Thank you' or 'If you don't mind' or 'I'm sorry.' Everybody needs to be told that they are respected or appreciated, and if that means going overboard with people on whom you will depend if your baby has an emergency, so be it. Put yourself in their position. Who would you go out of your way to make time for, the baby whose mother sent you flowers when you gave her baby a DPT shot without the baby even flinching, or the one who never remembers your name when she calls, let alone asks how you are, before haranguing you about getting the doctor to pick up the phone, AND I MEAN NOW!? What do you suppose is the medical professional's equivalent of a waiter spitting in your soup?

5. *Do Your Homework First.* Some conditions and questions about babies are so universal that your doctor will provide handouts on them to avoid having to tell the same story over and over again. My doctor has a shelf of one- and two-page flyers about such things as what to expect after a DPT vaccination, the pros and cons of the new chicken pox vaccine and how to care for a child with an ear infection. If the doctor's office gives you one of those flyers to read, READ IT! Nothing pisses off a busy person more than having a parent sit like a passive slug, expecting the doctor to parent her and the baby. I think it is also reasonable for the doctor to expect you to read at least one book about basic child care. Most of us have an entire library on our bedside tables devoted to that subject area, so this shouldn't be a problem. I just mention this because doctors seem to like talking to parents who have taken the initiative to find out how these little creatures work.

How Not to Need the Doctor So Often

Wouldn't it be an ideal world if the only encounter your little baby had with a doctor was to be measured and weighed? It is so gratifying to sit in the examination room with your naked baby in your lap and be told that he is in the eightieth percentile for height, the seventy-fifth percentile for weight and the ninetieth percentile for head circumference. Every little ounce gained and every fraction of an inch achieved feels like a miracle, a miracle that you helped create. And, being adults (or at least children in adults' clothing), we begrudgingly admit our gratitude for the various vaccinations that protect our babies from what used to be lethal diseases, even though we start dreading 'shot visits' a full week in advance. Our goal as mother medics is to keep all other visits to the doctor as few as the fates will allow.

We are not just victims here, though, Best Friends. There are some things many of us have learned (usually the hard way) that we can do to prevent some of the most common sources of illness and injury. By the time your child is five years old, you will probably have had to cope with one kind of emergency or other, but these guidelines just might save you one or two extra mad dashes to the accident and emergency department. Here is our list of the top-ten things you can do to help keep your baby healthy in this critical first year:

1. *Baby-Proof Your House*. Don't wait until the first tumble down the stairs or the first time you notice that the baby can open drawers and cabinets by himself to remedy these hazards. Trust us; they will do it sooner or later, so go ahead and install the locks, barriers and bumpers that any baby-proofing manual recommends. We are also big fans of turning down the thermostat on the hot-water heater because kids are drawn to taps like moths to a flame and scalding is a very real danger.

2. *Make Your House Baby Friendly*. There are a lot of conditions in your home that aren't even noticeable to you and your partner that can be dangerous or irritating to your baby. Allergens are the first things that come to my mind because I have children who sneeze and cough at the slightest airborne particles. Even babies who aren't by nature allergic may be sensitive to accumulated dust, animal fur or mould. Yes, Best Friend, this can only mean one thing: you must clean your house more often! No, I'm just kiddin' with you. I know that you run a sterile ship. But I've learned that these allergens need special attention. For

example, it's not the dog or cat's *fur* that makes us sneeze; it's the nearly invisible bits of dander that it sheds. If the baby seems to be stuffy even if he's not sick, put the animals outside for a while and see if it brings relief. (I have gotten so unsentimental about pets since my babies were born that I astonish myself, but there is no use pretending otherwise in front of my Best Friends.)

Curtains and carpets are other great sources of allergens. They just suck up all the dust and debris that floats down on them from the polluted air and hold on to it until the drycleaners has a 50-percent-off sale or until they rot and we throw them away. If your baby seems to be sensitive, consider wood floors with rugs you can wash from time to time and shutters on the windows instead of curtains.

We are all sensitive to certain fumes, like paint, nail polish remover or oven cleaner. Our babies, however, not being part of the drug experimentation generation that many of us belonged to, just may fail to appreciate the 'high' of aeroplane glue and gasoline fumes and would best be spared them.

Babies have very sensitive skin, and regular household soaps and detergents are probably too irritating for them. For the first few weeks of their life, newborns really don't need any kind of soap at all. A flannel and warm water should be enough to freshen up the little tyke. But, if you are obsessive, as I was, and are absolutely dying to use some enchanting-smelling cleanser on the baby, make sure it is not alkaline based and that it is formulated for newborns. Whatever you do, don't use that children's bubble bath you buy in the grocery store on them; you might as well run the baby through a car wash.

Most mothers-to-be who I know lovingly washed all their baby's clothes in Dreft or Ivory Flakes. You can go down the laundry detergent aisle every couple of weeks for your entire adult life and never notice these two brands, but when you get pregnant, something in your genetic code informs you that you need this special stuff. The theory, which I've just adhered to without any formal testing, is that regular clothing detergent can make babies get rashes because the residue stays in the clothes and irritates their skin. Why fight this tradition? It's sweet smelling and one more thing that shows you're in the sorority of mothers.

3. *Become an Obsessive Hand Washer.* Every flu season, all the TV ads lecture us again about the importance of washing our hands to keep the passing of viruses and germs to a minimum. Before I had children, I used to pass my hands under running water in a sort of polite way,

especially in public toilets where there were witnesses to my personal hygiene. Now that I am a mother, however, I scrub harder than Marcus Welby several times a day. I read someplace that we should wash with soap long enough to sing 'Twinkle Twinkle Little Star' from start to finish, which is pretty clever advice, because it is easy to teach your toddler when she is learning to wash up. Remember, your baby will be watching you and copying you for years to come. If you want her to wash her hands before snack time, especially since she has run her hands over the toilet seat several times in her 'I do myself' effort to go potty, you'd better be lathering up, too, whenever she can see you.

4. *Drive Properly*. When I'm driving and bored, I usually spy into the windows of the cars around me. There are two things that I often see that make me want to get out of my car with my tyre jack and break the offender's windscreen, grab the driver by the neck and slap him or her senseless: the first is people who let their children ride in the front seat while sitting on someone's lap or who let their kids stand on the seat and lean forward on the dashboard. What do these blockheads think, that seat belts are a fashion accessory? Don't they ever stop to think about where their precious baby's head will fly in the event of a sudden stop? I have just one thing to say to all you loving mummies who hold your babies in your arms during a drive because they cry in their car seats: if there is a collision, YOU ARE THE LAUNCHER AND YOUR BABY BECOMES THE MISSILE. Your body weight will push your baby through a windscreen faster and harder than its own little body could ever do on its own. Leave the baby in the car seat no matter what. If he won't stop crying, turn the radio up loud and sing along to try to keep from getting too frantic.

The other group of offenders who spit on the most fundamental rules of motherhood are people who smoke in the car while riding with their children. As far as I'm concerned, they are riding around town in a poisonous iron lung with wheels. (For the record, I am also offended by the multitudes of drivers who pick their noses, but they are dangerous only to our sensibilities, not to our children, so I won't say more about them here.) I don't think anyone should ever smoke around children, but a car is probably the most disgustingly claustrophobic place to commit this crime.

Even the most careful and best-intentioned mums can be seen trying to drive their cars and minister to their babies at the same time. I confess to several counts of driving at speeds of at least forty-five, steering with one stretched finger and practically climbing into the backseat to find the dropped dummy and return it to the empty and howling mouth. Admit it, Best Friends: we know better than this, and it doesn't hurt to be reminded that it's this kind of unthinking behaviour that can get us into the biggest trouble imaginable. Pull the car over to find the baby bottle that is rolling around under the front seats or to mop up the baby urp that the car's motion has brought up from your baby's last meal.

Short of begging you to reread the Highway Code and take a defensive driving class, I have only one other thing to mention about cars and mothers and a baby's well-being: *Never let the petrol tank get below a quarter full.* Stopping to buy petrol is even more annoying than going to the post office to buy stamps, but it has to be done regularly. You should have learned this lesson in pregnancy, but it bears repeating because you should never have to wonder if you have enough gas to get to the doctor or the hospital or a bomb shelter or the midnight madness sale without stopping for a fill-up. Single folks can do whimsical and wacky things like run out of gas in dangerous parts of town after dark. Such artsy, whimsical, left-brain behaviour has absolutely no charm when exhibited by mothers. Get over it; your Holly Go lightly days are more extinct than Pompeii.

5. *Expect the Worst to Happen.* Yes, your baby *will* learn to roll over the first and only time you leave him on the changing table while you get a clean vest from the laundry basket on the floor. Yes, your baby *will* pull herself up for the first time using the toilet for support and fall forward. And yes, I happen to know from my own horrendous experience that a cruising baby *will* immediately find that cup of coffee you left for a second on the coffee table while you ran to answer the phone and pull it down on himself. (To this day, I believe God gave me a free one here because that coffee just happened to be at room temperature. Ohhhhh thankyouthankyouthankyou!)

One of the single most important lessons I have learned in avoiding a baby catastrophe regards man's best friend. I don't care how much you adore all dogs and how much the owners reassure you that their dog 'just loves kids', NEVER let your baby's face near a dog's face. Nine times out of ten, the dog will bite your baby in the face. Okay, I admit it, I made up those statistics, but it's only because it is so critical to me that you take my advice without waiting to first test it out. Even the nicest, oldest, sweetest, littlest dog can bite quickly and aggressively (as in, it's time to call the plastic surgeon). The dogs can't really be blamed; it's just a threatening gesture for *any* other animal to put its face in the dog's face. Babies absolutely adore doggies, so this rule against getting close to them may be difficult to enforce, but you just have to trust me; it's not worth the possible price.

Isn't it interesting how becoming a mother makes all of your own mother's predictions of doom suddenly seem rational? All that 'Get-down-from-there-you'll-break-your-neck' talk sounds like sage advice rather than the mindless nagging you thought it was when you were a kid. Just wait a few years; you'll be dispensing the same advice (in the same voice!) your mother so annoyingly gave you.

6. *Be Prepared*. In addition to a full tank of petrol, there are several other things that you should have in your kit as a mummy medic. The following list is intended to supplement the obvious things that all the baby books tell you about, like Calpol.

- *Put* All *Important Phone Numbers at* All *Phones*. Not only should you have a card with the number of your baby's doctor near the kitchen or desk phone, you should also have it and all other emergency numbers at *every* phone so you don't have to run far to find them. The other important numbers are your partner's work number, 999 (as self-evident as this seems, baby emergencies don't inspire much logical thinking and a little reminder wouldn't hurt), the nearest twenty-four-hour pharmacy, the nearest helpful friend or relative and a cab company's phone, in case you don't trust yourself to drive to the doctor and an ambulance isn't necessary, like when my Best Friend Sondra held her baby in the backseat and caught his projectile vomiting in a beach towel while I drove them to the doctor's office.

- *Use a Warm Mist Vaporizer at the First Sign of Stuffy Nose or Cough*. They can't hurt, and they almost always help. I just love those things, especially the ones that have a little well to hold liquid Vicks. Dry air makes dry noses and lungs, and dry noses and lungs get swollen and clogged with mucus, so making the baby's room as humid as a tropical rain forest can work wonders.

- *Ear Thermometer*. I am such a fan of this invention that I would personally thank the manufacturers if I ever met them. They are so quick and unintrusive, and, unlike rectal thermometers,★ don't usually cause a spontaneous release of poo. Besides, they allow us

★ Doctors in the UK do not recommend that parents take a rectal temperature. An underarm reading is next best, after an ear reading.

nervous Nellies to take a temperature without having to take a sedative.

- *Boo Boo Bunnies*. These cute little creatures are basically flannel fabric wrapped around a plastic ice cube. Keep one or two in your freezer to apply to the inevitable bumps on the head or pinched fingers. My kids love them, and I have used a couple on my own puffy eyes after an all-nighter with a sick baby. Can't you just see me lying there with two pastel bunnies perched on my face?

- *Calpol*. Calpol (liquid paracetamol) is usually a mum's best friend in relieving her baby's fever. Sometimes, however, the fever is accompanied by vomiting, and when that happens, the medicine doesn't stay in the baby's tummy long enough to work its magic. Don't freak out if your baby throws up in pastel colors; it's probably just the Calpol coming back at you. There is another entrance for that medication, as alarming as the prospect might seem to the faint-hearted among us, and that is the baby's rectum. Listen, you're talking to a mother of four who has never taken a rectal temperature in her life, but if your baby has a fever of 105 degrees and can't keep anything in her stomach, you, too, will have the intestinal fortitude required to get that suppository right where it belongs. (And if you simply can't, make your partner do it.)

- *Nasal Aspirator.*★ When your baby has a stuffy nose, she can't pull out a handkerchief and have a good blow. She can't even sniffle yet. It's your job as a mummy medic to blow her nose for her, and for that you need one of those rubber bulbs. Ask your nurse for a demonstration. Some of us are too intimidated to use the things, especially while the baby is actively demonstrating her dislike for people sticking things up her nose, but it's worth overcoming your reluctance because it gives immediate relief to the baby. My Best Friend Jane once saw her Haitian nanny suck the baby's mucus gently out with her own mouth! Jane screamed at first, certain that this exotic woman was performing some voodoo breath-stealing ritual, but in a flash, the woman was spitting into a tissue and the baby was breathing comfortably. Is that heavy-duty or what? And guess what? If your baby were suffering and you didn't have a nasal aspirator, you'd probably improvise, too. By the way, if you are

★ These are not recommended for use at home.

sucking out white mucus, it may not be a sign of infection but rather the accumulation of breast milk or formula, so check with your doctor.

- *Small Dropper.* We all know that I am the queen of Western medicine. Few things make me feel more in control of my baby's health than running into a pharmacy with a prescription from the doctor. I admit that I am a tad sceptical about homeopathic treatments (okay, REALLY sceptical; heck, I actually *like* the smell of hospitals), but there was one little trick my doctor taught me when my three-week-old daughter caught a cold from her beloved big brother. (Second babies always get sick sooner than first babies since it's those first babies who round up all the germs and bring them home to share with the competition.) He told me to express a little breast milk, and, while it was still close to body temperature, to suck up some of the milk in the dropper and trickle a tiny bit down each of the baby's nostrils. The milk moistens swollen membranes and helps wash some of the dried-up gunk out. Breast milk is perfect because the baby likes the taste, it doesn't irritate the nasal lining and doctors don't usually give decongestants or antihistamines to infants. Go ahead and try it. Remember: desperate times require desperate measures.

weird but Normal

Contrary to our expectations, babies are not simply adults in smaller bodies. They still aren't completely baked, so to speak. Their bones aren't fused where ours are, their circulatory and digestive systems are more sensitive and the wiring in their brains can seem very screwy to the uninitiated. Brand-new parents are notorious for placing emergency calls to their doctors to report strange baby phenomena, only to be reassured that all the babes are doin' it. Here is a list of the top-ten most common things the Best Friends and I all thought indicated something terribly wrong with our babies, at least until a more experienced mother or the doctor informed us otherwise. Feel free to consult your baby's doctor about anything that looks unusual or concerns you, but don't say we didn't warn you about the ones that peg you as a neophyte.

1. *Pointy Heads and Flat Faces.* You all know that babies generally make their exit from your body headfirst. Nature depends on that

relatively hard sphere, which is the biggest part of the baby, to finish stretching your cervix and vagina and make way for the rest of the body. Think of the head as the coring machine that digs through mountains to make tunnels, and you'll get the idea. The softest parts of the head, the facial features and the very top of the head (called the fontanelle), often get squished in the journey, leaving babies who look like coneheads or Edward G. Robinson. It's no big news, but let us reassure you that your newborn looks nothing like what your one-month-old will look like. As I said before, I honestly cannot tell my babies apart by their hospital newborn pictures. I don't really recognize any of them, and when one of them finds a picture and asks, 'Mummy, who's this?' I invariably reply, 'It's you, Sweetie Pie, the most beautiful baby who was ever born.'

2. *Twitches and Jerks*. Babies startle easily and in a whole-body sort of way. If you pick a newborn up without swaddling him first, he will seem to grab out with his arms and legs like a monkey falling from a tree limb. They also shudder in their sleep for no apparent reason. This herky-jerky stuff is all to be expected of these tiny little people testing out all their synapses.

3. *Pulsing Heads*. The first time my husband noticed the top of the baby's head gently moving up and down, I thought he was going to have a stroke. It reminded him of too many horror movies where that kind of pulsing can only mean one thing: an alien is about to burst out. Sorry, no aliens here. That heartbeat on the head is due to the fact that the baby's skull hasn't fused on top and sometimes you can see the veins under his newborn skin.

4. *Crossed Eyes*. Have you ever peered into your precious baby's face, only to notice that his eyes are slowly crossing? Don't go running to your local Lenscrafters yet. Babies are just getting this vision thing after nine (ten) months of near darkness, and it takes them a few months to be able to track objects near and far with both eyes simultaneously. Plus, it might just be a tad your fault, too, since most mothers stick their own faces so close to their irresistible infants' that their noses touch, and the baby's eyes have to cross just to keep sight of you.

5. *Sleeping with His Eyes Open*. No, your baby is not staring at you and trying to fake you out by acting like he's asleep, nor is he having a moment of demonic possession. Sometimes when they are sound

asleep, their eyelids part and you can look inside. Don't worry; even if the eyes seem to be darting around the room and backwards in the baby's head, this is what Rapid Eye Movement (the kind of deep sleep that you haven't had since giving birth) looks like in a baby.

6. *Cartoonish-Looking Sex Organs*. New babies often dazzle their unsuspecting parents with almost comically large testicles or labia (the lips of the vagina). Dads may preen with pride over their endowed sons and mothers may be concerned by their daughters' certain 'lack of proportion', but these phenomena are short-lived. They are a result of the mother's hormones travelling across the bridge provided by the placenta and settling in the baby before the umbilical cord was cut. Tiny babies are known to secrete milklike liquid from their breasts, and some baby girls have a bloody discharge that can resemble a baby period. None of this means the early onset of adolescence; it's just that hormone thing again. I told you motherhood was not for wimps!

7. *Baby Dandruff*. Lots of babies get dry, flaky skin on their heads. You know, the stuff that our mums called 'cradle cap'. Even if the baby doesn't have much hair to speak of, he can still get baby dandruff, since it's a 'skin thing', not a 'hair thing'. Even the biggest worriers among us are pretty certain that dandruff is not a serious health risk, but that doesn't make it less disconcerting because IT DIMINISHES OUR PERFECT BABY'S BEAUTY, and that's almost as serious. We smear the tops of their heads with gentle baby lotions, only to end up with infants with the greasy pompadour of Danny Zucco. We pick the big pieces off, but there is no visible improvement and, to make matters worse, we risk causing an infection up there. Doctors will often tell you just to leave it alone and not worry about it, but they don't understand that all your relatives are coming out in four days for the baby's christening, and he simply cannot make this kind of first impression. Our advice: use a baby washcloth with some baby oil on it to slough off some of the flakes. Rinse it well with warm water, put a little lotion on it and comb whatever hair there is artfully over the flaking part, much the way a middle-aged man combs his longer hairs over his bald spot. Or, if all else fails, put a hat on it.

8. *Birthmarks*. Contrary to the image created by such clichés as 'She had the perfect skin of a baby,' little babies often have all sorts of bumps and blotches on their skin. The good news is, most of them go away, even those scary ones called strawberry birthmarks that seem to grow

with each new day. By the time your child is ready for school and the embarrassment you are dreadfully certain such a mark will encourage among the other little five-year-old heathens, a strawberry birthmark should be going, going, gone.

My first baby had birthmarks on the nape of his neck and on his forehead. They were reddish purple, sort of butterfly shaped and flat. My mummy Best Friends told me the one on his neck was called a 'stork bite' and the one on his forehead was called an 'angel's kiss'. (Ahhhhh.) They gradually disappeared over the first year, but even after they had gone, they would show up vividly every time he cried energetically. It was years before I stopped looking for them as a sort of mood barometer.

Babies of colour are frequently born with bluish birthmarks right around their tail bones. These, too, fade with time. They are known in the vernacular as 'Mongolian spots', but I think it's time we found a more charming name.

Not every birthmark goes away, however. My youngest daughter has a mole-like mark at the top of her left cheek. If you are picturing a future Cindy Crawford, let me get more specific and say her left *butt* cheek. But hey, she can start her own supermodel rage when she grows up. In ten years, everyone will be using eyebrow pencil to make a dot at the top of their heinie.

Birthmarks, while overwhelmingly harmless, still should be watched by your baby's doctor to make sure that they stay safe. Well-baby checkups are more than frequent enough for this task, so there is no need to place any after-hours panic phone calls unless the birthmark is bleeding or starting to form a 666 pattern on the back of his head.

9. *Technicolour Poos.* Baby poos don't look like everybody else's, either in colour or consistency. They tend to be thin, but not watery, until the baby starts eating solid foods. Sometimes they even have the consistency of cottage cheese or puréed pumpkins. A newborn's first bowel movements, called meconium, can range in colour from tyre-rubber black to spinach green. This is completely normal. Later the nappy contents start to resemble a kind of pumpkin paste, especially in babies who are breastfed. The big thrill comes after you are moving your baby on to solid foods and you feed it strained beetroot. Those veggies come out almost the same color they went in. The first time new mothers witness this special effect, they feel faint for a moment and then start suspecting a haemorrhage. Don't worry: it's not blood – it's beetroot. Another funny poo food that you will feed your baby

sometime during this first year is raisins. No matter how thoroughly the baby seems to gum or chew those little devils, they show up in the nappy completely intact, as though they had been stirred in straight from the box.

10. *Funny Weenies.* Baby boys in this country are usually circumcised.* For some parents, this is a religious decision; for others, the reasons are aesthetic. I still get faint thinking about the times when my sons were taken from my hospital room to have 'it' done, so I will spare us all the details. My point is, after the healing is complete, you may think that the penis is too exposed or not exposed enough. If anyone thinks that we mummies don't closely investigate such things, they are mistaken. Anyway, I used to mentally compare my sons' penises with each other's and with my friends' baby boys. Some looked like pigs in a blanket and some looked like rocket ships. By the time boys are about eight years old, they aren't very likely to let Mum sneak a peak at the privates very often, but my most recent glimpses into the matter have led me to conclude that they all start looking much more alike as the years go on. Now I just have to sit back and wait for adolescence to begin so that we can start worrying about penis presentability all over again. But then, I guess that will be *their* job, right?

When Baby Gets Sick

My Best Friend Chris's partner called the other night, and I immediately heard the strain in his voice. Someone close to him had died, he was being brought up on RICO charges, Chris was having an affair with her pottery teacher. I knew something awful had happened. With some trepidation, I asked in a hushed voice, 'Is everything all right?' 'The baby has a temperature of 105 degrees,' he replied. My next enquiry was not about the baby's health, not that I wasn't deeply concerned about the little beauty. Instead I asked, 'And what about Chris? Is she going to be all right?' After enduring several of these episodes with my own kids, I had faith that the baby would recover nicely, but I wasn't at all optimistic about my Best Friend. When a new baby, especially a firstborn, gets her first cold or flu, the parents feel as though they have had their souls ripped out and held for ransom.

When her baby gets sick, a mother's first sensation is utter vulner-

* Boys in Britain are circumcised only for religious or cultural reasons at birth.

ability. Any illness, even a tiny sniffle, is perceived by a mother as a threat to her very existence. The bottom line for all of us who have been bitten by the baby love bug is this:

IF ANYTHING HAPPENS TO MY BABY, I WILL HAVE TO KILL MYSELF.

We can't help but play out every sickness to its very worst possible conclusion, and then we know a fear of loss that is stark and paralysing. Common sense has nothing to do with much of our behaviour because the stakes are too high to have any bearing on emotion. I'm not telling you this to scare you. You need to know that, if this happens to you, you are not the first mummy to sit down in the middle of the floor and weep. We've all looked into our babies' eyes and seen their plea for help, and we've all been willing to take on any amount of pain or torture if it might spare our babies a moment of discomfort. It's an awful experience, but there is a silver lining to this cloud and that is the joy you should feel that you are able to love someone so very much that you would gladly give your life for her. Makes you take another look at your own mother, doesn't it?

I recall so many times that I was so worried and frightened that I couldn't even speak. My husband would do all the talking to the doctors and nurses while I attended to the baby with a focus that could have bored a hole through steel. Take note of this: if you are nervous and upset, you should get someone to be with you while you are going through this first illness. The baby's father is the logical first choice, since he cares as much as you do, but there are times when a Best Friend or other relative is at least as good, if not better. If you have a mummy friend who can talk you down and give you support, call her immediately. But even a friend who has never held a child, let alone birthed one, can be a godsend because she is there to take care of YOU, not the baby.

Call the doctor. An illness that is making the baby vomit, feverish, shiver, unable to breathe well, emit green or putrid anything from any orifice, cough repeatedly or anything else that your instincts tell you is wrong, is worth a call, even after office hours. Remember, doctors may not love being awakened in the middle of the night, but they accept it as part of the job. Don't be put off if the answering service makes it sound like a big deal to reach your doctor and have her get back to you. It's an even bigger deal that your baby is sick and everyone should be prepared to jump through whatever hoops are necessary for your baby's comfort and your sanity.

There are a few things that can happen when a baby gets sick that look more serious than they usually are. I mention them so that if your baby experiences any of them, you can calm yourself by repeating this mantra: 'Vicki says this is normal, Vicki says this is normal.' One of those things is a very high temperature. Babies can run fevers that would have us adults packed in ice in the emergency wards. One hundred and four- and even 105-degree temperatures are serious, but not usually dangerous on their own. It will amaze you how quickly Calpol will bring the baby's temperature right back down to normal, and the baby will be smiling and acting as though nothing had happened. Of course, you must call your doctor when your baby has a fever, because they all have their own fever protocol, but just remember that babies run hotter than we do.

Projectile vomiting is another terrifying, but not usually dangerous, sick-baby trick. If you haven't seen this before, it will blow your mind. A little baby will open its mouth to chuck up and the stuff will fly five feet across the room, as if it had been launched from a cannon. Even babies who aren't sick but who have gulped a lot of air during a feed can do this trick, but you should have your doctor check it out ASAP to rule out anything more serious.

The most important thing to keep in mind regarding both vomiting and fever in babies is that they can lead to dehydration very quickly: much more quickly than with us big folk. If you are breastfeeding, do it as often as the baby will join in; and if you are bottle feeding, keep sterile water or one of those electrolyte liquids on hand and offer it as often as you can.

mummy medic

If you thought that you were unprepared to be a mother, you ought to be going into shock right about now over the realization that you are expected to be a doctor, too. First, as we said before, you are probably the best diagnostician in the world of illness in your baby. Sure, you may be a little overzealous in your concerns, but you sure aren't apt to *miss* anything. Second, unless your baby is sick or hurt enough to require hospitalization, once he has been treated by the doctor, he goes home with you. That means that you must administer all medications, you must change all dressings, you must give progress reports that make sense to the doctor, you must give cool baths or whatever other treatment the doctor has instructed and – most important of all – you must reassure and soothe this tiny baby who can't understand why the universe seems to have turned against him.

If you have a sick baby who needs a mummy medic, you must shut down all other parts of your life until the baby is well. As far as I'm concerned, a sick baby is the same as a sick mummy and you should feel no guilt about calling your office and telling them you are too ill to come in today. (We'll never tell!) The baby will need to sleep a lot, and chances are great that the only place he will do that for any length of time is in your arms. Fine, you hold that baby forever if you have to because I don't believe you can spoil a baby, and I'm damn sure you can't spoil a sick kid of any age. Call your family and Best Friends for reinforcements. You take care of the baby, and they can help take care of you. Remember, you will need to keep your strength up to provide the care the baby needs, and this is even more so if you are the milk manufacturer as well.

Babies sometimes seem to get more 'babyish' when they are sick. They may need to feed or cuddle more, they may stop sleeping in their cots and they may start acting shy or frightened of any human but you. Don't worry one bit about this. You can go back to old routines when everybody is feeling better. This is how mothering is: two steps forward, one step back. Sounds sort of like the cha-cha, doesn't it?

12

Going Back to Work

If you want to make Mother Nature laugh, tell her your plans for having a baby, recovering and returning to work all within your allotted maternity leave, be it six weeks or six months. It's such precious naïveté when women, invariably pregnant with their first child, pull out a calendar and show how they will be home resting for the first week after delivery; in the second week, they will slowly begin to resume some of their work at home with the help of E-mail and faxes; then they will begin a mild fitness programme in week three or four, so that by the time they return to work, they are fitting into their old wardrobe. During that time, they will interview several capable (and affordable) baby-sitters or crèches and have selected the best of the best for their own baby. At first, they will work an abbreviated schedule, with the full support of their boss and colleagues, so that they are home for the afternoon feed and in time to make dinner for the family. All this time, however, they will be reachable by phone for any professional business that might come up. They will pump their milk at the office so that the baby has all the benefits of breast milk *and* the inspiring example of a mother who works outside the home. They are woman; hear them roar.

Those of us standing on the other side of that river, so to speak, just nod along and encourage them. It's like the pain of labour: why should *we* be the ones to ruin the dream? They will soon have to step into the water for themselves, and if they are lucky they won't drown. They can't yet see the whirlpools and currents below the surface and have no idea how perilous the fording will be. In the meantime, we guilty Best Friends keep repeating 'Come on in – the water's fine.'

My Best Friends Donna and Amy G. had their babies within three weeks of each other and both started back to work last week. Donna works in sales, a job she adores, and Amy is in the publishing business, which has always been her career dream. And how do they feel about being back at work? AWFUL! How will you feel if your plans include going back to work outside the house sometime in the next six months? AT LEAST AS AWFUL!

There are so many considerations that you didn't even know existed when you were pregnant. How could you ever have imagined the adoration you feel for your baby and how emotionally and physically painful it is to be separated from her? It's an entirely unique sense of interdependence. You could never have anticipated the effects of sleep deprivation in your life: how it makes you stupid, foul-tempered and addicted to sugary snacks. Then there is the breastfeeding aspect: you may have finally mastered it and are actually enjoying it, and now you face the prospect of spending much of your time bonding with an electric breast pump in the ladies' room instead of cooing over your baby as she suckles. And where in the world does someone find loving, responsible and affordable child care? The prospect of leaving your baby, the core of your existence, in the care of someone other than yourself is terrifying, even if Daddy is the one who becomes the carer.

About half of all mothers return to work within the first year after giving birth, and another big chunk will return when the child is old enough for nursery school, so you know it can be done. Not only can it be done, it can actually be fulfilling and an essential part of your life, but we Best Friends feel it's our duty to tell you:

IN THE BEGINNING, GOING BACK TO WORK WILL NEARLY KILL YOU.

The Decision to Go Back

For many of us, there is one single, overriding reason why we go back to our jobs outside of the home – the money! It isn't really about anything other than that: either we are the primary breadwinners in our family, or our income is essential to fill in cost-of-living gaps left by our partner's income. There is no big philosophical discussion to be had about our need for fulfilment outside the realm of motherhood or our commitment to our contributions outside the home. We need the money to pay the bills, which are growing now that there is an extra member of the family.

Sometimes the only reason a woman returns to her job is because it has a great insurance plan: a very enticing thing for the mother of a baby with a lifetime of ear tubes, braces, stitches and broken arms ahead of him. If you don't know it already, having a child without health insurance is like golfing in the rain: lightning is sure to strike you down; you just don't know when. If you don't already know your doctor better than you know your minister or your manicurist, you will shortly.

Perhaps the biggest group comprises those of us who are part of a two-income family, who are as trained and educated in our careers as our partners and who enjoy both the work and the extra layer of comfort (you know, like a holiday every other year or cable TV) that comes with combining two salaries. We were raised to expect to be able to do it all, and we waltzed into motherhood assuming that, with the help of a good Filofax, we can work, parent, partner, recycle and serve in the local soup kitchen at Christmas.

During pregnancy, we continue to labour (no pun intended) under the illusion that motherhood will have little or no effect on our jobs or careers. Two of the teachers at my kids' elementary school are newly pregnant, and they are optimistically planning to effortlessly deliver during the summer holidays and then smoothly return to work when school resumes in the autumn. Little do they realize that their impending motherhood has barged into the workplace without their knowing it. They are already working harder than their nonpregnant colleagues to fit morning sickness into their curriculum and not let their smell aversions interfere while the kids are making piggy banks with scraps of newsprint dunked in liquid starch.

Actually, this is just one of many acts of courage that make me so proud to be a woman. I don't have a single Best Friend who dropped the ball professionally when she was pregnant, no matter how roughed-up she felt. They all just forged on as if pregnancy added some weight resistance to the exercise but didn't make it impossible to do. I just love people like my Best Friend Mary, who could interview a member of the president's cabinet, go throw up in the rest room, touch up her lipstick and walk right into the editing room, armed with dry biscuits, bottled water and indigestion tablets in her satchel. Or my Best Friend Rosemary, who would spend three hours on the phone fiercely protecting her client's rights in some complicated contract negotiation, then close the door to her office and sleep like Rip Van Winkle while the rest of the office went to lunch, waking up ready to battle again, except this time with a crease from the sofa upholstery on her cheek. It's a shame we don't get the hint that working motherhood is going to be a juggling act from our working pregnancy experience, but we mummy-optimists somehow cling to the belief that everything will get easier once we get these babies out of our bodies. Mother Nature is nearly splitting a gut right about now.

Telling the Boss

Almost as soon as we learn that we are pregnant, we start worrying about how this news will go over at work. Many of us don't even mention the miracle for several months, until we think that people are whispering about how we've let ourselves go by getting so pudgy. Everybody knows that all but the most enlightened workplaces (like, maybe, Gloria Steinem's office or the staff of NOW) look suspiciously at pregnant women and the disruption they promise to bring. Sure, there are equal-rights protections and guaranteed maternity leaves, but the unspoken agenda is that it's going to cost the company or office lots of time, money and convenience to carry your weight (which we all know is ample these days) while you're launching this baby of yours. It's interesting that, even when we had negotiating power before accepting employment, very few of us dickered over the terms of our hypothetical maternity leave. Vacations, company cars, telephone credit cards might all have been negotiated, but not one mention is usually made of what kind of protection the company would afford us when we became pregnant and had families.

Almost no one goes into the personnel office or to her superior with the news of her pregnancy and simultaneously announces that she will be quitting her job when the baby is born. Even if that is what we intend to do, it's a bonehead announcement because we don't want to do anything to jeopardize our benefits or paid maternity leave. Word to the wise: make sure to know all maternity provisions in your employee handbook and under the law before you tell your boss you're pregnant. If he or she is misinformed and you are, too, then you might miss out on some crucial benefits and protections.

We don't want prejudice about our impending motherhood to get in the way of any promotions or raises, either. If we can bear to keep the thrilling news to ourselves, it is generally a good idea not to tell anyone at work that we're expecting until our colleagues can see the baby move from their position across the desk. Just to be fair to the employer, give them a couple of months, at least, to start scrambling around for someone to fill in during your absence. Believe your Best Friends when we say you may be gone longer than you think.

Most of us, however, still can't imagine why in the world we would up and quit a job in this time of rampant unemployment just because a baby is coming. There are, we remind ourselves, all sorts of creative ideas that can help a woman have a career and a baby or two, too. We can try job sharing or abbreviated work schedules. We can set up a home office like the lady in the computer commercial who is so adept at teleconferencing and the internet that she practically runs the world in her nightshirt and fuzzy slippers. Our partners, too, are a tremendous asset, aren't they? They were raised with the higher consciousness of their feminist mothers and understand that they are expected to co-parent this child, right down to changing her nappies and comforting her after she's had a vaccination. Maybe our employers have even had the social conscience to set up a crèche on the premises. What a breeze that would make life for the mummy with a job! Right? Yeah, right.

The Real Picture

There are good days and there are bad days for mothers who work outside the home. The good days are pretty much what your active fantasy life has conjured up for you since the minute you found out you were pregnant. The bad days are like nothing you could ever imagine. Try this little scenario on for size.

The baby is five months old and teething. You have been back on the full-time schedule for a month now, your boss having decided that you were taking too long to return your calls on those Fridays when you were supposedly 'working from home'. (Admit it: you *did* take a few of those hours to get your hair coloured, drop off dry cleaning and go to Costco for a new baby swing.)

Your partner has the flu, and you suspect that only desperation is protecting your immune system. The baby was awake all night with what you figured must be teething pain, but now that it's morning and you are raving with fatigue, you are convinced is really a double ear infection. The baby-sitter doesn't come till lunchtime because your partner has adjusted his work schedule so that he can take care of the baby in the mornings. You have a staff meeting at 9:00, and you will definitely be missed if you don't show. The baby clearly needs to go to the doctor, and no parent would send a sick child to the doctor without the mother or father present in case he gets a shot or something equally traumatic occurs. Your partner, the father of your child, is useless, and you can't really argue with his 102-degree temperature (although you are secretly convinced that if the tables were turned, *you* would manage to rally and get that baby to the doctor, even with a temperature of 110). You eventually decide to leave the miserable baby with the miserable partner, praying that nothing happens that would demand quick action or clear judgement from Daddy. You will get to that staff meeting, look alert and involved for the sixty minutes required, then you will think of some excuse to leave the office, at which point you will take the baby to the doctor.

In the meeting, you are so concerned about the baby that you can't help but hear and see him crying in discomfort. All these maternal feelings conspire to trigger your let-down reflex, and you feel the front of your blouse getting wet. Naturally, in your distraction and exhaustion this morning, you neglected to slip any breast pads into your bra (and you aren't even sure you have any more since you emptied the box yesterday), so you look like someone who has had two growing bull's-eyes drawn on her chest.

With a crimson face, you sprint out of the meeting and grab the breast pump and all its tubes and bottles. After ten minutes of looking for the gasket to one of the nursing funnels and finding it in your paper clip bowl, you sit behind a closed door at your desk and try to express your milk. Understandably, you feel a bit pressured at this fragile moment, since you know everyone in the staff meeting is waiting for you. The phone rings twice, but you can't answer it without losing the suction on your breasts because both of your hands are holding plastic baby bottles with clear plastic funnels drawing so hard on your breasts that with every tug your nipples stretch at least three inches in length. All of a sudden, the baby that pervaded your consciousness only moments ago is so far from your thoughts that you stare at his framed picture on your desk to try to remind your body why you are going to all this trouble in the first place.

It is now nearly ten o'clock. You have missed the staff meeting and will be late for the doctor if you take a moment to explain to your boss and co-workers why you evacuated the meeting as if the room had been on fire. Besides, your boss is a man, and he starts looking queasy and fidgety any time you mention anything about breasts being used as a food source. By the way, you are sweating like a pig at this point because (1) you have your jacket on to cover up the milky targets on your blouse; (2) your hormones are still off-kilter and you get the occasional hot flush; and (3) you are so nervous about the baby needing his mother and his mother not being there for him that you could shatter into a thousand pieces.

You call your partner on your way home, and the answering

machine picks up. You know that can only mean one of two disasters: he has passed out from his fever and the child is unsupervised or – the baby is sicker than when you left him and your partner is at the hospital with him right this very minute. For a moment, you notice how terribly you are driving, and you thank heaven that mothers, unlike pilots, are not required to get a certain amount of sleep before getting behind the wheel. If that were the case, you'd be living on public transport.

When you arrive home, you find both your baby and partner still there, just as you left them. Evidently, your partner felt that answering the phone would be the straw to break this camel's back, so he left all calls to the answering machine. As soon as the baby sees his beloved mother, he turns from a quiet and calm little angel into a screeching orangutan. You are bouncing him around the room, singing songs and crying, too, when the phone rings. It's your assistant calling to tell you that UPS has lost that overnight letter you sent yesterday, and she was wondering if you had the receipt for it in your briefcase because it's nowhere in your office. You try to think where it could be, but the baby's cries are like needles piercing your eardrums and it takes all your self-restraint not to tell your assistant that you hate UPS, you hate your job, you hate her for interrupting you during this obvious crisis and, most of all, you hate your sick partner for not doing something to rescue you from this nightmare.

After the doctor's visit and a stop at the pharmacy, where it takes forty minutes to fill a prescription for antibiotics, you deposit the baby home where, if fortune is smiling on you, the baby-sitter is waiting. (I'm not even going into the very real possibility that she has caught the flu from germs your partner has spread all over the house and can't come to work for the next several days. It would just cause you to become unnecessarily hysterical.) You change your shirt, grab two Snack-Well's and a Diet Coke and get back into the car to go back to work. All you can feel is a dull sense of failure and misery at the prospect of wasting the rest of the day in some stupid job that doesn't mean anything in the grand scheme of things while your precious child, a child who could be the Messiah for all you know and is definitely your greatest contribution to the universe, is sick and motherless.

Perhaps it will help you deal with this terrifying prospect if we take it apart and look at it one piece at a time.

Child Care

Dads Are a Possibility . . .

I know this is a strange notion, but if you can't be there all the time to take care of your precious new baby, you might consider relying on the other person in the universe who loves her as fiercely and devotedly as you do: her father. We all know that the ineptitude that many men show around new babies is just a ploy to avoid any unnecessary exertion, just as when they ask things like, 'Honey, do you know where we keep the scissors?' They are as capable as you are at everything but the breastfeeding.

You should have begun thinking when you were still pregnant about who would care for your baby while you worked. As we mentioned earlier, this is the time for both you and your partner to study your employer's position regarding maternity and paternity leave. I know a man who just took a three-month leave from his job as a schoolteacher to help his partner care for their newborn twins. Yes, he was pointed at by nearly every other man on campus as though he were the oddest thing they had ever seen, or else gay, but he has been gone and receiving a salary for a couple of months now, and we Best Friends applaud him.

Traditionally, if the dads take any time off from work to help with the new baby, it is at the time of delivery and when his new family comes home from the hospital. If your partner can get a chunk of time off to help with the baby, you both might want to consider postponing that leave until the baby is a month or two old. As hard as it might be for you to adjust to motherhood during those first few weeks, it truly gets harder around the passage of the first month. For the first couple of weeks, the baby usually sleeps more than he will later, when he opens his eyes and realizes he's not in Kansas anymore. You will still be stunned and sore, and initially you will surrender simply to lying around and doing little more than feeding and changing the little darling. About a month or so later, when you are able to walk without feeling like your uterus is going to slip out of you and on to the floor and you have some control over the milk in your gigantic breasts, you might really benefit from having your partner around to help you tentatively find your way back into the real world. You might actually start back to work, or you can use this time to prepare for the big reentry.

Both my Best Friends Donna and Amy G., who just returned to work, have partners who are at home caring for the baby right now. One is a chef and the other is an actor, and they feel that they can take this leave for their babies, at least for the next few months. These guys are both doing a great job. They care for the babies, take them out to the park and to visit friends. I must add a pinch of reality to this frothy picture, however; both of them have hired housekeepers to do the cleaning and cooking. No judgement here; I love housekeepers, but I just want to make sure you are seeing the picture clearly. Also, when there is a shot to be administered, both Donna and Amy G. take off from work to take the baby on this dreaded visit. I don't know exactly what it is about fear and pain that we mums find so irresistible, but we can't bear to let our babies face them without their mummies by their sides. By the way: as far as I can tell, these men are not hamstrung by postnatal depression, trying to lose twenty to thirty pounds of baby fat and getting blisters on their nipples. But I am beginning to sound bitter, aren't I?

Amy G. and Donna both give the same answer when asked how it feels to know their babies are home with their daddies: they are reassured, they are happy for the babies and for their partners but mostly they are JEALOUS. They are bugged beyond human tolerance several times a day when they call home and Daddy tells them something adorable or amazing that the baby just did *that Mummy wasn't around to see*. They feel denied something that is every mother's right, at least according to those blissed-out pregnancy books that have poisoned our minds. We told you this motherhood gig is a tough one. If it makes you feel any better, there are plenty of mummies who are home witnessing these miracles for themselves who dream of getting dressed in clothes that match, leaving the baby and the messy house and going into a world where no one talks baby talk or has baby urp on her shoulder.

Other Members of the Family

When my Best Friend Julie returned to work as a manicurist, her mother took care of her baby boy. A grandma, aunt or other relative can be a godsend when you are facing the end of your maternity leave. The good things about them are that they love your baby like kin because, well because he is kin. The chances are very good, too, that if your potential baby-sitter is family and has a prison record, you've already heard about it. Now that you are a mother, I don't need to tell you how frightening it is to think that you may leave your baby in the care of someone who might steal him. It's a phobia for all of us working mums.

Even those of us who have spent hours in therapy trying not to be like our mothers will unwittingly emulate our poor, maligned mums when it comes to caring for our new babies. Sure, we may breastfeed, and almost none of our mothers did, but other than that, we probably have our mothers' attitudes about whether babies with runny noses should go outside, whether newborns always need a hat (even in the middle of summer) and how often we need to wash our hands in flu season. I remember my Best Friend Stacie once had a baby-sitter who boiled some herb she found growing in Stacie's yard and fed the 'tea' to her baby for colic! I guarantee, this is not something a grandma would do, at least not unless she did it to you, too.

As your active imagination might predict, there are some sticky parts to this caregiving option, too. For one thing, most of us are still struggling to express our independence from our mothers and mothers-in-law. If they are caring for our babies, it is very tempting to nitpick and criticize their mothering skills, since we never really got a chance to nitpick and criticize them when they were mothering us.

Or, if we don't find every parenting choice to be grounds for a shrill confrontation, we go overboard the other way and revert to being babies ourselves. Face it: if your mother is a good nurturer, cuddler and coo-er, it's impossible to watch her do it to your baby all day long and not want a little for yourself, especially after a hard day at work. Either way, you will eventually want to claim your position as Boss Mother, and that might be hard to do when the Dowager Mother is so deeply involved in your life.

My mother-in-law helped my sister-in-law take care of her children every day of their young lives. They never once experienced a teenaged girl with homework in her arms showing up on the doorstep to baby-sit, talk on the phone and watch TV. After I had my children and was ready to go back to work, I mentioned to my beloved sister-in-law how incredibly fortunate she was to have her mother helping her every step of the way. She smiled very sweetly and said, 'So how come I want to move to New Jersey and not leave a forwarding address?' Evidently, the price she paid for such tender loving care was a certain lack of privacy and having to hear her mother's opinion on everything from when the baby should be baptized to how much fabric softener should go in with the baby clothes. That very same mother-in-law came to stay with me when each of my babies was born, and I luxuriated in her loving, self-sacrificing and ever-attentive ways. Of course, if she had been my mother rather than my mother-in-law, it would have been a totally different story.

A PERSON WHO GETS PAID

You have tremendous freedom to set the rules when you pay someone to take care of your baby. The nanny or au pair understands that you are the boss, even if you are somewhat inexperienced at this mothering stuff, and she will agree to nearly every stipulation you make. Of course, once you leave the house, it's another matter. I don't care how good your nanny is, she is doing things her way when you aren't looking. That's why it's a good idea to use the job interview with a potential nanny to pose hypothetical situations for her. If her impromptu responses are similar to what you think you would do under those circumstances, she is a good candidate. Don't ever hire someone thinking that you will change her; it doesn't work with partners, and it doesn't work with nannies and au pairs.

As a member of the California Bar Association, it is my duty to remind or inform you that it is against the law to hire anyone to work in your home (or anywhere else in the United States) who is not either an American citizen or authorized to hold a job by virtue of a green card or work permit.★ That said, depending on where you live, you will probably consider nannies or au pairs who were not born in this country, since they are the people who are willing to put in the long hours for less-than-spectacular wages. It's a very hard call for some working women because, after paying for child care, their income is often negligible. My Best Friend Lisa, after the birth of her second child, looked into the cost of hiring someone to care for her children while she went back to work and decided to get herself registered as a childminder. The money she saved plus the money the other parents paid made staying home a real option for her. Of course, Lisa is a woman of extraordinary calm and extraordinary faith. Oh yeah, and she moved to Utah a year ago to escape all those babies.

Most of us find our nannies, childminders or au pairs through the Best Friends' Grapevine. We mention to a Best Friend's nanny that we need help, and she sends one of her friends to us. Sure, there are plenty of agencies and placement services, but they are often very expensive,

---

★ In the UK, the law says that you can only hire an au pair from the EU. Anyone else you employ has to have a valid visa.

so find out their commission before asking them to send you any candidates. Here in the rarified child-care atmosphere of Los Angeles, the leading agencies charge a fee equal to the nanny's first month's salary, BEFORE TAXES!!

After four kids and countless nannies, I could write a book on the things I have learned about the species. (Hey, there's an idea!) For now, however, I want to tell you just the most essential rules.

1. Never hire a nanny or au pair without having her work for two weeks on a trial basis. You must see her in action to really judge her ability. Some of the best talkers are the worst nannies, and vice versa. Yolanda, Colombia's answer to Mary Poppins, looked so dour in her interview, I only tried her out because I was so sleep deprived. She ended up being a part of our household for four years.

2. Require documentation that the nanny has tested negative for TB These certificates are strangely easy to get on the streets, so it might be a good idea to send a serious candidate to your own doctor. It's one thing for your baby to catch a cold from your nanny (blood-chilling as that thought is), but it's inexcusable to risk exposing a baby or child to a disease that is still popping up in countries all around the world.

3. If the nanny is working in your house, get her home address and phone number. Not only that, but go to the house and call the number to make sure they are accurate. I am humiliated to admit it, but I once hired a woman who went to church with the nurse in my paediatrician's office. I figured, *nurse, church*, how could I go wrong? Well, one Tuesday when she was due back from her weekend off, she never showed up. I sat with my baby in my arms and wept on the front porch. (See what I told you about postnatal depression sneaking up on you?) I couldn't believe that she didn't love my baby enough to come back to him and I couldn't believe that I had to face still more sleepless days and nights after a Sunday and Monday from hell. Most shocking of all, I realized for the first time that I didn't even have her phone number, let alone know where she lived. What if I had come home to find her and my baby gone one day? What had I planned to do, call the paediatrician's nurse's church? I still feel anxious and nauseous when I think of my knuckleheaded risk.

4. Make it a habit to arrive home at unexpected times. You will want to know what your nanny and baby are doing when no one is looking.

Feel free to peek into windows or ask neighbours for their observations. Behaviour that might be called 'stalking' in another situation is completely acceptable where your baby is concerned. In fact, I think stalking is a sign of great parenting all the way through childhood and up until the kids move out of your house. Even by the time my kids were old enough to go to nursery school, I was frequently noticed hiding in the shrubbery, mud squooshing up the sides of my shoes, outside their play yards to spy on them. Come to think of it, I really could have used one of those army helmets with the bushes on the top. Even now, I will stop at my older kids' school on the pretext of bringing them a sweater just so that I can hide in the halls and watch them in class. It's not that I don't trust anybody; I just don't trust *myself* to trust only the right people. I certainly don't want to be a humanitarian at my babies' expense, nor should you.

5. 'Remember: the first nanny that you hire will not be your last nanny.' I remember when my friend Jerry, the father of three grown children, sagely told me this fact to comfort me when that nanny abandoned my baby and me. Intellectually, you will know the truth of this advice, but your emotions will refuse to believe it. Especially with our first babies, we new mums tend to be so uncertain and tentative about our mothering that we grow very dependent on capable and experienced nannies. It isn't long before we become convinced that the key to our success as mothers with jobs outside the home – heck, the key to the survival of ourselves and our babies – is worn on a chain around the neck of our beloved nannies. And, so convinced are we of our baby's innate irresistibility and charisma, we can't fathom that someone would let their relationship with the baby end without being struck dead. Believe it, Best Friend, they will leave – either because they feel like moving on or because you feel like moving them on. You will mourn. You will fear emotional injury to your baby. You will feel abandoned. You will be certain that you will never find another nanny. But trust us: you will find someone, and someone after that and someone after that. And you and your baby will grow and thrive and live happily ever after.

6. Make a plan for emergencies. First of all, mothers must be reachable by phone at all times. In this era of pagers, cellular phones and call forwarding, there is absolutely no reason that your nanny should not be able to speak to you immediately in an emergency. Remember, pagers are not just for crack salesmen anymore. If your

nanny can drive, and you don't live in New York City or around the corner from the emergency ward, it might be a good idea if she has access to a car – her own, yours, your neighbour's – while she is caring for your child. I don't know about you, but I am a sceptic where 999 is concerned. I once called it when someone was breaking into my mother's apartment and I was put on hold forever. In fact, I never did actually speak to a human being, so there is not much chance that I'm going to be relying on those folks if my baby is feverish or bleeding. The best plan is to contact the person most likely to be able to help you or your nanny in an emergency. Have the numbers for your GP, the fire department and so on listed in big print ('mature' nannies and 'mature' mothers are farsighted, and you don't want either of them to be running around looking for reading glasses at a time like this). The nanny should carefully describe the baby's condition to the professional. If a trip to the hospital is necessary, then she should ask whether she should drive the baby herself or wait for an ambulance. When my Best Friend Sally's little boy fell and hurt his head, the paramedics told her to start driving to the hospital and they would meet her on the highway! Her neighbour drove her and her son, they actually met up with the ambulance and the little boy received the care he needed when he needed it.

Nurseries

Here's the problem as I see it: most women who take maternity leave from their jobs to have a baby must return to their jobs in three or six months. While many of us are fortunate enough to have someone (paid or begged) to take care of the baby in our own homes, many of us are not. It's always as painful as amputation to leave your baby for your first day at work, and if you are leaving her at a nursery or childminder's home that you've only visited a couple of times, you feel like dying. If it's any consolation, this whole experience of leaving your child in day care gets much easier as she grows. They are very fragile and susceptible creatures those first few months, however, and you should be prepared to spend a lot of time choosing the best place for your baby.

Ideally, when a baby is under a year old and not walking, any group child-care situation should be as small a group as possible. Even if the larger nurseries tell you that the ratio of caregivers to babies is four to one, that is not the same as a setting that only has four children in it, total. Often it's not lack of attention that will be the problem; it's that bigger nurseries have proportionately more germs added to the atmosphere, and there are more changes in routine and personnel. One note: even though a stay-at-home mother with an immaculate home and only one other child to care for can sound like nirvana to a mother who needs child care so that she can go back to her job, it can be risky to rely on only one person. When that lovely stay-at-home mum gets bronchitis from the cold your baby shared with her, she will have to close her business for a few days, leaving you with a baby to care for during business hours. If you have someone else to step in, great, if not, you might be better off with a slightly larger set-up that is always staffed.

As with nannies in your home, make it a point to drop by the nursery unexpectedly. Go ahead and peek in windows or through partly opened doors to see how things go when there's no audience. If you get discovered, don't be embarrassed; every mother worth her salt does the same thing.

mummies in the workplace

It's no coincidence that most maternity leaves last for three months. In those three months, most of us have healed substantially, we are managing to feed our babies and care for them with confidence, and we are even ready to start getting our hair coloured and styled again. This is the precise moment when you realize you will not only survive this ordeal but perhaps regain some control and, heaven forbid, *style*. That's when they pull the rug out from under you! Just when you thought you got a schedule you could live with, you have to return to work and start all over again. You know that the first thing that you will cancel in your desire to fit everything into one twenty-four-hour day will be *the hair appointment*. I know for myself that I used to have luxurious, nearly waist-length hair and long manicured nails. In a process that was too gradual for me to notice, I started making less and less time for this top-drawer maintenance. And now, four children and three books later, I have shorter hair than Peter Pan and no fingernails whatsoever.

Don't hold out hope that your co-workers will actually appreciate the sacrifices you are making. In fact, you might even discover that there are some people in your workplace who are convinced that, simply by virtue of being a new mummy, you are not giving the job enough of your attention. Don't you just hate people like that? Guess what? They are right! But so what? You deserve some settling in time to get used to this working mother routine. Pretty soon you'll be running laps around all of them, or you'll win the lottery and be able to tell them to take their job and love it (or something that rhymes with 'love').

Most mothers I know, and certainly all of my mummy Best Friends, do their best to keep both their families and their employers from feeling that they are getting shortchanged. Since there is only so much time, the person who is perpetually shortchanged is the mother. She will stay up half the night finishing third-grade geometry mobiles but still get up to get the kids off to school because she knows that the day starts better for them if she does. She will attend to her outside job by working seven days a week, particularly early mornings and late nights when the children are asleep. Last night I had to stop my work to sit Siva with my son, whose parakeet had finally gone to heaven (after five hours of an agonizingly slow death, which my son watched).

This is the part of the book where I want to tell you to claim some time for yourself, because it will never be offered to you. I must confess, however, that I still don't have this handled in my own life, so feel free to dismiss everything I say. My husband and I have been on two romantic getaways in the nine years since we became parents. I don't know, we just feel so lonely and guilty without the tots that we almost always vacation with them. The one thing I do set time for is physical exercise. I need to get out and hike or run several times a week to stay somewhat fit, but more important, to blow off steam and feel that good old endorphin high. Since none of us seems to be able to make time for 'lunch with some of the Best Friends' anymore, these hikes have become ever more cherished by me. We always try to get a group together on Saturday and Sunday mornings early, before baseball practice and dance recitals begin. We talk about everything during these ninety-minute hikes: partners, children, schools, fertility crises, lack-of-partner crises, plastic surgery and how we can get the city council to build a youth centre to keep kids from hanging out where we can't see them. It's sort of a therapy/support/medical/civic group, with a lot of jokes thrown in.

Does the hamster in his wheel remind you of your life about now? There is no way in heaven that you can go to work, teach your baby simple phonics, keep your relationship fresh and sexy, pump or feed several times, go to the cleaners (remember, you are dressing for adults now that you're back at work), cook dinner and do a load or two of laundry in one day. And that's a good day. A bad day is when you need to do all those things and (1) the baby's sick, (2) you're sick or (3) your car is in the garage. Once again we tell you: surrender, Dorothy! This condition is not a temporary state. It is your life for the foreseeable future. Since no one should live like a drone, it's up to you to prioritize and get rid of the nonsense. Give yourself little breaks, like turning off the phone after 6:00 P.M., taking a bath with your baby after dinner, saving weekend afternoons for sex. If that means you eat out more often or that you neglect the housekeeping more than usual, good for you. In the end, you will not spend one moment on your deathbed wishing that you had kept a cleaner house.

13

The second Baby

Nearly everyone has a brother or a sister, and the stereotypical family has 2.4 children, so what's the big deal about having a second baby? Only the mother of a precious only child can know the conflict, guilt and anxiety that are attached to the decision to have another. First of all, we know deep in our hearts that it is virtually impossible to ever love another baby as much as we love our firstborn. There just isn't that much love in the world to go around. Second, who really has the time to care for more than one baby – or the money, for that matter? And how about facing pregnancy and delivery all over again? That prospect alone can send you running for your birth control.

Still, as their babies get within toddling distance of their first birthdays, most new mummies at least *consider* having another one. Perhaps it's simply because everyone else is doing it, or maybe you are starting to suspect that your baby is not going to stay a baby forever. As our babies learn to move away from us, first by crawling and then by walking, we begin to miss that newborn smell and the way they used to sleep on our chests with their little legs tucked up under them and their bottoms in the air like precious stinkbugs. My babies arrived every two years or less, so simple maths lets you know that I didn't waste much time in a normal hormonal state. My pattern went something like this:

> Have a baby, nearly drown in the undertow of motherhood, start to come back to life, lose the weight, throw the first birthday party, drink red wine at my husband's birthday party and accidentally become pregnant again.

If you don't believe this schedule is true, let me inform you that my husband's birthday is in March and I have three children born in November and December, two within one day of each other. Next time you're at your doctor's surgery, borrow his wheel and see for yourself what I give my husband for his birthday.

Anyway, I think I had the babies in such rapid succession because (1) It's what my own parents had done and I liked being so close in age to my darling brother; (2) I was already thirty-four and had a history of infertility when I finally had my first baby, and I didn't want to wait too long before trying again; (3) I knew that if I ever finally got rid of all the nappies and baby bottles, I might not have the courage to start up with all that again; (4) I wanted to guarantee that I would have children in my nest up until senility set in; and (5) I have a hard time concentrating on endeavours that are not of crisis proportions, and I worried that I would forget entirely that I was a mother unless I had so many kids that it was undeniable. In other words, if I finally got some control over the chaos brought by one child, I neurotically had to add another baby to the mix, just to keep the challenge alive.

I have very few Best Friends who have only one child, which is interesting because the few I do know have extraordinary kids and wonderful relationships with them. Families of three, or even two, clearly seem to work quite well. And even those who do have one child often came to that decision after repeated attempts to have another have just not worked out. It's often only after nature or circumstance has determined that they will be a 'triangular' family that they realize the charm, intimacy and relative ease of having a single child. Not that I'm trying to talk you into or out of anything. But it is raining today, and I do have one vomiting child resting on the couch, two who are cramped up in classrooms with closed windows that are just crawling with infection and a three-year-old who is so bored that she is upstairs trying out all my lipsticks. (I hope she's using just her own body for a canvas, but I'm too busy to keep running up to check . . .)

Sometimes we are faced with a second pregnancy simply because we didn't listen to the Best Friends when they told us that we could get pregnant *while we were breastfeeding and before we had our first postnatal menstrual period*. While the birth of a child is always a blessing and cause for celebration, it does help if you were at least *intending* to get pregnant again. Even if you weren't, lie because people will think you are really a bonehead if it's an accident.

The Ultimate Betrayal

Okay, so let's assume that you're on a roll with this mothering business, and you find out that you are pregnant again. It's pretty exciting news every time you get it. You just have to marvel that such a miracle has occurred again and that you and your partner have created another little human being. You have about an hour, at most, to revel in your good fortune, then it is time to realize that you might have just made the biggest mistake of your life. At least that's how you will feel much of the time. Your darling, perfect precious little firstborn will be so resentful of the intrusion of another person into your magic circle that he will hate you forever and need therapy before he's out of nappies.

What in the world made you think that having a brother or a sister would make your original baby happy? Someone to share your love and attention with? Someone to steal his toys or trash his room? Are you crazy? That's like saying that your partner's new girlfriend is welcome because she will be a good companion for you. You can hardly look into your baby's face without feeling overcome with guilt. Someone is going to break up your affair, and it's all your fault!

Don't expect to have these conflicting feelings all nicely worked out by the time the baby comes. As a matter of fact, it's safe not to expect to *ever* have them worked out. (Each of my kids is *still* convinced that he or she is being gypped of my attention and mothering by its siblings on a daily basis.) My Best Friend Sondra and I both checked out of the hospital with such haste after the births of our second babies that the doctors had barely cut the umbilical cords. We were so nervous about introducing the new babies to the little princes at home that we couldn't stand the anticipation one moment longer than necessary. We also sickened ourselves with worry that the firstborns would notice our brief absence and realize that they had been abandoned. We could only pray that they would forgive us for needing to give birth in a hospital instead of staying home with them. If I can get through to you at a stressful time like this, I would like to impart this one message: *After delivering your second baby, stay in the hospital as long as they will let you.* Your firstborn will be equally indifferent or resentful forty-eight hours later as he will be five hours later. By the time I gave birth to my fourth, my desperate husband had to break in to get me out of my hospital room, where I had barricaded myself with the flower arrangements and bedpans against the door. Well, almost; I did so love that room and the peace and quiet it provided.

There Isn't Enough Love in This World

Every mummy knows that no nonmother or mother-to-be is prepared for how much she will love her baby (whether it's love at first sight or a gradual affair) once she comes into her life. The feeling is so big and powerful that there are times when it threatens to break your ribs. It preoccupies your thoughts to the exclusion of almost anything else and can make you delirious or absentminded. So essential is that relationship to your well-being that you know that if, God forbid, something were to happen to threaten it, you would disintegrate into a pile of dust. Simple physics makes you certain that no human being can feel this emotion for two people simultaneously; you would crumble or break apart from the inside. Even though they are not admitting it to a single living soul, the truth is that all mothers must love their firstborn more than they love their other children; they just cover it up with feigned affection and forced kindness, right?

Wrong. It is true, however, that the exclusivity and intensity of your devotion to your first child is difficult, if not impossible, to recreate with a second child, unless you have the foresight to have your children about sixteen years apart. And you will never have the freedom to wrap your world around the newborn because you will still have the firstborn to care for. But love her you will, and as the children grow you will find that they each fulfil you in their own unique way. Don't you remember how your mother used to say, 'I love you all equally, but I love you all differently'? Well, she wasn't just placating you – it was the truth for her and it will be for you, too. I'm not going to jump ahead here to what you know eventually happens in all our slightly dysfunctional families, and that is Mum being 'closer' to one sibling than another. (That usually isn't a function of love, but rather a function of something else like comfort, convenience or guilt anyway.) There is a very good chance that you will enjoy your second baby more than your first because you have more confidence in your ability to care for her. You will be more familiar with which things are crises and which are no big deal, and you will probably be slightly less shocked by the way motherhood completely rocks your universe (although mummies' Alzheimer's does tend to make you forget the more painful parts of pregnancy and childbirth; otherwise, no one would have a second baby!).

Some of my Best Friends have told me that, as their second pregnancies were drawing to an end, they got incredibly sentimental about their relationship with their firstborn. They would say things like, 'This is the last Christmas where it's just Jake and us, so we're going to do something special,' or 'This might be my last chance to spend the whole day in the house with Alex.' It was almost as if they were hoarding up their precious moments with their first love in preparation for the inevitable intervention of the new baby. By the way, this isn't a sign of disloyalty to the new baby. It's just easier to care about the feelings of someone you already know than of someone you have yet to meet.

There isn't Enough Time in the world

This is true, but we mothers spend our lives trying to make more time. There is a rule of thumb that a second baby does not affect your life proportionately. In other words, having two kids is not just twice as hard as having one; it's harder than that. You just have to trust us on this. I don't know why it's true, but an equally true rule of thumb is that if you have three kids, caring for four kids isn't much different. I guess by that time you have given up all hope of control and sanity or have suffered such profound brain damage that you don't much notice the addition of another monkey to the barrel.

One of the main reasons that caring for two small children is so hard is that you not only have the regular care and feeding requirements that you have with a single baby, but now you have to deal with *their* relationship with each other. So, in addition to feeding, burping, going to Mother and Baby classes, and all the other tasks of mothering, you are also soothing a baby who has just been beaned by Big Brother or Sister with a rattle or something far harder, sharper and more dangerous. Then there is the time you must devote to coaxing your older child out of the baby's cot, where she is vehemently maintaining that she is a baby, too, and she doesn't want any new baby in her bed.

One of the biggest inside jokes of motherhood is the difference in how we document our first babies and all other babies. Firstborns have beautiful baby books with written observations, reflections and mile-stones. There are countless photos and videos of all the 'firsts' from eating solid foods to eliminating them into a potty. All babies who are not firstborn will find their baby books filled with empty pages. In fact, most of us end up using the books as file folders in which to throw such things as baptism certificates and medical progress reports. By my third baby, I didn't even try to fool myself into believing that I would eventually bring a baby book up to date. Instead, I just found a big hatbox and threw everything into it. Who has time to compose diary entries about 'Mummy's Dreams for Your Future' when mummy isn't sleeping enough to dream about anything these days?

Other people will certainly have all sorts of advice for you to help you get organized and prioritized and efficient-ized with the promise that being the mother-of-many will be like a day at the beach. We Best Friends would never lie to you like that. Some of us are just blessed with the ability to get two kids ready to go out and have them both be dressed in clean clothes with combed hair and big bows or braces. Others of us straggle in and out of places with howling children in mismatched outfits and faces that look permanently stained with popsicle. Neither style is any indication of how good a mother you are, so just do what you can. Being a mother is hard and endless work, and you just keep putting one foot in front of the other. And just when you think you can't take another step, out of the corner of your eye you will see the older child hug his new baby like he really means it, and you will weep and hear angels sing.

will Another Pregnancy Kill Me?

It appears that, contrary to what our good sense tells us, most of us are built to withstand more than one pregnancy. While everyone and her pregnancy are unique, there are some things that are more often true than not.

1. Your Second Pregnancy will Go Much Faster than the First.

The second child needs nine (ten) months to gestate, just as the first did, but chances are you will be so busy caring for your first child and trying to integrate him into your life somehow that huge chunks of time will pass when you actually forget you are pregnant. I bet you can't say that about your first pregnancy!

Remember how careful you were with yourself in your first pregnancy? How you allowed the checkout guy to load your groceries into your car for you or stayed out of kitchens with microwaves in them? Giving yourself such special attention drew your attention to the pregnancy, and probably made it seem to last forever. There is no time for such fussiness with second babies. You are not only lifting your own groceries, you are setting your thirty-pound firstborn on your growing secondborn in your belly and carrying both of them over hill and dale every day. And if you don't take your pregnant self into the kitchen and use the microwave every now and then, no one in the family is going to get a hot meal.

2. Your Pregnancies will be more Alike than Different.

Sure, you may carry one baby higher or wider than another, or you may have a pudgier face with a girl than with a boy, but most of the major characteristics tend to be similar. For example, if you got morning sickness (also known as 'progesterone poisoning') with the first baby, be ready to get it again with subsequent pregnancies. It might be worse or it might be milder, but you will probably have the joy of experiencing it again in some form.

You might be the kind of pregnant woman who has food cravings or aversions. While the type of food will probably change from pregnancy to pregnancy, you will probably remain a person who feels especially strong, one way or the other, about food.

My Best Friends and I noticed that we tended to put on about the same amount of weight with each child, give or take four or five pounds. In my case, it didn't matter if I ate everything in sight (as I did with my first baby) or if I was so busy that I forgot to eat (as I did with my fourth baby); I still gained around thirty-eight (all right, forty!) pounds every time.

While it is generally the case that labours get shorter and more efficient with each baby a woman has, the *kind* of labour she has will often be similar with each one. If you are one of those mums who can squat in a rice paddy and deliver a baby, you will, barring extraordinary circumstances, be just as successful with each baby. Unfortunately, the inverse is also true; if you were plagued by such things as 'failure to progress' in your first labour, you have a statistically higher chance than your rice paddy Best Friend of having the same thing happen in your next labour.

Since the Best Friends are always willing to give a nod to old wives' tales, we mention this last truism for you to note or ignore: If you got symptoms of postnatal depression after the birth of your first baby, you will probably get them again after your next baby comes. We're not telling you this to be party poopers, but rather to remind you to pay attention to these feelings now and start looking for solutions because you will need these problem-solving skills again in this lifetime.

3. Your Family and Friends will Take Your Pregnancy for Granted.

When a woman is pregnant with her first baby, everyone around her acts like it's their first baby, too. You'd think they'd never given birth themselves or known anyone who had given birth before you. Every little development is met with great congratulations. Every little discomfort is pitied and fretted about. Well, I hope you got all that spoiling out of your system with your first baby, because nobody wants to know about your second go-round. Been there, done that. Unless you are growing sextuplets or kittens in there, you just aren't all that compelling anymore.

Partners are particularly guilty of this nonchalance. The same darling man who lived to get you nectarines in the middle of the night when you couldn't think of anything else you could stomach will actually ask you to get up and scramble him some eggs after you've just thrown your brains out with your second battle with morning sickness. You are definitely on your own for all antenatal visits. Most critically, those little emotional outbursts and crying jags that were tolerated (even if just barely) and indulged by your mate during the first pregnancy are a total bore and annoyance this time. The bottom line is this: a woman gets 'Precious Vessel' status once with each partner, so either suck it up or get yourself a new partner.

4. Most of the Lasting Damage Is Done by the First Pregnancy.

If you are hesitant to have another baby because you don't want to put still more mileage on your breasts, your vagina or even your feet, take it from us: a second pregnancy won't make that big a difference. One of the first signs of this truth appears shortly after you get pregnant for the second time. Within ten minutes of taking the pregnancy test, you will notice that you already look five months pregnant. Trust us, the baby isn't growing faster this time; it's your stomach muscles and uterus demonstrating how much the first pregnancy took its toll, no matter how many crunches you did to get back in shape.

Some of my Best Friends tell me that their breasts didn't really bite the dust until their second or third pregnancies. They admit that the first one pretty much robbed them of their perkiness and perch, but they insist that things just went steadily downhill with each subsequent baby. I'm not sure I agree with them here. I think that what really happens is we get amnesia about our droopy darlings as soon as they get all full and lively again with the next pregnancy. We fail to realize that this is just a temporary state of vitality, and that Cinderella's footmen will turn back into field mice again, so to speak, once the breastfeeding is finished. Even worse, but true nonetheless, is the fact that we are older with each successive pregnancy, and gravity is pulling on all sorts of body parts.

As for the vagina, that brave but fragile tunnel through which most babies enter the world, well, here's what my doctor told me: I went to his office one day in the middle of my fourth pregnancy and announced that I wanted to deliver the baby by C-section. He was a little startled to hear this because my second and third babies had been delivered vaginally and there was nothing to suggest that this one wouldn't follow suit. My thinking was much more farsighted than just the successful delivery of the baby – I wanted to avoid traumatizing my private parts again. I had been doing pelvic floor exercises for five years by that point, and I didn't think I could possibly squeeze my pelvic floor tightly enough to withstand yet another assault. My doctor, the kindest and least patronizing person on the planet, softly explained to me that I had lost that battle five years earlier with the birth of my first baby. I may not have the insides of a nineteen-year-old virgin, but I wasn't going to get any worse, and I would have four beautiful babies to show for it. He didn't give me the C-section, but he did do some artful episiotomy stitching afterward. And, ever the optimist, I am still doing pelvic-floor exercises.

Gosh, after what I've just told you about our dainty bits, who really even cares that your feet only get bigger after the first pregnancy? It seems a tad anticlimactic at this point, doesn't it? Oh well, it's true. You may have needed to buy bigger shoes once you got pregnant and had your first baby, but you won't have that excuse for a shopping frenzy ever again.

Will My Baby Ever Forgive Me?

The answer is yes and no. Yes, there will be times when your various children love one another madly and are grateful to have someone special beside them to face the world. Of course, when siblings discover one another, the first thing they usually do is gang up on their mother, but let's not even go there yet. My experience is that my kids are an allied force in the world most of the time, but as soon as you put me into the mix, they start beating the heck out of one another. They don't seem to mind sharing anything, except Mum (oh yeah, and their Barbie Dream House and their Nintendo 64).

No, they will never overtly forgive you for taking their only childhood away, mostly because it's not a kid's nature to cut her mum a break in any area, at least not until she has had children of her own. Then it will hit her like a ton of bricks that she was judging Mum way too harshly all those years. I've given up trying to have much influence on my children's relationships. I draw the line at any hitting that is going to require stitches and any teasing that is within my earshot and driving me crazy. All you have to do is ask your own friends how they like their siblings to realize that some are devoted to each other, some haven't spoken since that disaster four Christmases ago, and still others go in and out of being close. Who knows why we don't all grow up to be as close as the March girls in *Little Women*? Sibling rivalry goes all the way back to Cain and Abel, so there's no reason to think you'll be the exception.

Perhaps a better way to look at the challenges faced by a first-born when a new baby comes home is as a sort of boot camp for life. As all grown-ups know (and still secretly resent), all toys are not theirs, all love is not showered on them, they don't always get to be first and they don't get to win every game. It's a tough break, but it's going to happen sometime so why not learn how to cope now? My third child, my second son, has at age five already defined his life by how miserable he is having a big brother. No matter what the battleground, his big brother is going to cream him and always has. Sometimes it just breaks my heart, like when he is sobbing because his brother 'always touches me last'. But I suspect that this little drama still has several scenes to go before we will know if having this omnipotent older brother has ruined the little one's life or given him the keys to the kingdom.

Let's be pragmatic here. Think of your old age when your children have grown up and left your house (you hope). If you have one child, a phone call every day is an awful lot to expect. But if you have several children, they can share the burden of being nice to you. I'm sure that there will be times when at least one of my kids can't stand the sight of me, and it's rather comforting to think that I would still have three others who would let me rattle around in their lives. My plan, after my kids are gone, is to buy an R.V. and drive from one child's house to the next. I will park in their driveway for a few weeks or months at a time and try to be essential to them in some way. Then, just when they are ready to call social services on me, I will move off to another one's driveway. They will all stay close to each other because they will spend so much time on the phone discussing what a nut and burden their mother turned out to be and pawning me off on each other for the major holidays.

Coping with Sibling Rivalry

The first thing people will ask upon the birth of your second child is 'And how does little Johnny like his new baby sister?' If you are asked this during the first week the new baby is in your house, the combination of wishful thinking and prematurity will conspire to make your answer, 'Oh, he just loves her! He doesn't seem to be jealous at all!' Just you wait, Mummy dear. Any child under the age of five who doesn't go through a period of actively resenting the new baby is shockingly repressed or not sufficiently connecting with reality. Even children who are too young to talk will clearly make known their disapproval of the new arrival. Don't kid yourself into thinking that the transition in your house will be smooth just because you have vowed to sacrifice yourself in any way necessary to meet everyone's needs. We all kill ourselves trying to avoid any inconvenience to our firstborns, and we all fail miserably.

Never Trust the Older Child

Because you won't know when your older little darling will first express her resentment, it is wise to expect it at any time. It's like when an infant rolls over for the first time; he doesn't send out announcements first, so you must always be ready. My own mother once trusted me with my brand-new baby brother, since I was kissing him and cooing to him, but she turned away for a moment, and turned back to find a howling infant with bright red teeth marks on his cheek. My own firstborn used to hug his new sister so sweetly . . . and then start squeezing tighter and tighter until he was nearly strangling her. Even seemingly innocent play near the new baby is guaranteed to end in disaster. If your older child is playing with blocks in the same room as the new baby, no matter how large the room or how unaware of the baby he seems, it is a certainty that one of those blocks will connect with the baby's head. I don't know how it happens, but it always does. Trust me!

'When Is the New Baby Going to Leave?'

The first few days of having a new baby around can be novel and amusing to a firstborn. It's kind of like death, in that in the beginning, you aren't really capable of fathoming how long it's going to last. Once the senior baby gets an inkling that this new little creature is here to stay, he will set about trying to find a way to get rid of it. One way, of course, is to hurt it. As we said before, almost all firstborns try to hurt their siblings at some time, so just be on guard for it and don't let it shock you. This is no indication of how the two of them will get along in the future and shouldn't be allowed to dash all your dreams of a loving family.

Another way to make the new baby go away is to take its place as the baby of the family. Be prepared for your toddler to want to breastfeed again, for your preschooler to want to sleep in a cot again, and for everybody's toilet training to regress. I call this the Baby Huey Syndrome, when a child who is obviously too old for certain behaviour indulges in it. Think of a five-year-old trying to fit into a high chair or buggy. They can't resist trying them out. Even kids as old as six or seven wish that a baby bottle still tasted as good as they remember (don't we all?) and will demand to try one of the newborn's. You may suffer some embarrassment or worry during this period, like when your nursery school child comes to the dinner table in one of the baby's nappies, but your child is no goofier or more poorly adjusted than any other kid who has just been pushed off the throne. Let them do what they have to do with as little comment or interference from you as possible. I find too much discussion about it with the child to be tiresome, so I don't personally recommend any conversation that begins like this: 'Darling, Mummy understands and validates your need to . . .'

Particularly sophisticated firstborns of any age will soon figure out that if they keep you occupied with their needs 100 percent of the time, then you won't have any time for the new baby and he will disappear. Since new babies are very clever, too, and have all sorts of critical needs like food, warmth, soothing, the firstborn usually must learn to add extra urgency to his own humble needs. If the new baby is crying with hunger, the old baby should break something or look like he's about to fall off the dining table. When the new baby is getting her nappy changed, the old baby should begin to tinkle on the carpet. And when all else seems to fail, they can both resort to constant, high-pitched screaming until Mummy really loses it. Unless you run a man-to-man defence, meaning that each child has his or her own caretaker, you will just have to endure this period of adjustment with as little lasting brain damage as possible. In the meantime, we have this one bit of advice:

WHEN ALLOCATING YOUR PRECIOUS ATTENTION TO YOUR BABIES, ERR ON THE SIDE OF THE OLDER CHILD.

This goes against your natural instincts a lot of the time, but we really believe this rule will help you in the long run. The new baby needs you, certainly, but the only thing that can *only* be provided by you is breast milk; the rest of the time she needs those 'loving arms'. That means Daddy, Grandma, or any trustworthy baby-sitter can fill in with the cuddling and rocking part while you try to stay active in the older baby's life. This will break your heart at times, but heartbreak, and a lot of it, seems to go with this mothering territory. You know that already, so don't act surprised now.

Think of it this way: the new baby has no frame of reference by which to measure her treatment. She doesn't know how you spent the entire first three months of her older sibling's life cocooning with him as if the world outside held no attraction whatsoever, and that, by comparison, the new baby is getting shortchanged BIG TIME. Let her grow up thinking that it is natural to be thrown into a car seat and ferried around all day while her older brother or sister gets taken to preschool, to play with friends and to birthday parties. Let your second-born be the first baby in your family to experience a playpen. (It really is safer in there, out of the bigger baby's reach, anyway.) Babies really are resilient little beings and will adjust to nearly anything.

By the time I had my third baby, I had a three-year-old and an almost-two-year-old already at home. My father told me, with keen powers of observation, that I was busier 'than a one-legged man in an ass-kicking contest'. Never was a truer statement made. I recall, both nostalgically and guiltily, how I spent the nights getting to know No.3, because the daylight hours were reserved for the older two. He was so beautiful in the gentle glow of the night-light, and I would breastfeed him for hours while he stared at me with those inky grey eyes that newborns have. Then, come morning, he was handed off to the baby-sitter for nearly the whole day while I desperately tried to maintain a sense of normality for the other two babies in my life. I even fed each new baby while hiding in my bedroom or some other place out of the sight of the older child in an attempt to avoid jealousy. Am I sure that I did the right thing? Not yet, but I'm still not sure about any parenting decisions I've ever made. My best guess, however, is that ultimately, it made the addition of each new baby a little easier.

Unlike those tractable newborns, however, firstborns notice *every single* instance when they are not being treated like the Last Emperor.

Not only do they feel uncertain and neglected, but they have no choice but to deduce that having a sibling does, indeed, mean there is less mummy-love to go around. Kids not only crave attention, they crave and thrive on ritual and predictability. If they have to queue up behind the new baby often enough, they get jealous, AND they get thrown off-balance by the interruption of their precious routines. The world is a scary place, and the one gift we can try our best to give our babies is the right to depend on us for continuity and familiarity. A new baby coming into your home can throw the firstborn's entire little life up in the air. For the second-born, the truism holds: Ignorance is Bliss. Besides, in no time at all, the older baby will be going off to school, and the baby will get Mummy all to herself.

Top-Ten Things New Mothers Don't Do

10
New mothers don't leave the house on a moment's notice.

9
New mothers don't eat meals sitting down.

8
New mothers don't read anything longer than what can be digested during a visit to the toilet.

7
New mothers don't know about any of the movies nominated for a Best Picture Academy Award.

6
New mothers don't like other people's children, especially around their precious angels.

5
New mothers don't listen to any news stories that involve harm to small children.

4
New mothers don't end each day with a satisfying sense of a job well done.

3
New mothers don't wear anything that must be dry-cleaned or ironed.

2
New mothers don't listen to Howard Stern anymore.

1
New mothers don't sleep long enough to experience one single dream from start to finish. OR

1
New mothers don't remember their former personal grooming regimen. OR

1
New mothers don't remember anything. (I think that's everything . . .)

POStScriPt

Nine years later, I can still remember my first baby's first birthday in every detail. Naturally, I overdid it. My husband and I were so excited that we actually arose before dawn and pushed a Little Tykes car (you know, like the Flintstones drove) into the baby's room to wake him up. Standing there in the dark, except for the little night-light's weak glow, we clapped our hands and sang 'Happy Birthday' until we got him as festive as we were. Then, while his daddy put him in his new wheels, I just stood there and cried. I couldn't believe, and still can't, that we had made it this far. The tiny little boy who had come three weeks early into this world, who had aged his parents at least a decade and who refused to walk a step until two days before his birthday, was standing there smiling at us and making our rib cages strain to contain the love we felt.

That first year can be heaven and hell for new mothers, often simultaneously. Your baby's growth is evident in how she looks and what she does. Not as apparent, but maybe just as incredible, is your own growth. You still may not be sure you have a handle on this mothering job, but you suspect you'll do just fine. It's time to realize that all this upheaval in your life is never going away; it's the new 'normal', so you can stop holding your breath and get on with the fun.

When my first baby was this age, I couldn't imagine having the strength to go through it again, but I already knew I would.

Happy Birthday to you, Best Friend! We just knew you'd be great at this!

index